Lecture Notes in Computer Science 14114

The series Lecture Notes in Computer Science (LNCS), including its subseries Lecture Notes in Artificial Intelligence (LNAI) and Lecture Notes in Bioinformatics (LNBI), has established itself as a medium for the publication of new developments in computer science and information technology research, teaching, and education.

LNCS enjoys close cooperation with the computer science R & D community, the series counts many renowned academics among its volume editors and paper authors, and collaborates with prestigious societies. Its mission is to serve this international community by providing an invaluable service, mainly focused on the publication of conference and workshop proceedings and postproceedings. LNCS commenced publication in 1973.

Simon McIntosh-Smith · Michael Klemm ·
Bronis R. de Supinski · Tom Deakin ·
Jannis Klinkenberg
Editors

OpenMP: Advanced Task-Based, Device and Compiler Programming

19th International Workshop on OpenMP, IWOMP 2023
Bristol, UK, September 13–15, 2023
Proceedings

 Springer

Editors
Simon McIntosh-Smith (iD)
University of Bristol
Bristol, UK

Michael Klemm (iD)
OpenMP ARB
Beaverton, OR, USA

Bronis R. de Supinski (iD)
Lawrence Livermore National Laboratory
Livermore, CA, USA

Tom Deakin (iD)
University of Bristol
Bristol, UK

Jannis Klinkenberg (iD)
RWTH Aachen University
Aachen, Germany

ISSN 0302-9743   ISSN 1611-3349 (electronic)
Lecture Notes in Computer Science
ISBN 978-3-031-40743-7   ISBN 978-3-031-40744-4 (eBook)
https://doi.org/10.1007/978-3-031-40744-4

This Springer imprint is published by the registered company Springer Nature Switzerland AG
The registered company address is: Gewerbestrasse 11, 6330 Cham, Switzerland

Preface

The OpenMP API is a widely used application programming interface (API) for high-level parallel programming in Fortran, C, and C++. The OpenMP API has been supported in most high-performance compilers and by hardware vendors since it was introduced in 1997. Under the guidance of the OpenMP Architecture Review Board (ARB) and the diligent work of the OpenMP Language Committee, the OpenMP specification has evolved to version 5.2, which was released in November 2021. It supports parallelism at several levels: offloading in heterogeneous systems; task-based processing across processors; and vectorization in SIMD units. It also goes beyond parallel computing by support for processor affinity and through policies and mechanisms for using memory and for matching directives and functions to computing environments.

Many of these advances were realized through major new features in version 5.0: context selectors and the declare variant construct and metadirectives that use them; the requires directive; memory allocators and support for deep copy of pointer-based data structures; acquire and release semantics; task (memory) affinity; the descriptive loop construct; reverse offloading; affinity display; and first and third-party tools interfaces. OpenMP version 5.0 also significantly enhanced many existing features, such as implicit declare target semantics, support for task reductions, discontiguous array shaping in target updates, and imperfectly nested loop collapsing. Versions 5.1 and 5.2 refined these capabilities and augmented them for increased expressiveness and improved ease of use.

With version 5.2 of the OpenMP API specification, the OpenMP ARB undertook a great effort to regularize OpenMP directive syntax. While this effort involved deprecation of existing syntax, it makes the OpenMP API easier to understand and to apply. The new features that OpenMP API version 5.2 introduced include: the ompx/omx sentinel and API prefix for OpenMP extensions; extensions to metadirectives for Fortran programs; improvements to memory allocators; and additions to the OpenMP tools interface.

While these changes are small advancements, work has already well advanced for the definition of the OpenMP API specification version 6.0 and has been documented in Technical Report 11, published in November 2022. It contains previews of new loop transformations (reverse and interchange directives, and the apply clause); memory scopes for atomic and flush operations; extensions to memory allocators; device selection via traits; and further refinements of the OpenMP language. The OpenMP Language Committee has made great progress in defining the feature for threads to create tasks to be executed by threads in a different parallel team and to enable free-agent threads to execute tasks in addition to the threads explicitly created for that team. For heterogeneous programming, the OpenMP Language Committee continues to explore worksharing across target devices.

The OpenMP API remains important both as a stand-alone parallel programming model and as part of a hybrid programming model for massively parallel, distributed memory systems with homogeneous manycore nodes and heterogeneous node architectures, as found in leading supercomputers. As much of the increased parallelism in exascale systems is within a node, OpenMP will become even more widely used in top-end systems. Importantly, the features in OpenMP versions 5.0 through 5.2 support applications on such systems in addition to facilitating portable exploitation of specific system attributes.

After the first meeting in 2005, in Eugene, Oregon, USA, meetings have been held each year, in Reims, France; Beijing, China; West Lafayette, USA; Dresden, Germany; Tsukuba, Japan; Chicago, USA; Rome, Italy; Canberra, Australia; Salvador, Brazil; Aachen, Germany; Nara, Japan; Stony Brook, USA; Barcelona, Spain, and Auckland, New Zealand. In 2020 and 2021, IWOMP continued the series with technical papers and tutorials presented in a virtual conference setting, due to the SARS-CoV-2 pandemic. Each workshop draws participants from research and development groups and industry throughout the world. After hosting a hybrid event in Chattanooga, TN, USA, we are delighted to resume an in-person IWOMP at University of Bristol, UK. We are grateful for the generous support of sponsors that helps make these meetings successful; they are cited on the conference pages (present and archived) at the IWOMP website.

The evolution of the specification would be impossible without active research in OpenMP compilers, runtime systems, tools, and environments. The many additions in the OpenMP versions 5.0 through 5.2 reflect the contribution by a vibrant and dedicated user, research, and implementation community that is committed to supporting the OpenMP API. As we move beyond the present needs, and adapt and evolve OpenMP to the expanding parallelism in new architectures, the OpenMP research community will continue to play a vital role. The papers in this volume demonstrate the use and evaluation of new features found in the OpenMP API. These papers also demonstrate the forward thinking of the research community, and highlight potential OpenMP directions and further improvements for systems on the horizon.

The IWOMP website (https://www.iwomp.org/) has the latest workshop information, as well as links to archived events. This publication contains the proceedings of the 19th International Workshop on OpenMP, IWOMP 2023. The workshop program included fifteen technical papers, two keynote talks, and tutorials related to the OpenMP API. All technical papers were peer reviewed by at least three different members of the Program Committee. The work evidenced by these authors and the committee demonstrates that the OpenMP API will remain a key technology well into the future.

September 2023

Simon McIntosh-Smith
Michael Klemm
Tom Deakin
Bronis R. de Supinski
Jannis Klinkenberg

Organization

General Chairs

Simon McIntosh-Smith   University of Bristol, UK
Michael Klemm   AMD & OpenMP ARB, Germany

Program Committee Chairs

Bronis R. de Supinski   Lawrence Livermore National Laboratory, USA
Tom Deakin   University of Bristol, UK

Publication Chair

Jannis Klinkenberg   RWTH Aachen University, Germany

Local Arrangements and Registrations Chairs

Tim Lewis   Croftedge Marketing, UK

Steering Committee

Matthias S. Müller (Chair)   RWTH Aachen University, Germany
Eduard Ayguadé   BSC, Universitat Politècnica de Catalunya, Spain
Mark Bull   EPCC, University of Edinburgh, UK
Barbara Chapman   Stony Brook University, USA
Bronis R. de Supinski   Lawrence Livermore National Laboratory, USA
Rudolf Eigenmann   University of Delaware, USA
William Gropp   University of Illinois, USA
Michael Klemm   AMD, Germany
Kalyan Kumaran   Argonne National Laboratory, USA
Simon McIntosh-Smith   University of Bristol, UK
Kent Milfeld   TACC, USA
Stephen L. Olivier   Sandia National Laboratories, USA
Ruud van der Pas   Oracle, USA

Alistair Rendell	Flinders University, Australia
Mitsuhisa Sato	RIKEN Center for Computational Science, Japan
Sanjiv Shah	Intel, USA
Oliver Sinnen	University of Auckland, New Zealand
Josemar Rodrigues de Souza	SENAI Unidade CIMATEC, Brazil
Christian Terboven	RWTH Aachen University, Germany
Matthijs van Waveren	OpenMP ARB & CS Group, France

Program Committee

Eduard Ayguadé	Technical University of Catalunya, Spain
Mark Bull	University of Edinburgh, UK
Ludovic Capelli	EPCC, UK
Sunita Chandrasekaran	University of Delaware, USA
Florina M. Ciorba	University of Basel, Switzerland
Tom Deakin	University of Bristol, UK
Johannes Doerfert	Argonne National Laboratory, USA
Alex Duran	Intel Iberia, Spain
Deepak Eachempati	HPE, USA
Jini George	AMD, USA
Mary Hall	University of Utah, USA
Joachim Jenke	RWTH Aachen University, Germany
Jannis Klinkenberg	RWTH Aachen University, Germany
Michael Kruse	Argonne National Laboratory, USA
Kelvin Li	IBM, USA
Chunhua Liao	Lawrence Livermore National Laboratory, USA
Stephen Olivier	Sandia National Laboratories, USA
Swaroop Pophale	Oak Ridge National Laboratory, USA
Mitsuhisa Sato	RIKEN Center for Computational Science, Japan
Thomas Scogland	Lawrence Livermore National Laboratory, USA
Xavier Teruel	Barcelona Supercomputing Center, Spain

Contents

Beyond Explicit GPU Support

OpenMP Infrastructure and Evaluation

OpenMP and AI

Advising OpenMP Parallelization via A Graph-Based Approach with Transformers

Tal Kadosh[1,2], Nadav Schneider[2,3], Niranjan Hasabnis[4], Timothy Mattson[4], Yuval Pinter[1], and Gal Oren[5,6(✉)]

[1] Computer Science Department, Ben-Gurion University of the Negev, Beersheba, Israel
uvp@cs.bgu.ac.il
[2] Israel Atomic Energy Commission, Tel-Aviv, Israel
{talkad,nadavsch}@post.bgu.ac.il
[3] Electrical & Computer Engineering Department, Ben-Gurion University of the Negev, Beersheba, Israel
[4] Intel Labs, Hillsboro, USA
{niranjan.hasabnis,timothy.g.mattson}@intel.com
[5] Scientific Computing Center, Nuclear Research Center – Negev, Negev, Israel
[6] Computer Science Department, Technion – Israel Institute of Technology, Haifa, Israel
galoren@cs.technion.ac.il

Abstract. There is an ever-present need for shared memory parallelization schemes to exploit the full potential of multi-core architectures. The most common parallelization API addressing this need today is OpenMP. Nevertheless, writing parallel code manually is complex and effort-intensive. Thus, many deterministic source-to-source (S2S) compilers have emerged, intending to automate the process of translating serial to parallel code. However, recent studies have shown that these compilers are impractical in many scenarios. In this work, we combine the latest advancements in the field of AI and natural language processing (NLP) with the vast amount of open-source code to address the problem of automatic parallelization. Specifically, we propose a novel approach, called OMPify, to detect and predict the OpenMP pragmas and shared-memory attributes in parallel code, given its serial version. OMPify is based on a Transformer-based model that leverages a graph-based representation of source code that exploits the inherent structure of code. We evaluated our tool by predicting the parallelization pragmas and attributes of a large corpus of (over 54,000) snippets of serial code written in C and C++ languages (*Open-OMP-Plus*). Our results demonstrate that OMPify outperforms existing approaches — the general-purposed and popular ChatGPT and targeted PragFormer models — in terms of F1 score and accuracy. Specifically, OMPify achieves up to 90% accuracy on commonly-used OpenMP benchmark tests such as NAS, SPEC, and PolyBench. Additionally, we performed an ablation study to assess the impact of different model components and present interesting insights derived from the study. Lastly, we also explored the potential of using data augmentation and curriculum learning techniques to improve the model's robustness and generalization capabilities. The dataset and source code necessary for reproducing our results are available at https://github.com/Scientific-Computing-Lab-NRCN/OMPify.

S. McIntosh-Smith et al. (Eds.): IWOMP 2023, LNCS 14114, pp. 3–17, 2023.
https://doi.org/10.1007/978-3-031-40744-4_1

Keywords: NLP · Code Completion · OpenMP · Shared Memory Parallelism · Transformers · S2S Compilers · Code Representations

1   Introduction

There is an ever-growing need to develop parallel applications these days. The ever-growing demand for computing power is leading to various types of complex architectures, including shared-memory multi-core architectures. A part of the demand arises from the recent HPC as a service (HPCaaS) paradigm that has become widespread and available to a broader community of developers [3]. The services offered as HPCaaS usually depend on the CPU core count and the duration of compute usage. Furthermore, the number of cores per CPU node has increased over the years — for example, from dozens of physical cores available in GCP's C2 family [2] to hundreds of physical cores available in GCP's future C3 family [8].

Despite the growing need to write parallel programs, introducing shared-memory parallelization into code remains challenging due to numerous pitfalls. Besides the fact that parallelizing serial code requires extensive knowledge of the code structure and semantics, it also requires the programmer to avoid parallelization pitfalls, such as the need to synchronize simultaneous reads and writes to the same variables (leading to race conditions), as well as making sure that the workload is distributed evenly across the threads and the system resources (load balancing). In addition, it also requires a high degree of human expertise to comprehend fine details and abstract correlations between variables and different code segments [1]. It is then unsurprising that the number of parallel programming experts is relatively tiny compared to the growing community of users who can benefit from parallel programs.

The complexity of writing parallel programs is partly addressed by source-to-source (S2S) compilers [13–15], which are compilers that translate code from one programming language to another while preserving the code semantics. These compilers analyze the code for data dependencies that could prevent parallelization and automatically insert appropriate parallelization APIs (such as OpenMP *pragmas*) into it. Nevertheless, these compilers have several major drawbacks [22,33,34], such as long execution times and limited robustness to the input, even when optimized on runtime [27]. More importantly, these compilers require manual development and maintenance efforts, for instance, to support a new programming language or a new specification of parallel programming APIs.

Recent advances in deep-learning-based Natural Language Processing (NLP) models, like the Transformer architecture [38], offer potential solutions to the limitations of S2S compilers. These models, known as large language models (LLMs), have been successfully applied in programming-related tasks. For instance, Codex (based on GPT) [12] and Google's ML-enhanced code completion tool [4], demonstrate the ability to generate code from natural language prompts and predict the completion of code fragments, respectively. These technologies, commonly integrated into programming editors and IDEs, show promise in reducing programming efforts.

Although AI-based programmer assistance tools already exist, to our knowledge, PRAGFORMER [21] is the only AI-based programmer assistance tool that can advise programmers in parallel programming. PRAGFORMER uses a Transformer-based architecture to predict if a given serial code could be parallelized (using OpenMP *pragma*) and if a *private* or a *reduction* clause could be applied to it. Specifically, it formulates this problem as multiple binary classification problems, where one problem tackles the need of determining if OpenMP *pragma* could be applied, while the other two tackle the need of determining the need for *private* and *reduction* clauses respectively.

While PRAGFORMER has shown an interesting perspective toward automated parallel programming, in our experiments with PRAGFORMER, we identified several of its limitations. One of its key limitations is the problem formulation; conceptually, if a serial code cannot be parallelized, then there is no need of determining a *private/reduction* clause. As such, we found that these three are not independent problems, and rather formulating the problem as a multi-label classification problem seems much more intuitive. We address this and a few other limitations in PRAGFORMER to propose a new model, named OMPIFY, that improves upon PRAGFORMER on several fronts. Our experimental evaluation on a corpus of 54,000 *for-loops* mined from GitHub revealed that OMPIFY outperforms PRAGFORMER and several state-of-the-art AI models for codes in assisting programmers in parallel programming.

The rest of this article is organized as follows. Section 2 describes related work and provides the necessary background of our work. Section 3 presents the research objectives. Section 4 describes OMPIFY and illustrates our proposed method. Section 5 evaluates our method against previous methods. Finally, Sect. 6 concludes this article and suggests possible extensions of this work.

2   Related Work

Initially, the approaches for translating serial code into parallel heavily relied on rule-based methods, which often had limited capabilities and robustness (Sect. 2.1). However, with the rapid advancement of deep learning techniques in the field of NLP, along with the easy availability of open-source code, there have been some approaches to apply deep learning techniques to source code (Sect. 2.2). These approaches, however, process source code as text (similar to NLP) and fail to fully exploit the potential of other code representations (Sect. 2.3). By incorporating multiple code representations that capture different aspects of source code, multimodal learning techniques can overcome the limitations of these approaches.

2.1   Rule-Based Methods

Several S2S compilers, including Cetus [14] and Par4All [13], have emerged in the last decade or so to insert OpenMP pragmas into code automatically. These tools rely on program analysis-based techniques to analyze and identify potential constraints (e.g., loop-carried dependencies) that may restrict the code from being parallelized. The general workflow of S2S compilers can be summarized as follows:

1. Create an abstract syntax tree (AST) [28], which is a tree representation of the code's syntactic structure. ASTs are constructed using source code parsers, such as *ANother Tool for Language Recognition* (ANTLR) [31] or *pycparser* [11], etc.
2. Apply data dependence algorithms [17] to ASTs.
3. Produce appropriate OpenMP directives based on the data dependence graph.

There are multiple drawbacks associated with the approach of generating ASTs and applying data dependence algorithms. Firstly, creating an AST with a parser can be a challenging task with limited robustness to input due to each programming language's unique syntactic structures that have evolved over the years. Thus, many S2S compilers cannot handle the diverse syntax of programming languages. Moreover, not all parsers are publicly available. As a result, some S2S compilers may fail to produce an AST and analyze the input code. Secondly, data-dependence algorithms can be time-consuming, particularly for large-scale code, since these algorithms are strongly dependent on the size of the AST, which in turn is influenced by the length of the code. Additionally, the static analysis, including the analysis of C/C++ pointers, array sections, virtual function calls, and other related factors, is inherently limited. Studies by Harel et al. [22] and Prema et al. [33] have demonstrated that S2S compilers may produce sub-optimal results and even degrade program performance in certain cases. Therefore, it is crucial to consider this major limitation in the application of data dependence algorithms.

2.2   Unimodal Machine-Learning Driven Methods

Rule-based methods also suffer from another important limitation – tools relying on these methods require manual programming efforts to add new rules to maintain and update them. However, recent AI-based programming assistance tools have demonstrated that it is possible to reduce manual effort by instead learning the rules from data. Specifically, with the powerful computing devices and vast availability of open-source code as data, these AI-based tools can learn programming rules such as syntax, typing rules [23], etc. Continuing this trend, in recent years, several Transformer-based models have been proposed for various programming-related tasks [19,29]. Typically, these models are pre-trained on massive code corpora containing multiple programming languages (PLs) and then applied to various programming problems [30], such as program completion, code search, bug finding, etc., as downstream tasks. One of the common pre-training tasks is masked language modeling (MLM) [16].

Previous work by Harel et al. [21] showed the possibility of applying Attention-based models (Transformer) to determine if code can be parallelized with OpenMP. In their work, they introduced PRAGFORMER, which is a transformer model based on DeepSCC [40], which itself is a *RoBERTa* model finetuned on a corpus of 225k code snippets written in 21 programming languages (such as Java, Python, C, and C++) collected from Stack Overflow.

In the parlance of AI-based models, PRAGFORMER formulates the parallel programming assistance problem as *Code Language Processing for Parallelization (CLPP)* task. Specifically, it breaks this task down into three sub-problems: given a serial code (*for-loop*), determine (1) if it can be parallelized (using OpenMP *pragma*), (2) if *private* clause (specifying a variable to be private to each thread in a parallel region) would be applicable to OpenMP *pragma*, and (3) if *reduction* clause (specifying an operator and a variable to reduce across all threads in a parallel region) would be applicable to OpenMP *pragma*. It then approaches these three sub-problems independently and formulates them as three separate binary classification problems.

Although PRAGFORMER shows great potential in using Transformer architecture to solve the shared-memory parallelization task, it still suffers from several deficiencies. Primarily, PRAGFORMER is based on *RoBERTa*, which is essentially a model for Natural Language (NL) understanding. Applying an NL model to a code-related task is sub-optimal compared to models pre-trained directly on code [30]. Additionally, PRAGFORMER regards source code as a sequence of tokens, ignoring the inherent structure of the code. Intuitively, structural information of code, such as variable dependence information, etc., should provide crucial code semantic information that could improve the code understanding process. Furthermore, the approach of separating the classifications is unintuitive since the tasks of predicting the need for OpenMP *pragmas* and data-sharing attribute clauses are highly correlated — there will not be a private or reduction clause if there is no need for OpenMP *pragma* at all.

2.3 Multimodal Machine-Learning Driven Methods

While the unimodal ML methods accept source code in only one representation (most commonly as a sequence of tokens), multimodal ML methods realize that other code representations may offer richer semantic information that could improve the accuracy of the models on programming-related tasks. Specifically, multimodel ML models also accept source code in other representations such as AST, control-flow graph (CFG), data-flow graph (DFG), etc. Consequently, many pre-trained machine learning models have been developed, with each model incorporating different code formats into the training process.

Feng et al. introduced CODEBERT [18], a bimodal Transformer model trained on programming languages and natural languages. They compared CODEBERT trained on samples from both representations, CODEBERT trained only on code, and ROBERTA, using the *CodeSearchNet* dataset [25]. Their results demonstrated the superior performance of CODEBERT trained on both language types for various programming-related tasks. Guo et al. developed GRAPHCODEBERT [19], a multimodal Transformer model trained on the *CodeSearchNet* dataset, incorporating input programs as natural language text, pro-

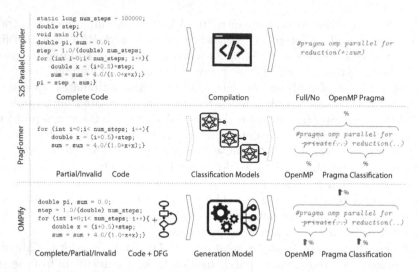

Fig. 1. Differences between S2S compilers, PRAGFORMER and OMPIFY.

gramming languages, and DFG. They showed that incorporating DFG improves code understanding compared to CODEBERT. Niu et al. proposed SPT-CODE [29], another multimodal model trained on natural language, programming language, and AST from the *CodeSearchNet* dataset. While CODEBERT and GRAPHCODEBERT utilize Transformer encoders, SPT-CODE employs a Transformer encoder-decoder architecture. Experimental results demonstrated the superior performance of SPT-CODE in code generation tasks.

Drawing inspiration from some of the design choices of multimodal models, we have designed the OMPIFY model also as a multimodal model. Figure 1 summarizes the difference between OMPIFY and related works.

3   Research Objectives

This paper draws inspiration from PRAGFORMER and approaches the parallel programming assistance problem as a *Code Language Processing for Parallelization (CLPP)* task. Nevertheless, we improve upon PRAGFORMER by posing the following research questions that are designed to evaluate the limitations of PRAGFORMER discussed earlier in Related Work (Sect. 2.2).

RQ1: *Which code representations impact the CLPP task?*

Given the discussion of different code representations, this question focuses on assessing the influence of various code modalities on code comprehension, particularly in CLPP tasks. We will evaluate the effectiveness of the previously mentioned multimodal models on our dataset.

RQ2: *Does the scope of the for-loop from input serial code matter for performance on CLPP task?*

Conceptually, the semantics of a *for-loop* from serial code heavily relies on its *context*. This question assesses the impact of different context lengths on the performance of various multimodal models on CLPP tasks.

RQ3: *Can code augmentation improve model's performance on CLPP task?*

We will investigate the potential of code augmentation techniques, specifically variable name replacement, to improve the performance of existing models on CLPP tasks.

RQ4: *Will multi-label classification based formulation for solving CLPP task perform better than* PRAGFORMER*'s multiple binary-classification based formulation?*

While PRAGFORMER employed three binary classification-based models to predict the requirement for an OpenMP *pragma* and whether it should include a work-sharing construct, we hypothesize that these predictions are interdependent and potentially benefit each other. We evaluate this hypothesis by formulating a multi-label classification problem and developing a single generative model for the CLPP task. We then compare our model against PRAGFORMER and other state-of-the-art multimodel models.

4   OMPify

This section describes the model architecture, its input, the code representations, and the fine-tuning process. OMPIFY predicts the need for both OpenMP *pragma* and shared-memory attributes (*private* and *reduction*) simultaneously, allowing the model to learn inter-dependencies between these tasks.

4.1   Model

OMPIFY (Fig. 2) is a Transformer-based, multimodal model that utilizes a graph-based representation of source code. OMPIFY is based on GRAPHCODE-BERT [19], a pre-trained model for programming languages that considers the inherent structure of the code by accepting source code along with its DFG. OMPIFY is composed of GRAPHCODEBERT and a fully connected layer. This architecture allows OMPIFY to perform multi-label classification, where each task is individually classified.

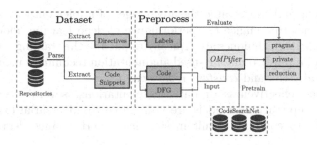

Fig. 2. Overview of OMPIFY training process.

4.2   Model Input

The model's inputs are two code modalities: the actual source code as a sequence of tokens and the serialized DFG.

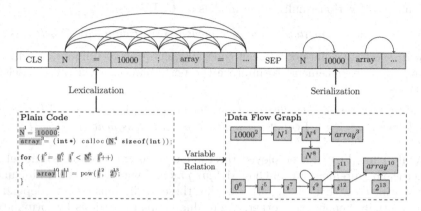

Fig. 3. The input format for a C code snippet.

- **Code Tokens.** As shown in Fig. 3, the first part of the input to OMPIFY consists of a sequence of code tokens. To generate a sequence of token IDs from code, we utilized the tokenizer provided by GRAPHCODEBERT.
- **Serialized DFG.** The second part of the input, which is the serialized DFG, is created by converting the code into an AST using TreeSitter parser[1]. We extract variables and their data dependence relationships from an AST to generate a DFG. The DFG nodes are serialized in the program ordered and serve as the model input.
- **Attention Mask.** Figure 3 provides an overview of the token connections, showcasing the interconnections between the tokens. Whereas the code tokens attend to each other during the self-attention mechanism [37], when dealing with DFG, we aim to disregard attention between variables that are not connected. To achieve this, we employed the masked attention approach described by Guo et al. [19].

4.3   Fine Tuning

Many studies have demonstrated the advantages of implementing data augmentation techniques to enhance the performance of deep learning models [36,39]. Data augmentation techniques are typically applied to the training set to increase the diversity of input. Commonly-used augmentation techniques include *variable renaming, dead store,* and *constant replacement.*

Despite the effectiveness of data augmentations, several studies [24,35] showed that deep learning models are vulnerable to adversarial examples, i.e., minor changes to code can result in significant performance degradation. To

---

[1] https://github.com/tree-sitter/tree-sitter.

address this issue, as many studies have suggested [20, 32, 39] leveraging a curriculum learning (CL) technique that involves the gradual introduction of data augmentation techniques. Specifically, we applied *variable renaming* as a data augmentation technique. We followed a gradual approach, starting with the original data without any augmentation during the first epoch. In each subsequent epoch, we augmented the original data by progressively increasing the proportion of renamed variables. Specifically, we applied a variable renaming strategy that gradually increased over epochs. In the second epoch, we renamed 10% of the variables per sample. This percentage increased to 20% in the third epoch, 30% in the fourth epoch, and 40% from the fifth epoch onwards.

5   Experimental Results

To evaluate the effectiveness of our proposed model, OMPIFY, we conducted several experiments to answer our research questions. All experiments were conducted on an NVIDIA A100 40 GB GPU. Furthermore, for the sake of consistency, we utilized the original implementations of the models as presented in their respective papers.

5.1   Dataset & Preprocessing

In our work, we developed a novel dataset, named *Open-OMP-Plus*, comprising more than 54,000 code snippets from C and C++ for OpenMP analysis (Table 1). The dataset was collected from https://github.com using the *github-clone-all*[2] script, which enables searching for repositories that satisfy specific criteria. We used this tool to locate all repositories that include C or C++ files and also feature the term "OpenMP" in their title, description, or README.

To minimize the noise in our dataset, we employed inclusion and exclusion criteria inspired by Harel et al. [21]. Specifically, we included only C/C++ files that contained OpenMP *pragmas* in their code. This criteria operates on the assumption that the developers were aware of OpenMP parallelization and that any non-parallelized loops intentionally have not been parallelized. We excluded duplicates, empty loops, and loops that used *barrier, critical,* or *atomic pragmas,* which can be bottlenecks on code execution and are not optimal samples.

Table 1. The distribution of each class for each programming language.

Description	C	C++
With OpenMP	14,906	8,241
Without OpenMP	17,193	14,323
Total	32,099	22,564

(a) Number of loops paralleled with OpenMP for each programming language.

Clauses	Amount
private	6,758
reduction	3,267
Total	10,025

(b) Number of common OpenMP shared memory attributes.

# Lines	Amount
< 15	40,745
16-50	10,607
> 50	3,311

(c) Code snippet length in *Open-OMP-Plus.*

---

[2] http://github.com/rhysd/github-clone-all.

Once we identified files that contained OpenMP pragmas, we parsed them using *pycparser* [11] parser, which converts the code into an AST format. Each sample in the dataset comprises several fields, such as the plain *for-loop* code, its corresponding *pragma* (if any), the AST of the *for-loop*, the AST of the functions called within the *for-loop*, the declaration of each variable used in the *for-loop*, all the assignment instructions from the context of the loop that involves each of the variables used in the loop, and the DFG of the *for-loop* and its extended scope. By analyzing the AST, we can extract code structures such as loops and identify the relevant functions and variables from its outer scope.

To evaluate the performance of our model, we divided the dataset into three sets: train, validation, and test, using standard 80-10-10 split. Additionally, we collected three benchmarks that were known to use OpenMP correctly, namely NAS [10], PolyBench [6], and SPEC [7], and used them to further test our model. To avoid fair evaluation, we removed from the training set any samples that could be found in the benchmarks.

5.2 Results

We now present the results of our experiments to answer the research questions. Note that the abbreviations used in this section represent specific metrics: **P** for Precision, **R** for Recall, and **Acc** for Accuracy.

RQ1: Code Modalities. To compare the various code modalities, we utilized three distinct models. CODEBERT was pre-trained on natural language (NL) and programming language (PL), SPT-CODE was pre-trained on PL and AST, and GRAPHCODEBERT was pre-trained on PL and DFG. To apply these models to *pragma classification* task, we added a fully connected layer of size two and a SoftMax layer at the end of these mod-

Table 2. Effect of different code modalities on the task of *pragma classification*.

Model Name	Metrics		
	P	R	Acc
PragFormer	0.826	0.780	0.830
CodeBERT	**0.848**	0.813	0.852
SPT-Code	0.812	0.784	0.831
SPT-Code (w/o AST)	0.792	0.786	0.820
GraphCodeBERT	0.836	**0.835**	**0.862**
GraphCodeBERT (w/o DFG)	0.834	0.833	0.861

els and fine-tuned them using our corpus, *Open-OMP-Plus*. Additionally, during the fine-tuning process, we trained SPT-CODE and GRAPHCODEBERT using two different settings: one with code alone and another with enhanced input that included code along with AST and DFG, respectively. Based on the results presented in Table 2, it can be inferred that the use of multimodal models, which combine code representations such as AST or DFG with the original code, has a positive impact on the performance of the model in the *pragma classification* task. However, despite being trained on the same dataset, i.e., *CodeSearchNet*, CODEBERT, SPT-CODE, and GRAPHCODEBERT achieved significantly different performance, with GRAPHCODEBERT outperforming others. This indicates that the DFG representation and pretraining tasks proposed by Guo et al. [19] were more beneficial this task. It is worth noting that while the use of AST in SPT-CODE improves performance compared to using only the code, the DFG in GRAPHCODEBERT has only a minimal impact on performance. This could be due to the DFG representation's inability to effectively capture the relationship between arrays and their indexing. As shown in Fig. 3, there is no direct connection between the array and the index variable i^{11}. In scientific codes, the relationship between the array and the index is often critical as it determines the feasibility of parallelization.

RQ2: Extended Scope. In this experiment, we aimed to investigate the impact of extended scope on the performance of OMPIFY in solving the CLPP task. To achieve this, we trained OMPIFY on two distinct corpora: one comprising only the *for-loop* structured block, and the other consisting of the extended version that includes the surrounding scope of the *for-loop*, incorporating assignments to variables used within the loop (Fig. 4). The results, as presented in Table 5, demonstrate the effect of including the outside scope in determining the necessity of OpenMP *pragma*. The observed increase in recall indicates that the model exhibits improved identification of *for-loops* requiring OpenMP *pragma*, resulting in fewer false negatives. This finding suggests that considering the outside scope provides valuable information for accurately identifying the need for *pragma* in *for-loops*.

Table 3. Effect of *context*.

Data Type	P	R	Acc
No Scope	**0.833**	0.831	0.860
With Scope	0.829	**0.844**	**0.863**

Fig. 4. Code length comparison.

RQ3: Data Augmentation. Through evaluating the impact of data augmentation techniques on performance, we investigated the effectiveness of PRAGFORMER and GRAPH-CODEBERT in the binary classification task of OpenMP *pragma* classification. The results of this experiment are presented in Table 4. We employed the *variable renaming* augmentation, where each variable was replaced with *var*, concatenated with a random index number. This augmentation is referred as *replaced* in the table. The

Table 4. Effect of data augmentation techniques.

Model	Augmen-tation	Metrics		
		P	R	Acc
PragFormer	original	0.793	**0.847**	0.841
	curriculum	0.825	0.815	0.848
	replaced	0.727	0.826	0.794
GraphCode-BERT	original	**0.851**	0.841	0.870
	curriculum	0.849	0.846	**0.872**
	replaced	0.838	0.781	0.843

results reveal the vulnerability of these models to adversarial examples created by fully replacing variable names, leading to degraded performance compared to the unmodified variables. However, by gradually introducing code augmentations using the curriculum learning method (referred as *curriculum* in the table), we observed improved accuracy.

RQ4: Multi-label Classification. Table 5 shows the results of PRAGFORMER, GRAPH-CODEBERT, and OMPIFY when applied to all the three tasks of *pragma* classification, classification of *private* clause, and *reduction* clause. Note that OMPIFY approaches all three tasks together as a multi-label classification problem, while PRAGFORMER approach each task independently. In the table, we present the result of OMPIFY for the combined task but split the results according to labels. The results

Table 5. Effect of multi-label classification problem formulation.

Model	Task	Metrics		
		P	R	Acc
PragFormer	*pragma*	0.793	0.847	0.841
	private	0.716	0.663	0.924
	reduction	0.632	0.598	0.953
GraphCode-BERT (Separated)	*pragma*	**0.850**	0.841	0.870
	private	**0.768**	0.684	0.937
	reduction	**0.690**	0.688	0.963
OMPify	*pragma*	0.849	**0.848**	**0.872**
	private	0.755	**0.689**	0.938
	reduction	**0.690**	**0.700**	**0.966**

convey that OMPIFY achieves significantly better performance compared to PRAGFORMER, with an improvement of 3.1% in *pragma* classification, underscoring the hypothesis that these three tasks are not independent. In addition, our model slightly outperforms the GRAPHCODEBERT model. The results show a significant improvement in recall for OMPIFY for all three tasks, with a major decrease in the number of false negative predictions. In our context, a false negative prediction means that a sample is incorrectly classified as not requiring *pragma*, *private*, or *reduction*. Therefore, the unified prediction strategy of OMPIFY can better identify samples that require *pragma*, *private*, or *reduction*. This suggests that the understanding of each task contributes to the overall prediction. For instance, if OMPIFY predicts the need for *pragma*, it will also influence the prediction of shared-memory attributes, which may also appear in the *pragma*.

Real-World Benchmarks. In order to test the performance of OMPIFY on real-world programs, we obtained C/C++ programs that were using OpenMP *pragma* from three scientific code benchmarks, namely, NAS, SPEC, and PolyBench. Table 6 shows the statistics of the collected programs. These benchmarks are manually-written as parallel programs using OpenMP, so they serve as a good test case for OMPIFY. As a comparison, we applied PRAGFORMER to the same test. Our model exhibited a significant increase in performance when compared to PRAG-FORMER (Table 7).

Moreover, given the recent popularity of ChatGPT [9] in programming-related tasks, we decided to evaluate it

Table 6. Benchmark statistics

Bench-mark	With OMP	Without OMP	priv-ate	reduc-tion
NAS	166	146	12	2
PolyBench	63	85	36	0
SPEC	157	1,000	1	0

Table 7. Comparison on different benchmarks.

Bench-mark	Model	Metrics		
		P	R	Acc
SPEC	PRAGFORMER	0.445	0.802	0.837
	OMPIFY	**0.572**	**0.854**	**0.894**
PolyBench	PRAGFORMER	0.703	0.301	0.648
	OMPIFY	**0.836**	**0.810**	**0.851**
NAS	PRAGFORMER	0.635	0.734	0.634
	OMPIFY	**0.731**	**0.886**	**0.766**
2500 examples	ChatGPT	0.401	**0.913**	0.401
	PRAGFORMER	0.815	0.721	0.817
	OMPIFY	**0.839**	0.818	**0.860**

on our CLPP task. For this evaluation, we randomly sampled 2500 test inputs from our test dataset. We then fed those test programs to ChatGPT (based on GPT-3.5) one by one and then used the prompt *"Generate the optimal OpenMP pragma if possible"* to check if ChatGPT's response matches with the expected label for the test program. Although ChatGPT performs well on various NLP tasks, it performed poorly in our specific task, often suggesting the use of OpenMP *pragma* even when it was not applicable.

6   Conclusions and Future Work

This paper aims to investigate the potential of multimodal models in accurately predicting the need for shared-memory parallelization in code. Our research discovered that incorporating additional code representations, such as ASTs and DFGs, significantly improves their performance compared to models that rely solely on the original code. Building upon this knowledge, we introduced a novel model called OMPIFY, based on GRAPHCODEBERT. OMPIFY takes advantage of the inter-dependencies between the task of predicting the need for parallelization and the prediction of shared-memory attributes, such as *private* and *reduction* variables. By leveraging these relationships, OMPIFY demonstrates enhanced accuracy and robustness in determining the need for shared-memory parallelization. In addition to developing the OMPIFY model, we also constructed a comprehensive database called *Open-OMP-Plus*. This database includes the *for-loop* itself and extends its scope to include assignment statements of variables found within the *for-loop*. By incorporating this extended scope, we demonstrate that OMPIFY can effectively utilize this additional information to improve its predictions further.

For future research, we aim to address several areas of improvement. Firstly, since the multimodal models analyzed in RQ1 were not pre-trained on C/C++ programming languages, there is a potential for enhancing their performance by pretraining them on datasets that include C/C++ code. This approach can contribute to better code understanding and comprehension. Additionally, in RQ4, we observed improvements in multi-label prediction. To further enhance this aspect, we intend to explore the conversion of the multi-label prediction problem into *pragma* generation. By generating *pragma*s directly, we can achieve more precise and fine-grained control over parallelization tasks. Furthermore, an important question arises regarding the correctness of the generated *pragma*s. To address this concern, we plan to investigate techniques and approaches for evaluating the accuracy and correctness of the generated *pragma*s.

Acknowledgments. This research was supported by the Israeli Council for Higher Education (CHE) via the Data Science Research Center, Ben-Gurion University of the Negev, Israel; Intel Corporation (oneAPI CoE program); and the Lynn and William Frankel Center for Computer Science. Computational support was provided by the NegevHPC project [5] and Intel Developer Cloud [26]. The authors thank Re'em Harel, Israel Hen, and Gabi Dadush for their help and support.

References

1. Automatic Parallelism and Data Dependency. https://web.archive.org/web/20140714111836/http://blitzprog.org/posts/automatic-parallelism-and-data-dependency
2. Compute-optimized machine family. https://cloud.google.com/compute/docs/compute-optimized-machines
3. High performance computing as a service market forecast. https://www.alliedmarketresearch.com/high-performance-computing-as-a-service-market
4. Ml-enhanced code completion improves developer productivity. https://ai.googleblog.com/2022/07/ml-enhanced-code-completion-improves.html
5. NegevHPC Project. https://www.negevhpc.com
6. PolyBench Benchmarks. https://web.cse.ohio-state.edu/pouchet.2/software/polybench/
7. SPEC-OMP2012 website. https://www.spec.org/omp2012/
8. The next wave of Google Cloud infrastructure innovation: New C3 VM and Hyperdisk. https://cloud.google.com/blog/products/compute/introducing-c3-machines-with-googles-custom-intel-ipu
9. ChatGPT. https://chat.openai.com/ (2023)
10. Bailey, D.H., et al.: The NAS parallel benchmarks. Int. J. Supercomput. Appl. **5**(3), 63–73 (1991)
11. Bendersky, E., et al.: Pycparser (2010)
12. Chen, M., et al.: Evaluating large language models trained on code. arXiv preprint arXiv:2107.03374 (2021)
13. Creusillet, B., et al.: Par4all: Auto-parallelizing C and Fortran for the CUDA architecture (2009)
14. Dave, C., et al.: Cetus: a source-to-source compiler infrastructure for multicores. Computer **42**(12), 36–42 (2009)
15. Dever, M.: AutoPar: automating the parallelization of functional programs, Ph.D. thesis, Dublin City University (2015)
16. Devlin, J., et al.: BERT: pre-training of deep bidirectional transformers for language understanding. In: Proceedings of the 2019 Conference of the North American Chapter of the Association for Computational Linguistics: Human Language Technologies, Volume 1 (Long and Short Papers), pp. 4171–4186. Association for Computational Linguistics, Minneapolis, Minnesota (2019). https://doi.org/10.18653/v1/N19-1423. https://aclanthology.org/N19-1423
17. Fagin, R., et al.: The theory of data dependencies: a survey. IBM Thomas J. Watson Research Division (1984)
18. Feng, Z., et al.: CodeBERT: a pre-trained model for programming and natural languages. arXiv preprint arXiv:2002.08155 (2020)
19. Guo, D., et al.: GraphcodeBERT: pre-training code representations with data flow. arXiv preprint arXiv:2009.08366 (2020)
20. Guo, S., et al.: CurriculumNet: weakly supervised learning from large-scale web images. In: Ferrari, V., Hebert, M., Sminchisescu, C., Weiss, Y. (eds.) ECCV 2018. LNCS, vol. 11214, pp. 139–154. Springer, Cham (2018). https://doi.org/10.1007/978-3-030-01249-6_9
21. Harel, R., et al.: Learning to parallelize in a shared-memory environment with transformers. In: Proceedings of the 28th ACM SIGPLAN Annual Symposium on Principles and Practice of Parallel Programming, pp. 450–452 (2023)

22. Harel, R., et al.: Source-to-source parallelization compilers for scientific shared-memory multi-core and accelerated multiprocessing: analysis, pitfalls, enhancement and potential. Int. J. Parallel Prog. **48**(1), 1–31 (2020)
23. Hasabnis, N., et al.: ControlFlag: a self-supervised idiosyncratic pattern detection system for software control structures. In: Proceedings of the 5th ACM SIGPLAN International Symposium on Machine Programming, pp. 32–42. MAPS 2021, Association for Computing Machinery, New York, NY, USA (2021). https://doi.org/10.1145/3460945.3464954
24. Henke, J., et al.: Semantic robustness of models of source code. In: 2022 IEEE International Conference on Software Analysis, Evolution and Reengineering (SANER), pp. 526–537. IEEE (2022)
25. Husain, H., et al.: CodeSearchNet challenge: evaluating the state of semantic code search. arXiv preprint arXiv:1909.09436 (2019)
26. Intel: Intel Developer Cloud. https://www.intel.com/content/www/us/en/developer/tools/devcloud/overview.html (2023)
27. Mosseri, I., Alon, L.-O., Harel, R.E., Oren, G.: ComPar: optimized multi-compiler for automatic openMP S2S parallelization. In: Milfeld, K., de Supinski, B.R., Koesterke, L., Klinkenberg, J. (eds.) IWOMP 2020. LNCS, vol. 12295, pp. 247–262. Springer, Cham (2020). https://doi.org/10.1007/978-3-030-58144-2_16
28. Neamtiu, I., et al.: Understanding source code evolution using abstract syntax tree matching. ACM SIGSOFT Softw. Eng. Notes **30**(4), 1–5 (2005)
29. Niu, C., et al.: SPT-Code: Sequence-to-sequence pre-training for learning the representation of source code. arXiv preprint arXiv:2201.01549 (2022)
30. Niu, C., et al.: An empirical comparison of pre-trained models of source code. arXiv preprint arXiv:2302.04026 (2023)
31. Parr, T.: The definitive ANTLR 4 reference. Pragmatic Bookshelf (2013)
32. Platanios, E.A., et al.: Competence-based curriculum learning for neural machine translation. arXiv preprint arXiv:1903.09848 (2019)
33. Prema, S., et al.: Identifying pitfalls in automatic parallelization of NAS parallel benchmarks. In: 2017 National Conference on Parallel Computing Technologies (PARCOMPTECH), pp. 1–6. IEEE (2017)
34. Prema, S., et al.: A study on popular auto-parallelization frameworks. Concurr. Comput. Pract. Exper. **31**(17), e5168 (2019)
35. Quiring, E., et al.: Misleading authorship attribution of source code using adversarial learning. In: USENIX Security Symposium, pp. 479–496 (2019)
36. Rebuffi, S.A., et al.: Data augmentation can improve robustness. Adv. Neural. Inf. Process. Syst. **34**, 29935–29948 (2021)
37. Vaswani, A., et al.: Attention is all you need. CoRR abs/1706.03762 (2017). http://arxiv.org/abs/1706.03762
38. Vaswani, A., et al.: Attention is all you need. Advances in Neural Information Processing Systems 30 (2017)
39. Wang, D., et al.: Bridging pre-trained models and downstream tasks for source code understanding. In: Proceedings of the 44th International Conference on Software Engineering, pp. 287–298 (2022)
40. Yang, G., Zhou, Y., Yu, C., Chen, X.: DeepSCC: source code classification based on fine-tuned roBERTa. CoRR abs/2110.00914 (2021). https://arxiv.org/abs/2110.00914

LM4HPC: Towards Effective Language Model Application in High-Performance Computing

Le Chen[1,2], Pei-Hung Lin[1], Tristan Vanderbruggen[1], Chunhua Liao[1(✉)],
Murali Emani[3], and Bronis de Supinski[1]

[1] Lawrence Livermore National Laboratory, Livermore, CA 94550, USA
liao6@llnl.gov
[2] Iowa State University, Ames, IA 50010, USA
[3] Argonne National Laboratory, Lemont, IL 60439, USA

Abstract. In recent years, language models (LMs), such as GPT-4, have been widely used in multiple domains, including natural language processing, visualization, and so on. However, applying them for analyzing and optimizing high-performance computing (HPC) software is still challenging due to the lack of HPC-specific support. In this paper, we design the LM4HPC framework to facilitate the research and development of HPC software analyses and optimizations using LMs. Tailored for supporting HPC datasets, AI models, and pipelines, our framework is built on top of a range of components from different levels of the machine learning software stack, with Hugging Face-compatible APIs. Using three representative tasks, we evaluated the prototype of our framework. The results show that LM4HPC can help users quickly evaluate a set of state-of-the-art models and generate insightful leaderboards.

Keywords: Language model · Programming language processing · High-performance computing

1 Introduction

Language models (LMs) are models designed to understand and generate human language. In recent years, large language models (LLMs) trained on large amounts of text data have demonstrated stunning capabilities in various natural language processing and visualization tasks. They have also been widely used to process programming languages due to the similarities between natural languages and programming languages. For example, GPT-4 [1] shows early signs of artificial general intelligence. Based on a large language model trained on code [2], GitHub provides an AI assistant for developing software.

Given the rise of LLMs, it is natural for researchers and developers in the high-performance computing community to start exploiting LMs for addressing various challenges in HPC, including code analysis, code generation, performance optimization, question answering, and so on. However, mainstream frameworks

S. McIntosh-Smith et al. (Eds.): IWOMP 2023, LNCS 14114, pp. 18–33, 2023.
https://doi.org/10.1007/978-3-031-40744-4_2

of LMs were originally designed to serve natural language processing. It is difficult for newcomers in HPC to quickly access HPC-specific datasets, models, and pipelines. For example, the current popular Hugging Face platform does not include dedicated pipelines for software analyses and optimizations. Another challenge is the entire field is evolving quickly, with new techniques emerging almost weekly, making it challenging for HPC users to keep up with the latest techniques and find relevant ones. Last but not least, there is a lack of standard, reproducible evaluation processes for LMs focusing on HPC-specific tasks. Therefore, it is difficult to have a fair comparison among different models for a given HPC task.

In this paper, we propose a framework (named LM4HPC) designed to serve HPC users as first-class citizens by including internal components and external APIs relevant to HPC-specific tasks. LM4HPC's components include models, datasets, pipelines, and so on, while the APIs allow users to interact with these components to finish given HPC tasks. We highlight the contributions of our work as follows:

- We design an extensible framework for including and exposing relevant machine learning components to facilitate the adoption of large language models for HPC-specific tasks.
- The framework provides a set of APIs to facilitate essential operations, including code preprocessing, tokenization, integration with new data, and evaluation.
- A set of pipelines have been developed to support common HPC tasks, including code similarity analysis, parallelism detection, question answering, and so on.
- We provide HPC-specific datasets such as DRB-ML, OMP4Par, and OMPQA to support various HPC pipelines.
- Our work introduces standardized workflows and metrics to enable fair and reproducible evaluation of LLMs for HPC-specific tasks.
- Using three representative tasks, we demonstrated how the framework can be used to test a set of language models and generate leaderboards.

2   Background

Language models (LMs) are machine learning models designed to comprehend and generate human language. They can be used to facilitate natural and intuitive interactions between humans and machines. Early generations of LMs, using recurrent neural networks (RNNs), showed inspiring results for various natural language processing (NLP) tasks. A transformative evolution by the Transformer [3] reveals remarkable potentials of LMs. Introduced by Vaswani *et al.*, transformer models utilize the attention mechanism to capture the dependencies between all words in an input sentence, irrespective of their positions. Compared to RNNs, transformers process data in parallel rather than sequentially and significantly improve the efficiency of model training and inference. Transformers further enables the inauguration of the large language models (LLMs). Compared to LMs, LLMs are trained on a vast amount of data and possess parameter counts on the order of billions or more, allowing them to generate more detailed and nuanced responses. Examples of LLMs include OpenAI's GPT-3, GPT-4 and Google's BARD. Nowadays, LLMs have shown remarkable capabilities in NLP tasks like translation, question answering, and text generation.

Table 1. Language models, associated training data and tasks

Model			Training data		Token Limit	Avail.
Name	Released	Size	Type	Size		
BERT	2018/10	340M	Text	3.5B words	512	Weights
CodeBERT	2020/11	125M	Mixed	2.1M(bimodal) 6.4M (unimodal)	512	Weights
Megatron	2021/04	1T	Text	174 GB	512	Weights
GraphCodeBERT	2021/05	110M	Code	2.3M functions	512	Weights
CodeT5	2021/11	770M	Code	8.35M instances	512	Weights
GPT-3	2022/03/15	175B	Mixed	500B tokens	4096	Weights
LLaMA	2023/02/24	7–65B	Mixed	1.4T tokens	4096	Weights*
GPT-4	2023/03/14	1T	Mixed	undisclosed	8k/32k	API*
BARD	2023/03/21	1.6B	Mixed	1.56T words	1000	API
Cerebras-GPT	2023/03/28	0.11–13B	Text	800 GB	2048	Weights
Dolly 2.0	2023/04/12	3–12B	Text	15k instr./resp	2048	Weights
StarCoder	2023/05/4	15B	Code	1T tokens	8192	Weights
StarChat-Alpha	2023/05/4	16B	Code	31k instr./resp	8192	Weights

Table 1 shows some example language models and their release dates, sizes, training data, input token length limits, and availability. LLaMA [4]'s weights can be obtained after filling out some form. GPT-4 has a waiting list to use its API. At the time of writing this paper, we have not yet obtained its access.

LMs are trained mainly by text data with a focus on NLP. The sources of the training data mainly come from books, web content, newspapers, scientific articles, and other text data in various natural languages. Latest LLMs have demonstrated rich skill sets in NLP including text prediction, common sense reasoning, reading comprehension, translation and question answering.

There has been a keen interest in deploying NLP techniques to programming language processing (PLP) tasks, such as code summarization, code generation, and code similarity analysis [5,6]. Previous studies have demonstrated successful applications of traditional language models to PLP tasks, showing the feasibility of this approach [7]. CodeBERT [8], for example, is a transformer-based model trained with a diverse range of programming languages and can be used for a variety of programming-related tasks. Similarly, CodeT5 [9] is a variant of Google's T5 language model, trained specifically on code datasets to perform advanced programming tasks like code completion, bug detection, and code summarization. Lately, StarCoder [10], a 15B parameter model trained with 1 trillion tokens sourced from a large collection of permissively licensed GitHub repositories, is developed to be a Large Language Model mainly for code generation or completion. StarChat-Alpha is a GPT-like chat model fine-tuned from StarCoder to act as a helpful coding assistant.

2.1 LMs for HPC

With the recent breakthroughs in Generative Pretrained Transformer (GPT) large language models [11], it has become increasingly intriguing to explore the application of large language models (LLMs) for HPC tasks. However, their deployment in the HPC domain is still relatively unexplored. This venture comes with various challenges, including:

1. Pipelines: Traditional language model frameworks like Hugging Face were designed to support natural language processing or compute vision problems. Expanding LMs to any new domain, including HPC, requires the addition of new pipelines designed to finish domain-specific tasks.
2. Datasets: The HPC domain encompasses an extensive amount of code spanning various fields, including biology and climate modeling. However, preparing this data for machine learning training, such as labeling parallelizable loops in HPC programs for parallelism detection, presents significant challenges. The scarcity of ready-to-use, pre-labeled HPC datasets poses a particular obstacle for training language models, especially large ones, highlighting the need for more shared resources in the community.
3. Pre-processing: Pre-processing in the context of LMs for HPC typically involves the conversion of source files into a sequence of tokens. However, the direct application of NLP tokenizers to code can be sub-optimal. For instance, an NLP tokenizer might split a variable name into two tokens, a scenario that is not desirable for PLP analysis. Also, models designed for processing source code may use graph representations, such as abstract syntax trees, to have better performance.
4. Input size limit: Language models often have limited input token lengths (such as 512 to a few thousand of tokens). HPC tasks often involve processing large-scale software packages with millions of lines of source code.
5. Evaluation: There is a pressing need for standardized and reproducible evaluation of different models in the context of various HPC tasks, using metrics suitable for domain-specific requirements.

3 Approach

To address the challenges discussed in Sect. 2, we introduce LM4HPC, a comprehensive framework that encapsulates a suite of machine learning components within user-friendly APIs. This framework is tailored for HPC users, simplifying the implementation process and making the robust capabilities of language models more accessible and user-friendly within the HPC community. The primary goal of LM4HPC is to reduce the complexities inherent in employing language models, thus enabling HPC users to leverage their powerful capabilities more effectively and efficiently.

3.1   LM4HPC Design Overview

Figure 1 provides the overview of the LM4HPC framework. It is built on top of multiple internal machine learning components with Hugging Face-compatible APIs. Higher-level components provide concepts and interfaces to users, while middle or lower-level components provide implementation support. Table 2 shows the example classes and functions in LM4HPC API, including those supporting HPC-specific language models, tokenizers for programming languages, datasets, inference pipelines, and evaluation. We elaborate on some essential components in the following subsections.

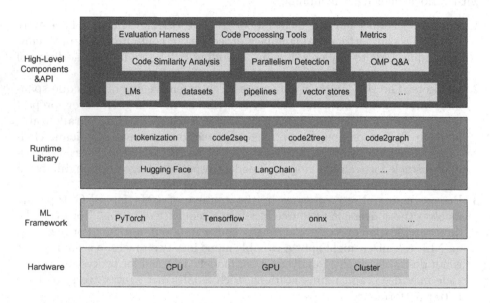

Fig. 1. Overview of the LM4HPC framework

3.2   HPC Tasks and Inference Pipelines

HPC users are interested in a wide range of tasks related to programming language processing. Table 3 outlines one way to categorize HPC-specific tasks. The purpose here is not to provide a comprehensive taxonomy of all tasks but a starting point for common tasks we are interested in supporting in our framework. Most tasks are self-explanatory by names and each may have further sub-tasks. For example, clone detection can be viewed as a specialized sub-task under code similarity analysis.

In the context of machine learning, a pipeline represents a sequence of data processing stages to complete a task. Our LM4HPC framework extends the pipeline function provided by Hugging Face, adapting it for HPC tasks. We have developed three inference pipelines: code similarity analysis, parallelism detection, and OpenMP question answering. Code similarity analysis determines the

Table 2. LM4HPC API: example classes and functions. Each class can be imported using "from lm4hpc import *" in Python.

LM4HPC classes	Description	Example API functions
hpcmodel	Fine-tune text-based (HF, OpenAI) and graph-based models, including local private ones, for HPC tasks	`hpcmodel.from_pretrained(model_name_or_path: Optional[str], *model_args, **kwargs)`
		`hpcmodel.save_pretrained(model_name_or_path: str, *model_args, **kwargs)`
		`hpcmodel.finetune()`
hpctokenizer	APIs to represent code in either tokenized text, trees, or graphs	`hpctokenizer.from_pretrained(model_name_or_path: Optional[str], *model_args, **kwargs)`
		`hpctokenizer.addtokens(contentsingle_word=False, strip=False, normalized=True)`
		`hpctokenizer.encoding()`
hpcdatasets	Load and process HPC datasets	`hpcdatasets.load(path: str, data_files: Union[str, List, Dict, None], **kwargs)`
		`hpcdatasets.split(dataset: hpcdatasets, partition: [float, float, float], **kwargs)`
		`hpcdatasets.shuffle(dataset: hpcdatasets, **kwargs)`
		`hpcdatasets.sort(dataset: hpcdatasets, **kwargs)`
hpcpipeline	Pre-built pipelines for common PLP tasks	`hpcpipeline(task: str, model_name_or_path: str, *model_args, **kwargs)`
hpceval	Evaluate the results of various models	`hpceval.compute(task: str, models_name_or_path: [[str]], data_files: Union[str, List, Dict, None], *model_args, **kwargs)`
		`hpceval.plot(shape: str)`

Table 3. HPC Tasks for Programming Language Processing: Categories and Examples

Code Analysis	Code Generation	Others
Compiler Analysis	Code Completion	Test Case Generation
Algorithm Classification	Natural Language-to-Code	Code Search
Code Similarity Analysis	Code Translation	Question Answering
Documentation Generation	Code Repair	Code Review
Parallelism Detection	Code Migration	Decompilation
Defect Detection	Compilation	IR-to-Source Translation

similarity between a pair of code snippets. Parallel detection is defined to check if an input code snippet can be parallelized or not using OpenMP. The OpenMP question answering pipeline is designed to use models to generate answers to OpenMP-related questions.

Tokenizers are responsible for preprocessing input into an array of numbers as inputs to a model. They are essential components used by pipelines. Most LM tokenizers are primarily designed for NLP tasks. For instance, given a function name `my_func`, a typical NLP tokenizer like BERT might split it into separate tokens (such as `'my'`, `'_'`, and `'func'`) while a code-aware tokenizer may treat the function name as a single entity to ensure a more meaningful representation.

To overcome this, we developed the LM4HPC tokenizer, leveraging the treesitter [12] and programl [13] library. Our tokenizer is specifically designed to handle the pre-processing of code data required for a language model. It includes tokenizers such as the ast-tokenizer. As a result, LM4HPC can accommodate models (such as augAST [14]) that require AST as input in the pipeline.

3.3　Datasets

Datasets are crucial for any machine learning application. Within the LM4HPC framework, we contribute HPC-specific datasets either by converting existing ones into Hugging Face-compatible formats or by creating new ones from scratch.

We have converted three existing datasets to be compatible with Hugging Face dataset API: POJ-104 [15], DRB-ML [16], and OMP4Par [14]. POJ-104 is derived from a pedagogical programming open judge (OJ) system that automatically evaluates the validity of submitted source code for specific problems by executing the code. This dataset is particularly useful for the code similarity task. The DRB-ML dataset contains 658 C/C++ OpenMP kernels derived from DataRaceBench [17]. We extended it to have labels indicating if a kernel is parallelizable or not. The OMP4Par dataset is an open-source benchmark composed of data from three resources: code crawled from GitHub, OpenMP benchmarks such as Nas Parallel Benchmarks [18] and Rodinia [19], and synthetic code. This dataset contains loops with labels indicating whether a loop is parallel and, if parallelizable, the corresponding OpenMP directive associated with the loop.

Furthermore, we have manually created a new OpenMP question answering dataset called OMPQA in order to probe the capabilities of language models in single-turn interactions with users. Similar to other QA datasets, we include some request-response pairs which are not strictly question-answering pairs. The categories and examples of questions in the OMPQA dataset can be found in Table 4.

Table 4. OMPQA: categories and examples of questions

Category	Count	Example Questions
Basics	40	What is a worksharing construct in OpenMP?
Examples	20	Give an example OpenMP C code for computing PI using numerical integration.
Compilers	24	In what language is LLVM written? How is a parallel region represented in Clang?
Benchmarks	23	What are the NAS Parallel benchmarks? Which benchmark assesses data race detection tools?

3.4   Integration with New Data

Language models derive knowledge from training datasets and store this knowledge in internal weights within the model's neural network architecture. However, incorporating new information into a trained model presents a challenge. Traditionally, one might fine-tune pre-trained models with their own data for specific tasks, but this approach requires substantial relevant data and can be resource-intensive. An alternative approach involves integrating new data as context information into a user prompt, but this is constrained by the limited input token lengths of current models.

To address this challenge, LM4HPC leverages the LangChain framework [20] to easily integrate new data. LangChain aggregates a wide variety of components to build applications using LLMs. Particularly, it provides APIs allowing LLM applications to store large amounts of text in semantic databases called vector stores. The way to integrate new data can be done in two steps. First, text data is chunked and embedded with an LLM before being saved into a vector store. Later, user prompts are matched with relevant chunks in the vector store using similarity analysis. The top-matched chunks are then injected into the original prompts to form a new prompt with relevant context information. By employing this new prompt, language models can generate answers that incorporate new and relevant user data while still staying within the token length limits.

3.5   Evaluation

An easily accessible harness for evaluating different language models on HPC tasks is crucial. Standard and reproducible results from such evaluations can provide researchers and developers with insightful starting points, helping them select suitable models for their specific needs and identify research opportunities.

In response to this need, we developed an evaluator API in LM4HPC. One challenge we encountered is the lack of standardized metrics for code evaluation. Unlike natural language tasks, where metrics such as BLEU, ROUGE, and METEOR are commonly used, the domain of code lacks such universally accepted measures of quality. We are adding various LLM metrics such as CodeBLEU [21] for code output. Another challenge is that language models may generate different answers for the same input in different inference runs. Evaluation should consider consistent sampling settings (such as temperatures) and control over random seeds to improve reproducibility.

Ultimately, many users are interested in seeing leaderboards that showcase mainstream models competing on common HPC tasks. To satisfy this interest, we create and release a set of test harnesses scripts to enable standard and reproducible evaluation for supported HPC tasks.

4   Preliminary Results

In this section, we evaluate the current prototype implementation of LM4HPC through experiments designed to generate leaderboards for three representative tasks: Code Similarity Analysis, Parallelism Detection, and OpenMP Question Answering. LM4HPC utilizes LangChain v0.0.174, Hugging Face's transformers v4.29.0 and datasets v2.12.0 as our runtime libraries. Details of the models and datasets will be discussed in subsequent subsections.

Our experiments were conducted on two machines: 1) a Google Colab VM with a 6-core Xeon processor operating at 2.20GHz, 83.5 GB main memory, 166GB HDD drive, and an NVIDIA A100 GPU with 40 GB memory. 2) a Dell workstation equipped with a dual Intel Xeon 6238 CPU operating at 2.10GHz, 128 GB main memory, 1TB SSD drive, and an NVIDIA Quadro RTX 6000 GPU with 24GB memory. The majority of our experiments were run on the Google Colab machine to leverage its superior GPU memory. However, we encountered difficulties running Cerebras-GPT on the Colab machine and were compelled to use the Dell workstation with larger CPU memory instead.

4.1   Code Similarity Analysis

The code similarity task is designed to measure the syntactic and/or semantic similarity between two code snippets. Such analysis information can be beneficial in various scenarios such as plagiarism detection, code reuse and refactoring, bug detection and repair, licensing compliance, malware detection, and so on.

Preparing Datasets and Ground Truth. Two datasets introduced in Sect. 3.3, POJ-104 and DRB-ML, are loaded through LM4HPC's datasets API for this experiment. For each pair of code snippets in the POJ-104 dataset, we assign a binary similarity label based on their functional labels. A similarity label of 1 signifies that the snippet pair shares the same functional label and we assign a similarity score of 1. Otherwise, the label is 0. We have processed the DRB-ML dataset using a similar methodology to generate code pairs and labels. The main difference is that the similarity ground truth for DRB-ML is derived from its own similarity score table [22], providing a precise and reliable similarity measurement between code snippets in the dataset.

Inference Experiments and Evaluation. We employ LM4HPC's code similarity pipeline to test various models. The default model for this pipeline is CodeBERT. We additionally select four models from Table for evaluation: GraphCodeBERT, gpt-3.5-turbo, Dolly 2.0 (12B), and Cerebras-GPT (13B). We set the maximum token length for the model output to 256. This limits the verbosity of the model and keeps its responses concise. Additionally, we set the temperature parameter to 0 when applicable. For models like Dolly 2.0 that require positive temperature, we set the temperature to be 1×10^{-6}. This setting ensures that the model's responses are consistent and deterministic, minimizing variability and uncertainty in its output.

Within LM4HPC, the approach of processing input code pairs depends on the type of the model employed. Models like CodeBert and GraphCodeBert are specifically devised and trained on a variety of programming languages. We directly feed a pair of code snippets to generate a similarity prediction. On the other hand, large language models like gpt-3.5-turbo, Dolly 2.0, and Cerebras-GPT are evaluated using the following prompt template: "Code 1: {...} Code 2: {...} Determine whether the two code snippets are similar. If the code snippets are similar, output 1; otherwise, output 0.".

Results. The Code Similarity Analysis leaderboards generated using the two datasets are shown in Table 5. Notably, gpt-3.5-turbo demonstrates superior performance. Two other models, StarChat-Alpha and Dolly 2.0, also exhibit commendable performance. Most large language models outperform traditional models (GraphCodeBERT and CodeBERT) that were specifically trained for code analysis. However, Cerebras-GPT struggled to comprehend the code and mostly returned arbitrary word tokens, indicating a lack of effective code understanding since it is mostly designed for natural language processing.

Table 5. Code Similarity Analysis Leaderboard: POJ-104 (left) and DRB-ML (right)

Model	Precision	Recall	F1	Model	Precision	Recall	F1
gpt-3.5-turbo	**78.4**	**74.2**	**76.2**	**gpt-3.5-turbo**	**82.4**	**81.3**	**81.8**
Dolly 2.0 12B	61.9	61.3	61.6	StarChat-Alpha	79.6	77.4	78.5
StarChat-Alpha	59.4	56.2	57.8	Dolly 2.0 12B	74.3	73.2	73.7
GraphCodeBERT	52.7	60.3	56.3	GraphCodeBERT	79.4	77.9	78.6
CodeBERT	51.5	59.4	55.2	CodeBERT	76.9	74.5	75.7
Cerebras-GPT 13B	0	0	0	Cerebras-GPT 13B	0	0	0

4.2   Parallelism Detection

The parallelism detection task aims to identify parallelism opportunities within a given code snippet. We utilized two datasets, OMP4Par and DRB-ML introduced in Sect. 3.3, for the experiment.

Preparing Datasets and Ground Truth. The OMP4Par dataset is specifically designed for parallelism detection. Its existing labeling scheme allows us to prepare the data for binary classification models. Similarly, we prepared DRB-ML dataset with a label indicating whether each code snippet is parallelizable using OpenMP or not.

It is worth noting that both datasets have undergone source code preprocessing steps, including comment removal and code snippet extraction. These steps are common practice [14] to ensure that code snippets are small enough to be fed into language models with limited input token sequence sizes. However, the resulting code snippets may lose their context information, such as variable declarations. This is a serious limitation of language models with limited input sizes when applied to process large source files.

Inference Experiments and Results. We selected six models to generate parallelism detection leaderboards. Four of them are introduced in Sect. . They take the code snippets in a prompt template: "As an OpenMP expert, you will analyze the given code snippet to determine if it can be parallelized. Code: {...}. Answer yes or no first:". The other two are augAST [14] and DeepSCC-based [23], which are pre-trained models using OMP4Par's training dataset. We fed code snippets to these two models to directly obtain predicted labels.

Table 6 presents the resulting leaderboards. The highest F1 score reaches 93.9, indicating that LMs can be very effective for detecting parallelism. However, the datasets contain small-scale code snippets that are significantly simpler than real HPC codes. Again, gpt-3.5-turbo outperforms all other models overall, including specially trained models like augAST and DeepSCC. AugAST performs better than gpt-3.5-turbo in terms of precision, suggesting it's more effective in predicting a positive class, which, in this case, is parallelizable code. Finally, Cerebras-GPT did not perform well in this code analysis task.

Table 6. Parallelism Detection Leaderboards: OMP4Par (left) and DRB-ML(right)

Model	Precision	Recall	F1	Model	Precision	Recall	F1
gpt-3.5-turbo	90.6	**89.3**	**89.9**	**gpt-3.5-turbo**	90.0	**98.9**	**94.2**
augAST	**92.1**	82.4	87.0	augAST	**91.4**	72.3	80.7
DeepSCC	82.7	81.4	82.0	DeepSCC	80.4	79.5	79.9
StarChat-Alpha	85.7	68.2	75.9	StarChat-Alpha	81.9	20.3	32.5
Dolly 2.0 12B	64.2	63.7	63.9	Dolly 2.0 12B	40.0	11.2	2.17
Cerebras-GPT 13B	0	0	0	Cerebras-GPT 13B	0	0	0

4.3 OpenMP Q and A

In this experiment, we utilized LM4HPC to evaluate the capabilities of several language models in answering questions related to OpenMP. This evaluation was conducted using the OMPQA dataset, introduced in Sect. 3.3.

Experiment Settings. Each model receives the question in the following prompt template: "You are an OpenMP expert. Please answer this question. Question: {question}". Two metrics are selected to evaluate the quality of answers: the Bilingual Evaluation Understudy (BLEU) and ROUGE-L metrics. BLEU is a precision-oriented metric measuring the overlap of n-grams between the generated text and a set of reference texts. ROUGE-L (Recall-Oriented Understudy for Gisting Evaluation - Longest Common Subsequence) calculates the longest common subsequence (LCS) that appears in a left-to-right sequence in both the system-generated and reference summaries, thus providing a measure of the coherence and fluidity of the generated text.

Results. Table 7 displays the Q&A leaderboard of several selected models. We additionally include the memory and execution time information. The experiments using gpt-3.5-turbo do not consume any local GPU memory since the model is invoked remotely through OpenAI's API.

Again, gpt-3.5-turbo unsurprisingly outperforms other LLMs. However, the highest average ROUGE-L F1 score of 0.259 indicates that all models have room for improvement in answering OpenMP questions. One reason is that many questions in OMPQA are open-ended and do not necessarily have a single correct answer. Also, the two metrics used do not sufficiently consider semantics.

Table 7. Q&A Leaderboard using the OMPQA dataset. The arrow indicates the performance changes when augmenting external knowledge base by LangChain.

Model	CPU Mem. (GB)	GPU Mem. (GB)	Time(s)	BLEU	ROUGE-L (AVG)		
					Recall	Prescision	F1
gpt-3.5-turbo+ LangChain	4.1	0	21.452	**0.147**↑	0.347↓	0.262↑	**0.259**↑
gpt-3.5-turbo	4.2	0	12.749	0.139	**0.446**	0.231	0.257
StarChat-Alpha	6.8	18.9	29.732	0.082	0.322	0.149	0.172
Dolly 2.0 12B + LangChain	27.4	39.8	7.217	0.084↑	0.228↑	0.232↓	0.182↑
Dolly 2.0 12B	27.1	39.2	8.147	0.06	0.208	**0.312**	0.148
Cerebras-GPT 13B	52.6	11.7	590.763	0.071	0.319	0.089	0.112

To enhance the capacity of large language models (LLMs) in accurately responding to OpenMP queries, we integrate the official OpenMP documentation into our process. We employ LangChain, a mechanism designed to efficiently store and retrieve language model embeddings, enabling us to accommodate large volumes of new data. To assess the efficacy of using LangChain to incorporate additional user data, we leverage its API to create a vector store. This vector store holds embeddings of text chunks derived from the OpenMP API Specification v5.2 (669 pages) and the OpenMP Application Programming Interface Examples v5.2.1 (575 pages). We then select two LangChain-supported models, GPT-3.5 and Dolly 2.0, to utilize the vector store as an additional resource for answering queries, thereby demonstrating the practical utility of our approach. The results indicate slight improvements in both the BLEU and ROUGE-L F1 scores, increasing from 0.139 to 0.147 and from 0.257 to 0.259, respectively. However, there are mixed results for recall and precision metrics. gpt-3.5-turbo has a better recall, 0.446, compared to 0.347 of the Langchain approach.

Further, we examine the effectiveness of the LangChain approach across different question categories. When addressing 'Basic' questions, the BLEU scores rise by 20.7% and 9.8% for gpt-3.5-turbo and Dolly 2.0, respectively. Additionally, we assess the LangChain performance using the CodeBLEU metric [21] for the 'Examples' category, observing a score increase of 6.1% and 12.2% for gpt-3.5-turbo and Dolly 2.0, respectively. These observations indicate that augmenting LLMs with documentation via LangChain improves performance for

'Basic' and 'Examples' categories. However, for 'Compilers' and 'Benchmarks' categories, the performance of gpt-3.5-turbo and Dolly 2.0 diminishes when utilizing LangChain, recording an average BLEU score drop of 8.0% and 7.9%, respectively. This drop is likely because our documentation does not include information relevant to compiler and benchmark topics.

We also manually investigated the answers generated by the models. Overall, StarChat-Alpha delivers competitive results compared to GPT-3.5. It seems to be a good choice for people who want to use open-source language models based on our experiments. Research has indicated that GPT-4 surpasses GPT-3.5 in a variety of domains. However, as of now, API accessibility for GPT-4 has not been made publicly available. We plan to assess GPT-4's performance as soon as it becomes accessible and incorporate it into our framework if it benefits HPC tasks.

5   Related Work

PyTorch and TensorFlow are the most popular frameworks, backed by Meta AI and Google, respectively. Both frameworks are similar in many respects, including 1) providing low-level APIs for development, 2) supporting a rich collection of libraries, and 3) maintaining dedicated hubs - PyTorch Hub and TensorFlow Hub - for providing pre-trained ML models. Hugging Face is a large open-source community that builds tools to enable users to build, train, and deploy machine learning models based on open-source code and technologies. Hugging Face is best known for its `Transformers` library, which exposes a collection of Python APIs to leverage state-of-the-art deep learning architectures for NLP tasks. With the goal to simplify end-to-end NLP tasks, Hugging Face `Transformers` offers a pipeline that performs all pre- and post-processing steps on the given input text data. The overall process of the model inference is encapsulated within these pipelines. With the pipeline, users only need to provide the input texts and the model for the task. The remaining connections among a model and required pre- and post-processing steps are hidden within the pipeline implementation.

There were various research works and developments to improve the ML ecosystem to be Findable, Accessible, Interoperable, and Reproducible (FAIR). These existing frameworks aim to make the models, datasets, or both FAIR. Among these frameworks, HPCFAIR [24] focuses on supporting model interoperability, search capabilities for datasets and models, and seamless integration into HPC workflows. The work in [25] extended this work to include support for interoperability across different framework implementations using ONNX and provision to retrain a model with transfer learning. However, HPCFAIR framework relies on users to handle data pre- and post-processing. In comparison, LM4HPC is equipped to manage data processing within the pipeline design and generate leaderboards for supported HPC tasks.

General LLMs are trained with data covering general knowledge and information that is usually collected from public domains. Domain-specific datasets can be collected for the training of a specialized model or the fine-tuning of a general-purpose model. MedQA [26] is an example of domain-specific datasets collecting question-answer pairs and textbooks from professional medical board exams. ExeBench [27], another domain-specific dataset for tasks in compilation and software engineering, contains millions of runnable and representative C functions collected from GitHub. In addition to collecting existing data, ML research has started automating dataset creation with LLMs' assistance. The developers of LaMini-LM [28] develop a large set of 2.58M instruction and response pairs based on both existing and newly-generated instructions. A handful of seed examples from the existing LLM prompts and 2.2M categories from Wikipedia from existing are submitted to the `gpt-3.5-turbo` to generate relevant instructions. Similarly, the responses for the generated instructions are also generated by the `gpt-3.5-turbo`.

6   Conclusion

In this paper, we presented our efforts to facilitate the application of language models for tasks specific to High-Performance Computing. We have developed the LM4HPC framework to encompass and expose relevant machine learning components via corresponding APIs. Our experimental findings suggest that GPT-3 performs competitively, despite not being specifically designed for HPC tasks. However, there is significant room for improvement in answering OpenMP questions. Furthermore, the input size limitation of language models adds complexity to certain tasks, such as parallelism detection. Finally, an obstacle to advancing the application of language models for HPC tasks is the absence of HPC-specific training and evaluation datasets.

Looking ahead, our future work will explore automated approaches to generating HPC-specific datasets. We intend to enhance LM4HPC's capabilities to support the fine-tuning of models for HPC-related tasks, including those related to the Message Passing Interface (MPI), and to provide performance analysis and optimization suggestions.

Acknowledgement. Prepared by LLNL under Contract DE-AC52-07NA27344 (LL NL-CONF-849438) and supported by the U.S. Department of Energy, Office of Science, Advanced Scientific Computing Research.

References

1. Bubeck, S., et al.: Sparks of artificial general intelligence: early experiments with GPT-4. arXiv preprint arXiv:2303.12712 (2023)
2. Chen, M., et al.: Evaluating large language models trained on code. arXiv preprint arXiv:2107.03374 (2021)
3. Vaswani, A., et al.: Attention is all you need. Advances in Neural Information Processing Systems 30 (2017)
4. Touvron, H., et al.: LLaMA: open and efficient foundation language models. arXiv preprint arXiv:2302.13971 (2023)

5. Chen, L., Mahmud, Q.I., Jannesari, A.: Multi-view learning for parallelism discovery of sequential programs. In: 2022 IEEE International Parallel and Distributed Processing Symposium Workshops (IPDPSW), pp. 295–303. IEEE (2022)
6. Flynn, P., Vanderbruggen, T., Liao, C., Lin, P.H., Emani, M., Shen, X.: Finding Reusable Machine Learning Components to Build Programming Language Processing Pipelines. arXiv preprint arXiv:2208.05596 (2022)
7. Devlin, J., Chang, M.W., Lee, K., Toutanova, K.: BERT: pre-training of deep bidirectional transformers for language understanding. arXiv preprint arXiv:1810.04805 (2018)
8. Feng, Z., et al.: CodeBERT: a pre-trained model for programming and natural languages. arXiv preprint arXiv:2002.08155 (2020)
9. Wang, Y., Wang, W., Joty, S., Hoi, S.C.: CodeT5: identifier-aware unified pre-trained encoder-decoder models for code understanding and generation. arXiv preprint arXiv:2109.00859 (2021)
10. Li, R., et al.: StarCoder: may the source be with you! arXiv preprint arXiv:2305.06161 (2023)
11. Brown, T., et al.: Language models are few-shot learners. Adv. Neural. Inf. Process. Syst. **33**, 1877–1901 (2020)
12. The PY-tree-sitter project (2023). https://pypi.org/project/tree-sitter-builds/. Accessed 15 May 2023
13. ProGraML: program Graphs for Machine Learning (2022). https://pypi.org/project/programl/. Accessed 15 May 2023
14. Chen, L., Mahmud, Q.I., Phan, H., Ahmed, N.K., Jannesari, A.: Learning to parallelize with openMP by augmented heterogeneous AST representation. arXiv preprint arXiv:2305.05779 (2023)
15. Mou, L., Li, G., Zhang, L., Wang, T., Jin, Z.: Convolutional neural networks over tree structures for programming language processing. In: Proceedings of the AAAI Conference On Artificial Intelligence, vol. 30 (2016)
16. Lin, P.H., Liao, C.: DRB-ML-dataset (2022). https://doi.org/10.11579/1958879
17. Liao, C., Lin, P.H., Asplund, J., Schordan, M., Karlin, I.: DataRaceBench: a benchmark suite for systematic evaluation of data race detection tools. In: Proceedings of the International Conference for High Performance Computing, Networking, Storage and Analysis, pp. 1–14 (2017)
18. Jin, H.Q., Frumkin, M., Yan, J.: The OpenMP implementation of NAS parallel benchmarks and its performance (1999)
19. Che, S., et al.: Rodinia: a benchmark suite for heterogeneous computing. In: 2009 IEEE international symposium on workload characterization (IISWC), pp. 44–54. IEEE (2009)
20. Chase, H.: LangChain: next Generation Language Processing (2023). https://langchain.com/. Accessed 15 May 2023
21. Ren, S., et al.: CodeBLEU: a method for automatic evaluation of code synthesis. arXiv preprint arXiv:2009.10297 (2020)
22. Chen, W., Vanderbruggen, T., Lin, P.H., Liao, C., Emani, M.: Early experience with transformer-based similarity analysis for DataRaceBench. In: 2022 IEEE/ACM Sixth International Workshop on Software Correctness for HPC Applications (Correctness), pp. 45–53. IEEE (2022)
23. Harel, R., Pinter, Y., Oren, G.: Learning to parallelize in a shared-memory environment with transformers. In: Proceedings of the 28th ACM SIGPLAN Annual Symposium on Principles and Practice of Parallel Programming, pp. 450–452 (2023)

24. Verma, G., et al.: HPCFAIR: Enabling FAIR AI for HPC Applications. In: 2021 IEEE/ACM Workshop on Machine Learning in High Performance Computing Environments (MLHPC), pp. 58–68. IEEE (2021)
25. Yu, S., et al.: Towards seamless management of AI models in high-performance computing (2022)
26. Jin, D., Pan, E., Oufattole, N., Weng, W.H., Fang, H., Szolovits, P.: What disease does this patient have? A large-scale open domain question answering dataset from medical exams. arXiv preprint arXiv:2009.13081 (2020)
27. Armengol-Estapé, J., Woodruff, J., Brauckmann, A., Magalhães, J.W.d.S., O'Boyle, M.F.: ExeBench: an ML-scale dataset of executable C functions. In: Proceedings of the 6th ACM SIGPLAN International Symposium on Machine Programming, pp. 50–59 (2022)
28. Wu, M., Waheed, A., Zhang, C., Abdul-Mageed, M., Aji, A.F.: LaMini-LM: a diverse herd of distilled models from large-scale instructions. arXiv preprint arXiv:2304.14402 (2023)

OpenMP Advisor: A Compiler Tool for Heterogeneous Architectures

Alok Mishra[1,3]([✉]), Abid M. Malik[2], Meifeng Lin[2], and Barbara Chapman[1,3]

[1] Stony Brook University, Stony Brook, NY 11794, USA
almishra@cs.stonybrook.edu, barbara.chapman@stonybrook.edu
[2] Brookhaven National Laboratory, Upton, NY 11973, USA
{amalik,mlin}@bnl.gov
[3] Hewlett Packard Enterprise, Spring, TX 77389, USA
{alok.mishra,barbara.chapman}@hpe.com

Abstract. With the increasing diversity of heterogeneous architecture in the HPC industry, porting a legacy application to run on different architectures is a tough challenge. In this paper, we present OpenMP Advisor, a novel compiler tool that enables code offloading to a GPU with OpenMP using Machine Learning. Although the tool is currently limited to GPUs, it can be extended to support other OpenMP-capable devices. The tool has two modes: Training and Prediction. It analyzes benchmark codes, generates every possible code variant on the target device, runs and gathers data to train an ML-based cost model in the training mode, which predicts the runtime of every code variant in the prediction mode. The main objective behind this tool is to maintain the portability aspect of OpenMP. Our Advisor produced code for several applications on seven architectures with four compilers, and accurately anticipated the top ten options for each application on every architecture. Initial results suggest that this tool can help compiler developers and HPC researchers migrate their legacy codes to the new heterogeneous computing environment.

Keywords: openmp · gpu · machine learning · cost model · compiler

1 Introduction

General Purpose Graphics Processing Units (GPGPUs), initially designed for graphics tasks, have become integral to HPC platforms and general-purpose computing over the last decade, combining their capacity for efficient data parallelism with low power consumption. The vast majority of HPC systems in use today are heterogeneous, with AMD or NVIDIA GPUs delivering high performance per unit of energy consumed. Programming updates are needed to enable efficient utilization of diverse hardware resources, such as GPUs and specialized processors, in order to cater to the rapid change in heterogeneous architecture in the HPC industry.

Many programmers are adapting their code to take advantage of GPUs. Unfortunately, it can be time-consuming and require extensive re-engineering

S. McIntosh-Smith et al. (Eds.): IWOMP 2023, LNCS 14114, pp. 34–48, 2023.
https://doi.org/10.1007/978-3-031-40744-4_3

to maximize a GPU's computational power while minimizing overheads. It will be much harder to develop code for systems with extreme heterogeneity and a large number of devices. Therefore, it is essential to create tools that will relieve the application scientists of the burden of such development. Despite the variety of programming models available, it is still quite challenging to optimize large scale applications consisting of tens-to-hundreds of thousands lines of code. Even when using a directive based programming model such as OpenMP [6], pragmatizing each kernel is a repetitive and complex task. OpenMP offers a variety of options for offloading a kernel to GPUs. However, the application scientist must still figure out all the intricate GPU configurations. To demonstrate the complexity of porting a kernel to emerging exascale hardwares, we use a kernel from the Lattice Quantum Chromodynamics (LQCD) [2] application, which is a computer-friendly numerical framework for QCD. One of LQCD's key computational kernels is the Wilson Dslash operator [15], which is essentially a finite difference operator, to describe the interaction of quarks with gluons. The Wilson Dslash operator, D, in four space-time dimensions is defined by Eq. 1.

$$D_{\alpha\beta}^{ij}(x,y) = \sum_{\mu=1}^{4}[((1-\gamma_\mu))_{\alpha\beta}U_\mu^{ij}(x)\delta_{x+\hat{\mu},y} + (1+\gamma_\mu)_{\alpha\beta}U_\mu^{\dagger ij}(x+\hat{\mu})\delta_{x-\hat{\mu},y}]$$

(1)

Here x and y are the coordinates of the lattice sites, α, β are spin indices, and i, j are color indices. $U_\mu(x)$ is the gluon field variable and is an $SU(3)$ matrix. γ_μ's are 4×4 Dirac matrices that are fixed. The complex fermion fields are represented as one-dimensional arrays of size $L_X \times L_Y \times L_Z \times L_T \times SPINS \times COLORS \times 2$ for the unpreconditioned Dirac operator, where L_X, L_Y, L_Z and L_T are the numbers of lattice sites in the x, y, z and t directions, respectively. The spin and color degrees of freedom, which are commonly 4 and 3, are denoted by the variables $SPINS$ and $COLORS$.

When we express Eq. 1 in C++, it has four nested `for` loops iterating over L_T, L_Z, L_Y, and L_X (as shown in Code 1.1). When we keep the values of L_T, L_Z, L_Y, and L_X at 16 each, the COMPUTE section of the code has over 5 million variable definitions, 1.2 billion variable references, over 150 million addition/subtraction, 163 million multiplication, and so on. Additionally, this function is called several times throughout the LQCD application. It is a herculean task for an application scientist to understand the physics, transform it

```
#pragma omp target
  for(int i=0; i<N_i; i++) {
    for(int j=0; j<N_j; j++) {
      for(int k=0; k<N_k; k++) {
        for(int l=0; l<N_l; l++) {
          /* ... COMPUTE ... */
}}}}
```

Code 1.1. Loops of Wilson Dslash Operator

into computer program, analyze the offloadable kernel, and then consider how to parallelize it to execute efficiently on an HPC cluster. To get the best performance out of a GPU, an application scientist needs a thorough understanding of the underlying architecture, algorithm, and interface programming model. Alternately, they could test out various GPU transformations until they find the most effective one. However, none of these strategies is very efficient.

1.1   Our Contribution

This paper presents **OpenMP Advisor**, a first-of-its-kind compiler tool that advises application scientists on various OpenMP code offloading strategies. This tool performs the following tasks to successfully address the challenges of effectively transforming an OpenMP code:

1. detect potentially offloadable kernel;
2. identify data access and modification in kernel;
3. recommend potential OpenMP variants for offloading that kernel to the GPU;
4. evaluate the profitability of each kernel variant via an adaptive cost model;
5. insert pertinent OpenMP directives to perform offloading.

Although the tool is currently limited to GPUs, it is extensible to other OpenMP-capable devices. In the rest of the paper, we first discuss state of the art work that is related to and precedes our work in Sect. 2. Then we define our OpenMP Advisor in Sect. 3. The experiments conducted for this paper are covered in Sect. 4 along with their analysis, and Sect. 5 concludes our work with discussions of our future goals.

2   Related Work

Many studies have looked into how to best manage GPU memory when data movement must be explicitly managed. For instance, Jablin et al. [10] provide a fully automatic system for managing and optimizing CPU-GPU communication for CUDA programs. Also OMPSan [1] performs static analysis on explicit data transfers are already inserted in OpenMP code. However, these studies do not address the issue of data transfer and the use of data reuse on GPU for implicitly managed data between different kernels. In one of our previous work [18] we proposed a technique for statically identifying data used by each kernel and automatically recognizing data reuse opportunities across kernels. In this tool, we make use of this method for data identification and management between the CPU and the GPU.

HPC applications are getting extremely heterogeneous, complicated, and increasingly expensive to analyze. Because of heterogeneity, a tool like OpenMP Advisor is required to help application scientists offload their code to GPUs. Other related research on automatic GPU offloading by Mendonça *et.al.* [16] and Poesia *et.al.* [22] can benefit from our tool by including our technique of data optimization and cost model in their framework, further reducing the challenges of using GPUs for scientific computing. However, developing a cost model is time-consuming, and almost all modern compilers adopt a simple "one-size-fits-all" cost function that does not perform optimally in the situation of extreme heterogeneous architecture. In order to create a portable static cost model for our OpenMP Advisor tool, we utilize our ML based cost model, COMPOFF [17] which offers a new portable cost model that statically estimates the cost of OpenMP offloading on various architectures.

3   OpenMP Advisor

We design and develop the OpenMP Advisor, a compiler tool which transforms an OpenMP code to effectively offload to a GPU. This tool detects OpenMP kernels, proposes several GPU offloading OpenMP variants, and predicts the runtime of each kernel using a machine learning based cost model. Although the Advisor's initial implementation, as described in this paper, assists application scientists in programming for accelerators like GPUs, it can be expanded to support all OpenMP-capable devices. The tool has two modes: **Training** and **Prediction** mode. In the training mode, the Advisor makes use of data collected from multiple devices and compilers. It takes all benchmark codes as input and generates all possible code variants to run on the target device. Then it collects data from all generated codes to train an ML-based cost model for use in prediction mode. In prediction mode the tool does not need any interaction with the target device. It accepts C/C++ code as input and returns the best code variant that can be used to offload the code to the specified device. The tool can determine the kernels that are best suited for offloading by predicting their runtime using a machine learning-based cost model as defined in Sect. 3.2. The following are the key attributes of the OpenMP Advisor.

1. **Portable** – The Advisor's key feature is its portability across compilers and HPC clusters, as demonstrated in Sect. 4, which included four different compilers and seven HPC clusters with different GPUs.
2. **Static** – Since HPC GPUs are not always available during development, the Advisor performs all of its analysis at compile time and does not require runtime profiling in the prediction mode.
3. **Minimalistic** – The Advisor generates different kernel variants by adding OpenMP directives and clauses to the application's "omp target" regions without changing the kernel's body.
4. **Correctness** – The Advisor ensures that the generated code adheres to the OpenMP programming model, but it does not alter the kernel body or guarantee its correctness. Consequently, despite its ability to predict the optimal scenario for GPU offloading, it generates the top 10 code variants and lets the application scientist select which code to utilize.
5. **Adaptable** – The Advisor is adaptable enough to accept new applications by training the model on a proxy application if collecting real-time data is challenging or impractical for the real world application.

We used the LLVM compiler project [14] to develop the OpenMP Advisor. Despite the fact that LLVM's strength lies in the LLVM-IRs, our requirement is to generate and return C/C++ code to the scientist. To do so, we need to be able to accurately insert OpenMP directives into a C/C++ file, which the LLVM-IR cannot guarantee. On the other hand Clang's AST closely resembles both the written C++ code and the C++ standard. Clang has a one-to-one mapping of each token to the AST node and an excellent source location retention for all AST nodes. Clang's AST is the best option for accurate source code information and inserting OpenMP directives into C/C++ files. Hence, we implemented the Advisor in Clang compiler (ver 14.0.0). Both the Training and Prediction modes have three major modules, which are explained in the following subsections - *Kernel Analysis*, *Cost Model* and *Code Transformation*.

3.1 Kernel Analysis

This is the first module which the Advisor calls in both the Prediction and Training mode. As the name implies, this module analyzes an OpenMP kernel. Overall, this module takes as input a C/C++ source file, analyzes it, and outputs all possible GPU offloading variants. This module is responsible for three tasks: *Identifying Kernels, Data Analysis* and *Variant Generation*.

Identifying Kernels — As the project's scope doesn't include automatically parallelizing the code, the user's input serves to identify a target region. An application scientist only needs to use the "`omp target` directive" to mark the region. We parse the clang AST to search for the `OMPTargetDirective` node, which is a subclass of the `OMPExecutableDirective` class and an instance of the `Stmt` class. We override the `OMPAdvisorVisitor` class's `VisitStmt` method and check each visited `Stmt` to see if they are the `OMPTargetDirective` node. Once a kernel is identified, we assign it a unique id and create an instance of the class "KernelInformation", in which we store information like, unique_id, start and end locations of the kernel, function from which the kernel is called, whether the kernel is called from within a loop and the number of nested `for` loops.

Data Analysis — The next step is to determine what data the kernel uses. We need to carefully manage data transfer between the CPU and GPU due to the high cost of transfers. We reuse our work on *Data Reuse Analysis* [18] to identify and utilize GPU data and improve overall execution time, since OpenMP doesn't specify how data should be handled in implicit data transfer. We use the Clang AST to implement "*live variable analysis*" for each kernel, concentrating only on variables used within a kernel. Our current approach only maps data between the CPU and GPU before and after the kernel. Managing data transfer during kernel execution is a future task. Before the variables are stored in the `KernelInformation` object, we classify them into five groups, based on how they are accessed before, during, or after the kernel:

- *alloc*: Variables *assigned within* the kernel for the first time. Data need to be mapped, but no data transfer is required.
- *to*: Variables *assigned before* but were only *accessed* within the kernel, not modified. Only host to device transfer of data is required.

- *from*: Variables *assigned within* and *accessed after* the kernel definition. Only device to host transfer of data is required.
- *tofrom*: Variables *assigned before*, *updated within* and *accessed after* the kernel definition. Data must be transferred both to and from the host and device.
- *private*: Variables that are defined and used *only within* the kernel. No data transfer is required.

Data labeled *alloc*, *to*, and *tofrom* are mapped in "omp target enter data" directives before the kernel, while data labeled *from* and *tofrom* are mapped in "omp target exit data" directives after the kernel.

Variant Generation — Finally, we generate a number of different kernel variants that can be used to offload the kernel to the GPU. We'll start by counting how many nested collapsible for loops are there. In the current implementation, we can check up to four levels of collapsing the for loops. We chose four nested loops (similar to Code 1.2) because the Wilson Dslash kernel has four for loops. Each of these for loops is given a unique Loop number ranging from $0 - 3$. Loop 0 is always expected to be distributed across all teams on the GPU.

```
#pragma omp target teams distribute collapse(1)
    for (int i = 0; i < N_i; i++) {   ¡= Loop 0
#pragma omp parallel for collapse(3) schedule(static)
    for (int j = 0; j < N_j; j++) {   ¡= Loop 1
      for (int k = 0; k < N_k; k++) {   ¡= Loop 2
        for (int l = 0; l < N_l; l++) {   ¡= Loop 3
          /* ... COMPUTE ... */
}}}}
```

Code 1.2. A variant of four nested "for" loops for GPU offloading

The variants are generated based on the collapse values used in `distribute` and `parallel for` directive, position of the `parallel for` directive, loop iteration's scheduling type and host-device data transfer. The total number of `for` loops and the position of the `parallel for` directive determine the maximum value of `collapse` that can be used in the `teams distribute` and `parallel for` directives. Suppose there are four `for` loops, as in Code 1.2. If the `parallel for` directive is at Loop 0, the "teams distribute parallel for" directive will be combined and thus the `collapse` clause for `distribute` directive doesn't exist. If the `parallel for` directive is located on Loop x (where $1 \leq x \leq 3$), then the maximum possible value of collapse for the `teams distribute` directive is x. While the maximum possible value of `collapse` for the `parallel for` directive is $(NUM - x)$, where NUM is the total number of for loops. The scheduling type of the loop iteration could be one of `static`, `dynamic` or `guided`. Using different permutations of these parameters, we could generate a variety of GPU offloading code variants. Once all of the variants have been generated, we use our static cost model to predict the runtime of each of these generated kernels.

3.2 Cost Model

A compile-time cost model is required to select the best option from all the variants generated by the Kernel Analysis module. Most modern compilers employ analytical models to calculate the cost of executing the original code as well as the various offloading code variants. Building such an analytical model for compilers is a difficult task that necessitates a lot of effort on the part of a compiler engineer. Recently, machine learning techniques have been successfully applied to build cost models for a variety of compiler optimization problems. For our tool we extended our previous work on COMPOFF [17] to be used as our cost model. COMPOFF is a machine learning based compiler cost model that statically estimates the cost of OpenMP offloading using an artificial neural network model. Their results show that this model can predict offloading costs with an average accuracy greater than 95%. The major limitation of COMPOFF was that they had to train a separate model for each variant. In our work, we add more training data and extend it to train a single cost model for all variants.

As soon as we know the prediction for the generated variant, we store it in the instance of the `KernelInformation` class so that the Kernel Transformation module can use it. But the biggest challenge in implementing an ML based cost model is the lack of available training data. To overcome this problem, we wrote additional benchmark applications (like the Pearson's Correlation Coefficient (correlation), Covariance (covariance), Laplace's Equation (laplace), Matrix-Matrix Multiplication (mm), Matrix-Vector Multiplication (mv), Matrix Transpose (mt)) and adopted some benchmarks from the Rodinia benchmark suite [4] (like the Breadth First Search (bfs), Gaussian Elimination (gauss), K-Nearest Neighbor (knn) and Particle Filter (particle)). The goal is to include a broader class of benchmarks that would cover the spectrum of statistical simulation, linear algebra, data mining, etc. We also developed a proxy app that has same number of loops and performs similar computation to our target app, the Wilson Dslash operator. Whenever it is difficult to collect data on real applications, proxy apps help us collect more data. More applications from various other domains will be added to this repository in the future.

3.3 Kernel Transformation

In the Kernel Transformation module we need to actually transform the original source code based on the analysis and predictions from the previous modules. For the given kernel, we generate every possible code variation in the Training mode. However, before we can generate code in Prediction mode, we must first address another crucial question. Which code should we generate? Should we only generated code for the fastest kernel? Regrettably, once the directives are in place, neither the Advisor nor OpenMP validate the kernel's correctness. This is in line with the OpenMP philosophy as well. As a result, we can only guarantee the correctness of the generated OpenMP directive in our framework.

So how can we overcome this problem? We could generate code for every possible variation, as we do during training, and let the user choose which one

```
0:  // Predicted Runtime: 1.2 s
1:  #pragma omp target enter data map(...)
2:  #pragma omp target teams distribute collapse(2)
    for (int  i = 0; i < N_i; i++) {
3:
        for (int j = 0; j < N_j; j++) {
4:  #pragma omp parallel for schedule(dynamic)
        for (int k = 0; k < N_k; k++) {
5:
            for (int l = 0; l < N_l; l++) {
            /* ... COMPUTE ... */
    }}}}
6:  #pragma omp target exit data map(...)
```

Code 1.3. Location of the seven generated code.

to use. But this means that users will be overwhelmed with information. Alternatively, we could ask the user to provide a number for the maximum number of codes to generate. The predicted runtime can be put as a comment before the kernel in every piece of code. The application scientist will then have more power to accept or reject the generated code. We will be able to produce a single code and provide it to the user once the issue of validating an OpenMP code for correctness is resolved. Until then, our Advisor will be able to generate the top best variants as specified by the application scientist. Regardless, we need to write a module to modify the existing source code and generate a new code. Clang provides the `Rewriter` [5] interface, whose primary function is to route high-level requests to the involved low-level `RewriteBuffers`. A `Rewriter` assists us in managing the code rewriting task. In the `Rewriter` interface we can set the `SourceManager` object which handles loading and caching of source files into memory. The `SourceManager` can be queried to obtain information about `SourceLocation` objects, which can then be converted into spelling or expansion locations. The `Rewriter` is a critical component of our plugin's kernel transformation module. The strategy used here is to meticulously alter the original code at crucial locations to carry out the transformation rather than handling every possible AST node to spit back code from the AST. For this we use the `Rewriter` interface, an advanced buffer manager that effectively manipulates the source using a rope data structure. For each `SourceManager`, the `Rewriter` also stores the low-level `RewriteBuffer`. Together with Clang's excellent retention of source location for all AST nodes, `Rewriter` makes it possible to remove and insert code very precisely in the `RewriteBuffer`. When the update is finished, we can dump the `RewriteBuffer` into a file to obtain the updated source code.

Finally, we create a vector of seven strings. The location of these seven strings are shown in Code 1.3. The first string (at #0) is always the comment that maintains the text — "`Predicted Runtime: ## s`". As the text suggests `##` is the predicted runtime for this particular kernel variant. This string is always placed before the kernel's start location. Then comes the `target enter data` construct (at #1). This directive handles what memory on the GPU needs to be created for the kernel and what data needs to be sent to the GPU before execution. This string is always placed right after the comments string. The next string (at #2) contains the OpenMP directive which specifies that this is the kernel to offload to the target. To gain maximum performance out of the GPU, we should always distribute

Table 1. Clusters and Compilers used in experiments

Cluster	GPU	Compiler	Version
Summit [20]	NVIDIA Tesla V100	LLVM/clang (nvptx)	13.0.0
		GNU/gcc (nvptx-none)	9.1.0
Corona [13]	AMD Radeon Instinct MI50	LLVM/clang (rocm-5.3)	15.0.0
Ookami [3]	NVIDIA Tesla V100	LLVM/clang (nvptx)	14.0.0
Wombat [21]	NVIDIA Tesla A100	LLVM/clang (nvptx)	15.0.0
Seawulf [23]	NVIDIA Tesla K80	LLVM/clang (nvptx)	12.0.0
		NVIDIA/NVC	21.7
Intel DevCloud [9]	Intel Xeon E-2176 P630	Intel/icpx	2021.1.2
Exxact	NVIDIA GeForce RTX 2080	LLVM/clang (nvptx)	14.0.0

the kernel across all the teams available in the GPU. Hence this string always contain the directive − "`#pragma omp target teams distribute`". The variant determines whether this directive contains any other clauses such as `collapse` or `map`,
and what will be the values of the clause. This string is always placed immediately before the kernel's start location, but after the `target enter data` string.
The remaining strings (#3, #4 and #5 if required by the variant) are placed just
before the start location of their nested `for` loop. If these strings are not needed
by a variant, they are left empty and no code is inserted in their location. The
last string (at #6) is the `target exit data` construct, which identifies the data
that must be released from the GPU or returned to the CPU. If not empty, each
of these strings is always terminated by a new line. Once these seven strings are in
their proper location, the code is dumped into a new C++ file and returned to the
application scientists, who can choose to accept or reject the best code based on
the kernel runtime provided in the comment.

4 Experiments and Evaluations

We used several clusters (on each using a single GPU) and compilers, as shown in
Table 1, to perform multiple experiments and evaluate our tool. For the purposes
of this study, we only use one GPU per node on the cluster. The management of
multiple GPUs is left for future research. The three modules explained in Sect. 3
need different experiments.

4.1 Experiment 1 - Data Analysis

First, we test our Advisor against all benchmark applications to determine
whether or not data is correctly identified and generated. In order to conduct
this experiment, we made use of our Advisor to generate code that used the
correct data between the host and the device. Additionally, we manually altered
each benchmark algorithm to map all data to and from the GPU. We executed

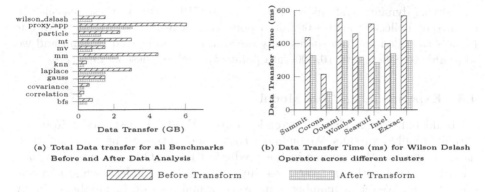

(a) Total Data transfer for all Benchmarks
Before and After Data Analysis

(b) Data Transfer Time (ms) for Wilson Dslash
Operator across different clusters

////// Before Transform   ▦ After Transform

Fig. 1. Data transfer Before and After Code Transformation

all the codes on each cluster, from Table 1, and collected data about the volume
and the duration of the data transfer. We found that the Advisor improved the
data management in all cases. Figure 1(a) shows the amount of data transferred
(in GB) between the CPU and the GPU before and after transformation for all
benchmark applications. After applying our transformation, we can clearly see
that the amount of data transfer has indeed been considerably reduced. Reduced
data transfer has an impact on all applications' data transfer times. Along with
reduced data transfer, the interconnecting bus between CPU and GPU (its version and number of lanes), affects the data transfer times of all applications.
On all the available clusters, we ran these applications and collected the data
transfer times. Figure 1(b) shows the data transfer time for the Wilson Dslash
Operator across different clusters.

4.2   Experiment 2 - Code Generation

In the second experiment, we use our Advisor to generate every possible code
combination using each of the Benchmark applications, as discussed in Sect. 3.1.
We used the compilers listed in Table 1 to compile all of these codes for various clusters. Some compilers (NVIDIA/nvc on Seawulf and LLVM/Clang 15 on
Wombat) do not support dynamic or guided scheduling on a GPU, resulting in
compilation failure. Apart from that, all of the codes successfully compiled and
ran on their respective clusters. We collected the runtime of each of the kernels
in this experiment, to be used by our cost model. We collected the data for the
Intel architecture a while ago, and we don't currently have access to the cluster
to conduct new experiments. As a result we had very limited data for Wilson
Dslash Operator and no data for our proxy_app on the Intel architecture. We
were unable to gather many data points for the Exxact machine (with NVIDIA
GeForce GPUs) due to the unavailability of compute nodes. Both these clusters has only around 2,000 data points each. Seawulf has NVIDIA K80 GPUs,
which is the slowest of the GPUs we're using in our experiment. So each kernel
runs longer on Seawulf than it would on any other cluster. On the other hand,
most variants of kernels failed to compile on Wombat due to their compilers not

supporting dynamic and guided scheduling on GPUs. Due to these reasons, we could only collect around 3,000 data points on Seawulf and Wombat. All our kernels compiled and ran successfully on Summit, Corona and Ookami and we were able to collect over 10,000 data points on each of these architectures.

4.3   Experiment 3 - Cost Model

To build our cost model, we extended our COMPOFF cost model from six variants to all 84 variants. We build our cost model in the testing mode and then use it to predict the runtime in the prediction mode. Our cost model utilizes an MLP model with six layers: one input layer, four hidden layers, and one output layer. We set the number of neurons on multiples of the number of input features rather than choosing a random number of neurons in each hidden layer or conducting an exhaustive grid search (number of neurons in the first layer). As a result, the first, second, third, and fourth hidden layers, with 33 input features, have 66, 132, 66, and 33 neurons, respectively. The weights of linear layers are set using the glorot initialization method, which is described in [7]. The bias is set to 0, and the batch size for training data is set to 16 in all runs.

$$RMSE(\bar{y}, y) = \sqrt{\frac{1}{N} \sum_{i=0}^{N} (\bar{y}_i - y_i)^2} \qquad NRMSE(\bar{y}, y) = \frac{RMSE(\bar{y}, y)}{(y_{max} - y_{min})}$$

$$(2) \qquad\qquad\qquad\qquad\qquad (3)$$

As the underlying optimization algorithm, we evaluate SGD (Stochastic Gradient Descent), Adam [12] and RMSprop [8]. We chose the RMSprop optimization algorithm as the underlying optimization algorithm, with an initial learning rate of 0.01 that is stepped down by a factor of 0.1 every 30 epochs and weight decay of 0.0001 for 150 epochs. We use the Root Mean Square Error (RMSE) loss function defined in Eq. 2, where $\bar{y}_i$ and y_i represent the predicted and ground truth runtimes, respectively.

We split the dataset used by all benchmark applications into two parts: training (80%) and validation(20%). The validation set do not occur in any learning for the model. The only augmentation applied to the training and validation data is Z-score standardization. The model is trained using the training set, and after that, testing data are given to the model to test its performance. In order to determine the standard deviation of the prediction errors, we compute the RMSE. The lower this value, the better our model. However, what constitutes a good RMSE is determined by the range of data on which we are computing RMSE. One way to determine whether an RMSE value is "good" is to normalize it using the formula shown in Eq. 3. This yields a value between 0 and 1, with values closer to 0 indicating better fitting models. Having a model with a normalized RMSE of less than 0.1 is considered successful in this study.

We observed strong correlation between actual and predicted data in Fig. 2, indicating that a simple MLP performs admirably in all our applications. It was anticipated that Intel and Exxact's model would perform the worst because of the lack of data. However, the model for Exxact performed better than Intel's due to the availability of more data for the proxy_app. Both Wombat and Seawulf

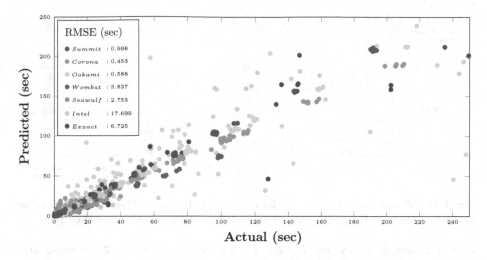

Fig. 2. Validation of Cost Model on different clusters

performed moderately well when compared to other models trained on a larger dataset. It is still an open question that how much data is enough data to train an ML model. We have observed from Fig. 2, however, that if we have more than 10,000 data points for our model, we will be able to train a model that is much more acceptable.

4.4   Experiment 4 - Prediction

Finally, for our final set of experiments we use our Advisor to predict the top 10 best variants for the Wilson Dslash Operator. Once the top 10 variants are identified we use the Code Transformation module to generate those 10 code variants and return them back to the user. The Advisor takes as input the base

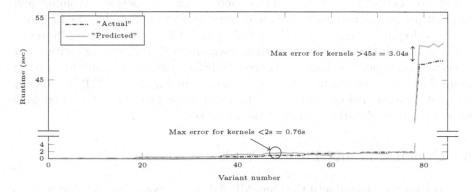

Fig. 3. Wilson Dslash operator's Actual and Predicted Runtimes (in sec) on Summit for all variants sorted by runtime.

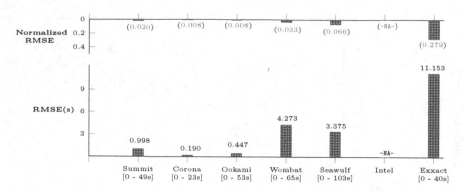

Fig. 4. RMSE and Normalized RMSE for runtime prediction of Wilson Dslash operator on different clusters (runtime range for each cluster is mentioned below their name).

Wilson Dslash kernel, where L_X, L_Y, L_Z, L_T are set at $32, 32, 32, 16$ each, and generates the top 10 best kernels as predicted by the cost model. As shown in Fig. 3, we plot the actual and predicted runtimes of all the 84 generated variants (sorted by actual runtime) of one such kernel when run on the Summit supercomputer. We can clearly see a strong correlation between the actual and predicted runtime for all the variants. The same correlation can be found in almost all kernels across all clusters. In Fig. 4, we display the Wilson Dslash operator's RMSE and normalized RMSE for each cluster. The range of runtimes (in seconds) for each cluster is mentioned below their name in the plot. We currently do not have access to the Intel cluster to conduct new experiments, and the Intel dataset contained very few data from the targeted Wilson Dslash kernel and none from our proxy_app. So, even if we make a prediction using this model, there is no way to validate it. Consequently, we did not conduct this experiment on the Intel architecture and the result is marked as $-NA-$. As expected on Exxact, the target kernel's RMSE increased significantly (11.153s) due to less data in its dataset. Even with a normalized RMSE of 0.279, it fell short of our expectation of 0.1. Nonetheless, this model demonstrated some correlation between the actual and predicted data. In contrast, Wombat and Seawulf performed reasonably well and were able to predict the top 10 kernel variants despite having an RMSE of 4.273s and 3.375s, respectively. However, with 0.033 and 0.066, respectively, their normalized RMSE was well within our expectation. As per our observation, their RMSE can also be improved by adding more data for these clusters. Finally, as shown in Fig. 4, the RMSE rates for Summit, Corona, and Ookami are less than one second each, and they were able to accurately predict the top ten kernel variants.

5   Conclusion and Future Work

In this paper, we introduced the OpenMP Advisor, a compiler tool that advises application scientists on various OpenMP code offloading strategies. Although the tool is currently restricted to GPUs, it can be extended to support other

OpenMP-capable devices. Using our Advisor, we were able to generate code of multiple applications for seven different architectures, and correctly predict the top ten best variants for each application including a real world application (the Wilson Dslash operator) on every architecture. Preliminary findings indicate that this tool can assist compiler developers and HPC application scientists in porting their legacy HPC codes to the upcoming heterogeneous computing environment. As a next step, we will extend our tool to 1) Data synchronization between host and device during kernel execution 2) Offload computation to multiple GPUs [11] via tasks 3) Predict the best variants for a variety of data sizes, and then use the OpenMP metadirective [19] directive to generate multiple directive variants for each range and 4) Extend the Advisor to other directive-based models, such as OpenACC. This tool is a first-of-its-kind attempt to build a framework for automatic GPU offloading using OpenMP and machine learning; as a result, there is plenty of room for improvement.

Acknowledgement. This research was supported by the Exascale Computing Project (17-SC-20-SC), a collaborative effort of the U.S. Department of Energy Office of Science and the National Nuclear Security Administration. This material is also based upon work supported by the National Science Foundation under grant no. CCF-2113996. This research used resources of the Oak Ridge Leadership Computing Facility at the Oak Ridge National Laboratory, which is supported by the Office of Science of the U.S. Department of Energy under Contract No. DE-AC05-00OR22725. The authors would like to thank Stony Brook Research Computing and Cyberinfrastructure, and the Institute for Advanced Computational Science at Stony Brook University for access to the SeaWulf computing system, which was made possible by a $1.4M National Science Foundation grant (#1531492).

References

1. Barua, P., Shirako, J., Tsang, W., Paudel, J., Chen, W., Sarkar, V.: OMPSan: static verification of OpenMP's data mapping constructs. In: Fan, X., de Supinski, B.R., Sinnen, O., Giacaman, N. (eds.) IWOMP 2019. LNCS, vol. 11718, pp. 3–18. Springer, Cham (2019). https://doi.org/10.1007/978-3-030-28596-8_1
2. Brower, R., Christ, N., DeTar, C., Edwards, R., Mackenzie, P.: Lattice QCD application development within the us doe exascale computing project. EPJ Web Conf. **175**, 09010 (2018). https://doi.org/10.1051/epjconf/201817509010
3. Burford, A., et al.: Ookami: deployment and initial experiences. In: Practice and Experience in Advanced Research Computing, pp. 1–8. ACM, New York (2021)
4. Che, S., et al.: Rodinia: a benchmark suite for heterogeneous computing. In: 2009 IEEE international symposium on workload characterization (IISWC), pp. 44–54. IEEE (2009)
5. Clang: Clang Rewriter class reference (2021). https://clang.llvm.org/doxygen/classclang_1_1Rewriter.html
6. Dagum, L., Menon, R.: OpenMP: an industry standard API for shared-memory programming. IEEE Comput. Sci. Eng. **5**(1), 46–55 (1998)
7. Glorot, X., Bengio, Y.: Understanding the difficulty of training deep feedforward neural networks. In: Proceedings of the Thirteenth International Conference on Artificial Intelligence and Statistics, pp. 249–256. JMLR Workshop and Conference Proceedings (2010)

8. Hinton, G., Srivastava, N., Swersky, K.: Neural networks for machine learning. Lecture 6a Overview of Mini-batch Gradient Descent, vol. 14, no. 8, p. 2 (2012)

9. Intel: Intel Developer Cloud (2021). https://www.intel.com/content/www/us/en/developer/tools/devcloud/overview.html

10. Jablin, T.B., Prabhu, P., Jablin, J.A., Johnson, N.P., Beard, S.R., August, D.I.: Automatic CPU-GPU communication management and optimization. In: Proceedings of the 32nd ACM SIGPLAN Conference on Programming Language Design and Implementation, pp. 142–151 (2011)

11. Kale, V., Lu, W., Curtis, A., Malik, A.M., Chapman, B., Hernandez, O.: Toward supporting multi-GPU targets via taskloop and user-defined schedules. In: Milfeld, K., de Supinski, B.R., Koesterke, L., Klinkenberg, J. (eds.) IWOMP 2020. LNCS, vol. 12295, pp. 295–309. Springer, Cham (2020). https://doi.org/10.1007/978-3-030-58144-2_19

12. Kingma, D.P., Ba, J.: Adam: a method for stochastic optimization. In: Bengio, Y., LeCun, Y. (eds.) 3rd International Conference on Learning Representations, ICLR 2015, San Diego, CA, USA, 7–9 May 2015, Conference Track Proceedings (2015). http://arxiv.org/abs/1412.6980

13. Laboratory, L.L.N.: LLNL - Corona (2019). https://hpc.llnl.gov/hardware/compute-platforms/corona

14. Lattner, C., Adve, V.: LLVM: a compilation framework for lifelong program analysis & transformation. In: International Symposium on Code Generation and Optimization, 2004. CGO 2004, pp. 75–86. IEEE (2004)

15. Lin, M.: Optimization of the domain wall dslash kernel in columbia physics system, p. 269 (2016)

16. Mendonça, G., Guimarães, B., Alves, P., Pereira, M., Araújo, G., Pereira, F.M.Q.: DawnCC: automatic annotation for data parallelism and offloading. ACM Trans. Archit. Code Optimiz. (TACO) 14(2), 13 (2017)

17. Mishra, A., Chheda, S., Soto, C., Malik, A.M., Lin, M., Chapman, B.: COMPOFF: a compiler cost model using machine learning to predict the cost of openmp offloading. In: 2022 IEEE International Parallel and Distributed Processing Symposium Workshops (IPDPSW), 30 May - 3 June 2022. IEEE (2022)

18. Mishra, A., Malik, A.M., Chapman, B.: Data transfer and reuse analysis tool for GPU-offloading using openMP. In: Milfeld, K., de Supinski, B.R., Koesterke, L., Klinkenberg, J. (eds.) IWOMP 2020. LNCS, vol. 12295, pp. 280–294. Springer, Cham (2020). https://doi.org/10.1007/978-3-030-58144-2_18

19. Mishra, A., Malik, A.M., Chapman, B.: Extending the LLVM/clang framework for openMP metadirective support. In: 2020 IEEE/ACM 6th Workshop on the LLVM Compiler Infrastructure in HPC (LLVM-HPC) and Workshop on Hierarchical Parallelism for Exascale Computing (HiPar), pp. 33–44. IEEE (2020)

20. ORNL: Oak Ridge Leadership Computing Facility - Summit supercomputing cluster (2017). https://www.olcf.ornl.gov/summit/

21. ORNL: Oak Ridge Leadership Computing Facility - Wombat cluster (2020). https://www.olcf.ornl.gov/olcf-resources/compute-systems/wombat/

22. Poesia, G., Guimarães, B., Ferracioli, F., Pereira, F.M.Q.: Static placement of computation on heterogeneous devices. In: Proceedings of the ACM on Programming Languages 1(OOPSLA), pp. 1–28 (2017)

23. Stony Brook University: Seawulf, computational cluster at stony brook university (2019). https://it.stonybrook.edu/help/kb/understanding-seawulf

Tasking Extensions

Introducing Moldable Tasks in OpenMP

Pierre-Étienne Polet[1,2]([⊠]), Ramy Fantar[2], and Thierry Gautier[1]

[1] Inria, CNRS, ENS de Lyon, UCBL, LIP, Lyon, France
pierre-etienne.polet@inria.fr
[2] Thales DMS, 06560 Valbonne, France

Abstract. This paper introduces a new approach to handle implicit parallelism in library functions. If the library already utilizes a third-party programming model like OpenMP, it may run in parallel. Otherwise, if the library remains sequential, OpenMP directives in client code cannot be used for direct parallelization. To express implicit parallelism and, in the meanwhile, dynamically adjust the parallel degree of a task when its starts, we propose to use moldable tasks. We handle this by introducing a new construct called `taskmoldable` that generates multiples tasks from a single function call and an iteration space. For the Lapack Cholesky factorization algorithm, our `taskmoldable` directive allows simple code annotation to express parallelism between tiles and improves programmability. Performance results on a beamforming application indicates that our moldable implementation is slightly faster by 5% in mean, than a parallel execution achieved with Intel MKL.

Keywords: Moldable task · OpenMP Task · Task Dependency

1 Introduction

The task programming model promotes seamless collaboration between application programmers and library developers, ensuring functional composition regardless of their respective choices during development. A work stealing scheduler from Cilk [6] has undergone theoretical analysis to provide guarantees for expected parallel time and space. A provable OpenMP-3.0 task scheduler should inherit these same guarantees. Furthermore, task models with dependencies have been subject to analysis within the same framework [14,30], allowing for the application of similar theoretical results to the OpenMP-4.0 dependent task model.

Although theoretical results have provided satisfactory findings, they are limited to a rigid task model that lacks consideration for the physical parallelism of the target machine during task creation. However, task management, including creation and scheduling, incurs overhead that significantly affects application performance. To mitigate this, researchers have proposed solutions such as lightweight task implementations (e.g., Cilk [6] for independent tasks, Kaapi [7,15]. for data flow dependencies), task throttling [1], high-performance work queue data structures for scalability [3,18], and caching task graph construction for multiple iterations [15,33].

S. McIntosh-Smith et al. (Eds.): IWOMP 2023, LNCS 14114, pp. 51–65, 2023.
https://doi.org/10.1007/978-3-031-40744-4_4

Parallel programs typically involve more arithmetic operations and memory accesses compared to their sequential counterparts. Although these extra overheads don't fundamentally alter the asymptotic number of operations, they do reduce practical efficiency. To mitigate these additional operations, it is crucial to align the parallelism level of the application with the hardware's degree of parallelism. It is important to note that the aforementioned solutions do not address these supplementary costs.

OpenMP efficiently adapts application parallelism to hardware through worksharing constructs. Parallel worksharing loops are automatically distributed among the threads in the current parallel region, ensuring balanced iteration space. The taskloop construct generates the right number of tasks based on the parallel region's size, limiting arithmetic overheads.

This paper proposes a new task generating construct for expressing hidden implicit parallelism in library functions. It allows to define *moldable tasks*, which can adapt their parallel degree to available resources, based on established theoretical scheduling concepts [20,29].

The following section motivates our proposal, focusing on concrete case studies. Section 3 provides detailed information about the `taskmoldable` directive and its key clauses. We then demonstrate the usage of the new directive in a classical Cholesky factorization and a beamforming application [16,28], concluding the presentation.

2   Motivation

A recently proposed linear algebra API [10] defined *batched API* to process a set of independent linear algebra subroutine calls on small matrices, with "*the aim of providing more efficient, but portable, implementations of algorithms on high-performance manycore architectures* [10]." They were present in commonly used APIs such as Nvidia cuBLAS, Magma [17] or Intel MKL.

A call to perform `batch_count` matrix multiplications on a set of input data is[1]:

```
1  gemm_batch(m,n,k,A,B,C,bc);
```

where each parameter is an array of size bc, the batch count, of the required parameter to call the BLAS gemm kernel, *i.e.* the call is equivalent to:

```
1  for (int i=0; i<bc; ++i)
2    gemm(m[i],n[i],k[i],A[i],B[i],C[i]);
```

The gemm_batch operation performs bc independent calls to the gemm BLAS subroutine where each gemm works with different parameters and data provided in the effective array parameters. Because the for loop resides inside the code body of the BLAS batch function it was not accessible to parallelize calls to gemm_batch using any OpenMP worksharing directives or the taskloop

---

[1] For simplicity, we omit some parameters such as the operations on matrices (transposition...), alpha and beta assumed to be 1, the leading dimensions or the info error parameter which are required to pass arguments to each underlying gemm kernel.

generating task construct. Our proposal aims at providing an OpenMP construct to expose the *implicit loop*, and its iterations, as a task generating construct.

The application developer knows that the gemm_batch is equivalent to executing the above implicit iteration loop. Thus the iterations may be partitioned in a disjoint set of N intervals $I_k = [b_k, e_k[$ such that $\cup_{k=0}^{N-1} I_k = [0, bc - 1]$, such that the batched gemm calls could be rewritten to:

```
1  for (int i=0; i<N; ++i)
2    gemm_batch(m+b_k[i],n+b_k[i],k+b_k[i],A+b_k[i],B+b_k[i],
3      C+b_k[i], e_k[i]-b_k[i]);
```

Therefore, the gemm_batch operation can be viewed as a list homomorphism [5]. Given a list l, a concatenation operator $\#$, and a function f assumed to be a list homomorphism, we can transform the call $f(l1\#l2)$ into calls to $f(l1) \oplus f(l2)$, where $\oplus$ is a reduction operator. In our case, the function f represents the structured block outlined following the OpenMP directive.

Overview of Moldable Task. The two main issues are defining the implicit loop iteration space (*e.g.* bc) and passing the effective parameters to the subcalls. We propose annotating the code with a new directive **taskmoldable** used to inform that the following structured block has an implicit loop to partition. The size of the iteration is specified by the clause **batch_count** and the transformation of effective parameters to the parameters of the subsequences calls is specified by the clause **access**.

```
1  #pragma omp taskmoldable access(linear: m,n,k,A,B,C) \
2                            batch_count(bc)
3  gemm_batch(m,n,k,A,B,C,bc);
```

In this example, the transformation is of kind **linear**, that is a default mapping function, that applies $M_X : i \to X + i$ to any variable X listed in the clause access to pass the parameter on the partition i. We called such transformation a *mapping function*. It could be defined by the user.

syrk: a list homomorphism with reduction. The proposed clause can be applied to list homomorphisms that involve reduction. Figure 1 illustrates a common call to the syrk subroutine in the left-looking Cholesky factorization [25], as seen in the Lapack netlib potrf. syrk computes $T = T - A \times A^T$ with T symmetric. The moldable task has dependence types in on A and inout on T. The computation $T = T - A \times A^T$ is equal to $T = T - \sum_i A_i \times A_i^T$ where A_i is the i-th tile of size $nb \times nb$ (except the last tile) as depicted in Fig. 1.

The moldable task in Fig. 1 expresses the fact that the call to syrk is a list homomorphism with respect to matrix A_i starting at position A+i*nb from A: This is an access strided{nb} with our proposal. Matrix T is fully accessed by all calls to syrk. It was possible to keep the original inout dependence-type, but to keep the possibility to reorder the accumulation depending on the predecessor tasks releasing the matrix bloc A_i the clause specifies that the dependence

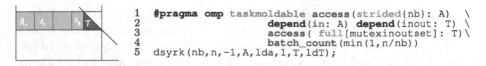

```
1    #pragma omp taskmoldable access(strided{nb}: A)   \
2                      depend(in: A) depend(inout: T) \
3                      access( full[mutexinoutset]: T)\
4                      batch_count(min(1,n/nb))
5    dsyrk(nb,n,-1,A,lda,1,T,ldT);
```

Fig. 1. Left: SYRK $T = T - A \times A^T$ in left looking version of the Cholesky factorization. Right: annotation with taskmoldable.

type on T expressed by generated task is mutexinoutset. Thus by accumulating the sequence of syrk calls on each A_i to the matrice T, we obtain the result.

The code that generates the explicit tasks from Fig. 1 is equivalent to the following, where bc is the batch count generated from the clause batch_count.

```
1    for (int i=0; i< bc; ++i)
2        #pragma omp task depend(in: A+i*nb) depend(mutexinoutset: T)
3        dsyrk(nb,n,-1,A+i*nb,lda,1,T,ldT);
```

The taskmoldable directive enables the expression of internal parallelism within library functions, including batched or non-BLAS subroutines. By reducing programming efforts, code annotations can result in highly parallel task-based programs. The next section focuses on presenting the taskmoldable directive and its associated clauses, which facilitates the extraction of more parallelism. Section 4 provides detailed accounts of three comprehensive case studies: the application of taskmoldable to matrix-matrix multiplication (gemm), the sequential Lapack left-looking Cholesky factorization [25] and a beamforming application [16, 28].

3 A New Directive: Taskmoldable

As the taskloop directive [22, 31], the **taskmoldable** directive is a *task generating construct*. It enhances the functionality of the taskloop directive by allowing the capturing of (implicit) parallel loops within any structured block through user annotations and parameter passing rules to generated tasks.

3.1 General Structure

The general structure of the directive is the following:

```
1    #pragma omp taskmoldable batch_count(<counter-list>) \
2        access( <data-mapping> [{args}] [<dependence-type>] : \
3            <list-item> )\
4        depend( <dependence-type> : <list-item> )\
5        <data-sharing attribute>\
6        num_tasks( <integer-list> ) | grainsize( grain-size-list)
7    {<structured block>}
```

When a thread encounters a taskmoldable construct, it creates an explicit task that partitions the implicit iterations defined by batch_count into chunks, each of which is assigned to an explicit task for parallel execution. Each chunk has an identifier from 0 to the maximal number of chunks - 1. The size of the chunk is computed before creating the explicit task. The data environment of each generated task is created according to the data-sharing attribute clauses on the `taskmoldable` construct, per-data environment ICVs.

The clause `access` is used to translate the variables to be passed to each explicit task. The effect is as if each variable in the list-item appearing in the structured block is rewritten by applying the data mapping function on the chunk id. The `data-mapping` is either a predefined identifier: `linear`, `strided{<integer expr>}` or `full`; or a user-defined identifier. Section 3.3 presents the data mapping function. Optionally, the clause `access` can specify the dependence-type of the generated tasks expressed on the variable.

Clause `batch_count` accepts a list of integers that are associated to an implicit nested iteration loops. For instance, $batch\_count(C_0, C_1, ..., C_{k-1})$ is associated with the implicit nested loops generating the tasks as illustrated in the following code. As for the taskloop directive, clauses `num_tasks` and `grainsize` limit the number of tasks generated at runtime. For `taskmoldable` directive, their parameters are a list of values applied on each loop of the nest.

3.2   Compilation

The compiler rewrites the `taskmoldable` directive to a code equivalent to the following skeleton:

```
1   #pragma omp task depend( weak-dependency-type: <list-item> )
2   {
3       _kmpc_omp_taskmoldable_size( C_0, .., C_{k-1},
4           num_tasks, grainsize, S_0, .., S_{k-1} );
5       for (int i_0=0; i_0<C_0; i_0+ = S_0)
6           for (int i_1=0; i_1<C_1; i_1+ = S_1)
7               ...
8               for (int i_{k-1}=0; i_{k-1}<C_{k-1}; i_{k-1}+ = S_{k-1})
9                   #pragma omp task depend( <inherited> )
10                  {<structured block. Variables of the 'access' list-item
11                      have been replaced by the mapping function called with
12                      (i_0,i_1,...,i_{k-1},S_0,S_1,...,S_{k-1}) as effective parameters>}
13  }
```

The moldable task is created with dependencies using the weak variant [14, 24] of the dependency type used in the depend clauses: e.g. a `depend( inout: A )` in the `taskmoldable` definition is translated to `depend(weak-inout: A)`. The objective is to postpone real dependencies on the child tasks (because those are making real memory accesses and computation) rather than to the moldable task which only creates tasks.

Then, the task calls the runtime function `_kmpc_omp_taskmoldable_size` to compute the size of the tasks in each dimension $S_0, S_1 ..., S_{k-1}$ from the sizes of the `batch_count` clause (dimension $C_0, C_1, ..., C_{k-1}$) and the values passed in clause `num_tasks` or `grainsize`.

3.3   Data Mapping Functions

A data mapping function is associated with an item using the `access` clause of the `taskmoldable` directive:

access(mapping_id [{<args>}] [<dependence-type>]: list-item)

The optional dependence-type argument is presented in the next section dealing with the expression of dependencies on generated tasks. The runtime defines the subset of the initial workload for each task. It provides a tuple start = $(i_0, i_1, ..., i_{k-1})$ that defines the beginning of the sub-iteration space it should process. The access clauses provide information to get the right data for each task. To do so the user provides a function called *mapping_id* where the declaration is defined as follows:

$$F(item, batch\_count, start, args...)$$

which is used to replace items from item-list each time it appear in the structured block.

We propose three basic mappings, strided{args} that take as argument a stride on each dimension, linear that assumes the data are linearly spaced and full that assume all task work on the same data. They are defined as follows:

$$strided(A, bc, start, strides) \rightarrow A + \sum_{u=0}^{|bc|-1} i_u * strides[u]$$
$$linear(A, bc, start) \rightarrow A + \sum_{u=0}^{|bc|-1} i_u * \prod_{v=0}^{u-1} bc[v]$$
$$full(A, bc, start) \rightarrow A$$

Items from list-item are expected to be pointers of types that allow pointer arithmetic.

An implementation of the linear *mapping_id* could be the following:

```
template<T> T* linear(T* A, int* bc, int* starts, int dim_count)
{
    int pos = 0; int size = 1;
    for(int u = 0; u < dim_count; u++)
    {
        pos += starts[u];
        size *= bc[u]
    }
    return A+pos;
}
```

The runtime tries to decompose the computation into N tasks where N is either provided by the clause num_tasks, or by default, computed automatically: The dimensions of the split are even and computed by the runtime function _kmpc_omp_taskmoldable_size. Preliminary experimental results reported in Sect. 4.3 show that our proposition of compilation of moldable tasks could be applied to heterogeneous architectures.

3.4   Data Dependencies

Task generating constructs often require implicit synchronization to ensure the correctness of parallel executions. However, relaxing these synchronization requirements can enable better utilization of hardware resources. Sharing this goal, a recent proposal to enhance OpenMP, as described in [22], suggests extending the depend clause to include the taskloop construct.

The same issue appears with the taskmoldable directive. The main difference is that iteration loops are hidden from the annotation thus the expression of dependencies on generated task is different. Thanks to the data mapping function we are able to replace the item and the mapped item through the function, as defined in the above section. In that way, the generated task inherits the dependencies from the depend clause in the taskmoldable directive but on items rewritten by the data mapping function.

However, the programmer may optionally refine the way generated tasks declare dependencies through the access clause. This is illustrated in Fig. 1 where the generated tasks declare mutexinoutset dependencies on item T while the moldable task has declared dependency type inout on it. The interest here is to allows commutativity on the reduction operated by syrk in case of faster resolution of dependencies on the A_i.

We assume the availability of the weak-dependencies [24] to postpone real dependencies on the moldable task to the generated tasks. Without them, it is possible to inline the execution of the moldable task creation of the task generating tasks: at runtime, the taskmoldable directive is translated to the code that directly generates the explicit tasks in place of creating the task (that will generate the explicit tasks).

3.5   Implementation

We have created a customized runtime specifically designed to handle moldable tasks, allowing us to validate a prototype before integrating it into the LLVM OpenMP runtime. Thanks to our previous development work in the LLVM runtime, we have taken care to ensure an easier merge process.

The task entry point follows the code outlined in Sect. 3.2. To create a moldable task, we utilize the runtime function __kmpc_omp_task_moldable, which extends __kmpc_omp_task_withdeps to include task dependencies and additional mapping functions. These are stored in supplementary fields of the task data structure kmp_task_t.

We have also incorporated support for partitioning moldable tasks between CPUs and GPUs. If the user provides a GPU version of the list homomorphism function, the runtime divides the implicit iteration between CPUs and GPUs. Initial experiments regarding this feature are reported in Sect. 4.3. We briefly discuss how to integrate moldable tasks with targets in the following perspective.

The runtime should select a granularity for each moldable task, our implementation relies on previous executions of similar functions to compute an expected performance for each worker, then it creates one task for each worker that handles a subset of the moldable task proportional to its performance. Tasks running on GPU targets may be further split by the runtime to fit the memory constraints of the co-processor.

4   Evaluation

The two next sections illustrate our taskmoldable directive with two decompositions of the gemm matrix product, and how to produce a highly parallel

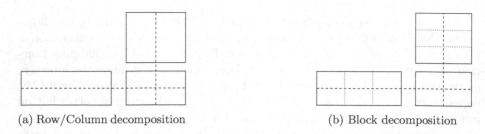

(a) Row/Column decomposition   (b) Block decomposition

Fig. 2. GEMM block decomposition.

Cholesky factorization from the sequential code of the Lapack netlib library. Then we present a beamforming application with performance evaluation.

4.1 Gemm Decomposition

The `strided{<optional-args>}` mapping function is well-suited when all data are stored in an array by spacing each consecutive partition with a constant stride. As an example, we will show how to generate two classical decomposition of gemm with the `taskmoldable` directive:

```
1  #pragma omp taskmoldable batch_count(m,n)\
2      access(strided{lda,0}:A)\
3      access(strided{0,1}:B)\
4      access(strided{ldc,1}:C)\
5      depend(inout:C) depend(in:A,B)
6  gemm( m, n, k, A, B, C );
```

The result of this decomposition, in case of even split, is presented as Fig. 2a. It can generate up to $m \times n$ independent tasks. In this case, the block decomposition only works with two dimensions thus the input matrices are split by row or by column but not in blocks. To allows full block decomposition we should handle dependencies between tasks and work on the third dimension of the gemm. The following code result in decomposition Fig. 2b. We describe dependency management in Sect. 3.4.

```
1  #pragma omp taskmoldable batch_count(m,n,k)\
2      access(strided{lda,0,1}:A)\
3      access(strided{0,1,ldb}:B)\
4      access(strided{ldc,1,0}[mutexinoutset]:C)\
5      depend(inout:C) depend(in:A,B)
6  gemm( m, n, k, A, B, C );
```

4.2 Lapack Cholesky Factorization

The Cholesky factorization algorithm is used in signal processing algorithms such as adaptive beamforming [13], it is also commonly studied in dependency graph generation. We worked on the block left-looking version of the algorithm which is implemented in the subroutine portf in Lapack[2], the associated code is sketched below[3]:

---

[2] https://netlib.org/lapack/.
[3] Code is rewritten in C to follow the guideline of the paper.

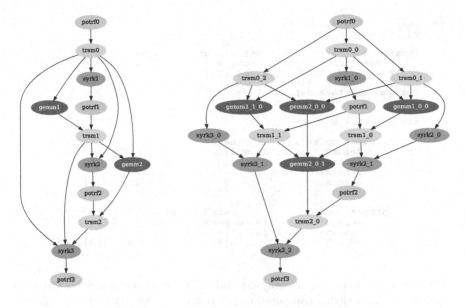

(a) Without moldability   (b) With taskmoldable

Fig. 3. Left looking Cholesky task graph with N/NB = 4

```
1   cholesky( N, NB, A, lda ):
2      for( j = 0; j < N; j += NB )
3      {
4         #pragma omp task depend(in:A[0][j]) depend(inout:A[j][j])
5         syrk( NB, j, -1, A[0][j], lda, 1 A[j][j], lda )
6         #pragma omp task depend(inout:A[j][j])
7         potrf( NB, A[j][j], lda )
8         if( j + NB < N )
9         {
10            #pragma omp task depend(in:A[0][j],A[0][j+NB])\
11               depend(inout:A[j][j+NB])
12            gemm( NB, N - j - NB, j, -1, A[0][j], lda, A[0][j+NB],
13               lda, 1, A[j][j+NB], lda )
14            #pragma omp task depend(in:A[j][j])\
15               depend(inout:A[j][j+NB])
16            trsm( NB, N - j - NB, 1, A[j][j], lda, A[j][j+NB], lda )
17         }
18      }
```

At each iteration, it updates a group of NB columns with their definitive
values. A graph of tasks generated with this code is provided as Fig. 3a. Whereas
the code is elegant and relatively simple, it does not express a lot of parallelism.

By seeing the calls to syrk, gemm and trsm as moldable tasks and adapting the granularity of the split we can achieve the same level of parallelism as
a right-looking implementation, the dependency graph is provided as Fig. 3b.
Furthermore, if we make the granularity finer, as presented in Sect. 4.1, more
parallelism can be generated on gemm and trsm function calls. The code is
provided below:

```
1   cholesky( N, NB, A, lda ):
2     for( j = 0; j < N; j += NB )
3     {
4       #pragma omp taskmoldable batch_count(j) depend(in:A[0][j])
5           depend(inout:A[j][j]) access(strided{1}:A[0][j]) \
6           access(full[mutexinoutset]:A[j][j])
7       syrk( NB, j, -1, A[0][j], lda, 1 A[j][j], lda )
8       #pragma omp task depend( inout: A[j][j] )
9       potrf( NB, A[j][j], lda )
10
11      if( j + NB < N )
12      {
13        #pragma omp taskmoldable batch_count((NB,N-j-NB,j))\
14            depend(in:A,B) depend(inout:C) \
15            access(strided{0,1,lda}:A[0][j])\
16            access(strided{0,1,lda}:A[0][j+NB])\
17            access(strided{lda,1,0}[mutexinoutset]:A[j][j+NB])
18        gemm( NB, N-j-NB, j, -1, A[0][j], lda, A[0][j+NB], lda,
19              1, A[j][j+NB], lda )
20        #pragma omp taskmoldable batch_count(N-j-NB)\
21            depend(in:A[j][j]) depend(inout:A[j][j+NB])\
22            access(strided{1}:A[j][j+NB])
23        trsm( NB, N - j - NB, 1, A[j][j], lda, A[j][j+NB], lda )
24      }
25   }
```

The key point here is that original code can be annotated with OpenMP directives[4] for parallelizing compared to restructuring algorithms to exploit parallelism between tiles [9]. This was possible thanks to advanced features such as dependencies between arrays [8,23].

4.3   Case of Study: Beamforming

We implement a beamforming algorithm design to work on rectangular arrays of sensors using only moldable tasks, the algorithm is composed of three main parts. First sensor data are converted from the temporal domain to the frequency domain with FFT1D. Then we apply dephasing coefficients to each input to compute the beams, thanks to the shape of the array we can decompose this step in two consecutive matrix multiplications. The final step is to convert complex values to energy by computing the absolute value of each element. Due to data pattern restrictions in the used libraries, we insert a transposition step between the FFT and the matrices multiplications. The pseudo-code is provided below, the values of parameters stride_x are user-defined, constant and depend on the in-memory representation of each array.

```
1   beamforming():
2     #pragma omp taskmoldable batch_count(fft_count) \
3         depend(in:Sensor_t) depend(out:Sensor_f)\
4         access(strided{fft_stize}:Sensor_t,Sensor_f)
5     fft1DExecBatch( fft_size, Sensor_t, Sensor_f, fft_count )
6
7     #pragma omp taskmoldable batch_count( fft_count )\
8         depend(in:Sensor_f) depend(out:Sensor_f2)\
9         access(strided{fft_size}:Sensor_f)\
10        access(strided{1}:Sensor_f2)
11    transpose( Sensor_f, Sensor_f2 )
12
13    #pragma omp taskmoldable batch_count(gemm_0_count)\
```

---

[4] Here we have presented C pragma directive - we also assume Fortran compatible directive.

```
14          depend(in:Sensor_f2,Dephase_x) depend(out:Pseudo_beam)\
15          access(strided{stride_S},Sensor_f2)\
16          access(strided{stride_X},Dephase_x)\
17          access(strided{stride_P},Pseudo_beam)
18      gemmStrideBatch( Sensor_f2, Dephase_x, Pseudo_beam, gemm_0_count )
19
20      #pragma omp taskmoldable batch_count(gemm_1_count)\
21          depend(in:Pseudo_beam,Dephase_y) depend(Beam)\
22          access(strided{stride_P}:Pseudo_beam)\
23          access(strided{stride_Y}:Dephase_y)\
24          access(strided{stride_B}:Beam)
25      gemmStrideBatch( Pseudo_beam, Dephase_y, Beam, gemm_1_count )
26
27      #pragma omp taskmoldable batch_count(abs_count)\
28          depend(in:Beam) depend(out:Energy)\
29          access(strided{1}:Beam,Energy)
30      abs( Beam, Energy, abs_count )
```

This code was executed on our custom runtime, it ran on a workstation with Intel Xeon 8253, 16 cores processor. It ran about 1M FFT of size 4K, 4K square GEMM of size 1024 and 256M abs values at each iteration. The implementation uses Intel MKL sequential on Intel CPU and OpenBlas on AMD ones, cuBlas and cuFFT are used for Nvidia GPUs.

Overhead of task managements : On this beamforming benchmark, at each iteration of the time step loop, the code generates 40 taskmoldable constructs decomposed into 4062 tasks. The number of dependencies is 103086 between all the tasks. We measure a mean creation cost of $360\mu s$ per moldable task; $4\mu s$ per task; and 140ns per dependency. Our moldable task runtime does not fit well with the analysis in [27] because the task granularity is not a free execution parameter: It is fixed by the runtime according to available resources and their performances. When more resources are used for the execution, the moldable tasks are decomposed into more finer tasks.

Moreover, we compare the performances of the moldable implementation using MKL sequential and a classical one using MKL parallel library. We find out that the moldable implementation is 5% faster, in mean, than the classical one, thus the overhead implied by the moldability and our runtime is negligible for this workload. Mean execution times over 100 iterations for different core count are provided in Table 1.

Table 1. Beamforming execution times

#core:	1	2	4	8	12	16
MKL parallel: (s)	15.9	8.7	4.4	2.3	1.7	1.3
Moldable (s):	15.3	7.8	4.0	2.0	1.7	1.2
Delta (%):	4	10	9	13	0	8

By adding two different RTX GPUs to the workstation, we show that the same code can scale on heterogeneous platforms, it implies to allow a task to execute different code for each target and to handle memory with the runtime.

Results of executions speed by adding GPUs are provided in Fig. 4 with results on a DGXA100 server. On the RTX platform, CPU-only execution ran in 28s, it was 14.7 times faster than sequential execution and 2.89 times slower than heterogeneous execution. On the DGXA100, CPU-only execution ran in 9s, we reach a speedup of 4.5 by adding GPUs.

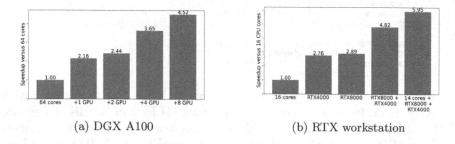

(a) DGX A100   (b) RTX workstation

Fig. 4. Beam-forming speedups

5   Related Work

Tasks based runtimes are used to schedule tasks on the fly. There are multiple runtimes available as OpenMP [12], StarPU [4], OMPSS [11], Kaapi [15] or PaRSEC [19]. Those runtimes aim to schedule dependent tasks with a lack of knowledge about task computational cost and without knowing tasks that will be scheduled in the future. None of them offer a moldable task concept that allows the expression of functions as a set of tasks. This criterion is absent in the classification of [32]. In [2] the authors theoretically analyze the upper bound on performance using an assumption that tasks are moldable without support in StarPU used by their application. Several moldable task schedulers are proposed and analyzed in scheduling literature [20,29] with *ad hoc* simulation or experimentation without any runtime support of moldable tasks.

The OpenMP task concept exists and had been extended to provide task creation from loop structures using taskloop [31], moreover, recent contributions open the path to data dependencies between tasks from different taskloops without the need for a global synchronization [22]. Furthermore, [21] provides a structure that allows OpenMP tasks to run inner loops as worksharing constructs, and [26] extensions allow more control over the parallelism generated inside a task that calls library code that uses openMP tasks. OpenMP does not provide a syntax to exploit the implicit parallel structure of library functions.

taskmoldable is a task generating directive. At runtime, it creates an explicit task that postpones real dependencies to its child tasks. Athapascan-1 runtime [14] allows this passing rule with the *postponed access mode*. Similar features are recently proposed under the term *weak-dependencies* in OMPSS [24]. With the absence of weak-dependencies it is always possible to directly create child tasks with an anticipated decision to decompose the moldable task.

6   Conclusion and Perspectives

The `taskmoldable` directive provides a means for users to leverage hidden parallelism in a function without sacrificing the performance of library-specific implementations or requiring an extensive restructuring of the function's internal design. Our evaluation and examples demonstrate how this directive enables the extraction of parallelism from a sequential Cholesky implementation. Furthermore, we achieve minimal overhead when handling moldable tasks in domain-specific workloads like beamforming, allowing us to compete with an MKL implementation.

Our ongoing research aims to expand the scope of our preliminary experimental results, encompassing CPUs and GPUs. This extension will enable users to annotate code, constructing performance models that guide the sizing of partitions. Additionally, we are exploring the integration of target clauses into the directive, facilitating heterogeneous computations based on moldable tasks.

Another future direction involves exploring how to express the moldability of more complex moldable code structures beyond nested loops. For instance, we aim to enable the perception of the entire Cholesky factorization as a moldable task.

Acknowledgements. Experiments presented in this paper were carried out using the Grid'5000 testbed (see https://www.grid5000.fr), supported by a scientific interest group hosted by Inria and including CNRS, RENATER and several Universities as well as other organizations.

References

1. Agathos, S.N., Kallimanis, N.D., Dimakopoulos, V.V.: Speeding up openMP tasking. In: European Conference on Parallel Processing (2012)
2. Agullo, E., Bramas, B., Coulaud, O., Darve, E., Messner, M., Takahashi, T.: Task-based FMM for heterogeneous architectures. Concurr. Comput. Pract. Exper. **28**(9), 2608–2629 (2016)
3. Arora, N.S., Blumofe, R.D., Plaxton, C.G.: Thread scheduling for multiprogrammed multiprocessors. Theory Comput. Syst. **34**(2), 115–144 (2001)
4. Augonnet, C., Thibault, S., Namyst, R., Wacrenier, P.-A.: StarPU: a unified platform for task scheduling on heterogeneous multicore architectures. In: Sips, H., Epema, D., Lin, H.-X. (eds.) Euro-Par 2009. LNCS, vol. 5704, pp. 863–874. Springer, Heidelberg (2009). https://doi.org/10.1007/978-3-642-03869-3_80
5. Bird, R.S.: An introduction to the theory of lists. In: Broy, M. (ed.) Logic of Programming and Calculi of Discrete Design. NATO ASI Series, vol. 36, pp. 5–42. Springer, Heidelberg (1987). https://doi.org/10.1007/978-3-642-87374-4_1
6. Blumofe, R.D., Leiserson, C.E.: Space-efficient scheduling of multithreaded computations. SIAM J. Comput. **27**, 202–229 (1998)
7. Broquedis, F., Gautier, T., Danjean, V.: LibKOMP, an efficient openMP runtime system for both fork-join and data flow paradigms. In: Chapman, B.M., Massaioli, F., Müller, M.S., Rorro, M. (eds.) IWOMP 2012. LNCS, vol. 7312, pp. 102–115. Springer, Heidelberg (2012). https://doi.org/10.1007/978-3-642-30961-8_8

8. Bueno, J., Martorell, X., Badia, R.M., Ayguadé, E., Labarta, J.: Implementing ompSs support for regions of data in architectures with multiple address spaces. In: Proceedings of the 27th International ACM Conference on International Conference on Supercomputing, pp. 359–368. ICS 2013, Association for Computing Machinery, New York, NY, USA (2013)

9. Buttari, A., Langou, J., Kurzak, J., Dongarra, J.: A class of parallel tiled linear algebra algorithms for multicore architectures. Parallel Comput. **35**(1), 38–53 (2009)

10. Dongarra, J., et al.: A proposed API for batched basic linear algebra subprograms (2016)

11. Duran, A., et al.: OmpSs: a proposal for programming heterogeneous multi-core architectures. Parallel processing letters **21**(02), 173–193 (2011)

12. Duran, A., Corbalán, J., Ayguadé, E.: Evaluation of openMP task scheduling strategies. In: Eigenmann, R., de Supinski, B.R. (eds.) IWOMP 2008. LNCS, vol. 5004, pp. 100–110. Springer, Heidelberg (2008). https://doi.org/10.1007/978-3-540-79561-2_9

13. Fuhrmann, D.R., San Antonio, G.: Transmit beamforming for MIMO radar systems using partial signal correlation. In: Conference Record of the Thirty-Eighth Asilomar Conference on Signals, Systems and Computers, 2004, vol. 1, pp. 295–299. IEEE (2004)

14. Galilée, F., Roch, J.L., Cavalheiro, G.G.H., Doreille, M.: Athapascan-1: on-line building data flow graph in a parallel language. In: Proceedings of the 1998 International Conference on Parallel Architectures and Compilation Techniques, p. 88. PACT 1998, IEEE Computer Society, USA (1998)

15. Gautier, T., Besseron, X., Pigeon, L.: KAAPI: a thread scheduling runtime system for data flow computations on cluster of multi-processors. In: Proceedings of the 2007 International Workshop on Parallel Symbolic Computation, pp. 15–23. PASCO 2007, Association for Computing Machinery, New York, NY, USA (2007)

16. Guerreiro, A.M.G., Neto, A.D.D., Lisboa, F.: Beamforming applied to an adaptive planar array. In: Proceedings RAWCON 98. 1998 IEEE Radio and Wireless Conference (Cat. No. 98EX194), pp. 209–212. IEEE (1998)

17. Haidar, A., Dong, T.T., Tomov, S., Luszczek, P., Dongarra, J.: A framework for batched and GPU-resident factorization algorithms applied to block householder transformations. In: Kunkel, J.M., Ludwig, T. (eds.) ISC High Performance 2015. LNCS, vol. 9137, pp. 31–47. Springer, Cham (2015). https://doi.org/10.1007/978-3-319-20119-1_3

18. Hendler, D., Shavit, N.: Non-blocking steal-half work queues. In: Proceedings of the Twenty-First Annual Symposium on Principles of Distributed Computing, pp. 280–289. Association for Computing Machinery, New York, NY, USA (2002)

19. Hoque, R., Herault, T., Bosilca, G., Dongarra, J.: Dynamic task discovery in parsec: a data-flow task-based runtime. In: Proceedings of the 8th Workshop on Latest Advances in Scalable Algorithms for Large-Scale Systems. ScalA 2017, Association for Computing Machinery, New York, NY, USA (2017)

20. Marchal, L., Simon, B., Sinnen, O., Vivien, F.: Malleable task-graph scheduling with a practical speed-up model. IEEE Trans. Parallel Distrib. Syst. **29**(6), 1357–1370 (2018)

21. Maronas, M., Sala, K., Mateo, S., Ayguade, E., Beltran, V.: Worksharing tasks: an efficient way to exploit irregular and fine-grained loop parallelism. In: 2019 IEEE 26th International Conference on High Performance Computing, Data, and Analytics (HiPC), pp. 383–394. IEEE (2019)

22. Maroñas, M., Teruel, X., Beltran, V.: OpenMP taskloop dependences. In: McIntosh-Smith, S., de Supinski, B.R., Klinkenberg, J. (eds.) IWOMP 2021. LNCS, vol. 12870, pp. 50–64. Springer, Cham (2021). https://doi.org/10.1007/978-3-030-85262-7_4

23. Paek, Y., Hoeflinger, J., Padua, D.: Efficient and precise array access analysis. ACM Trans. Program. Lang. Syst. **24**(1), 65–109 (2002)

24. Perez, J.M., Beltran, V., Labarta, J., Ayguadé, E.: Improving the integration of task nesting and dependencies in openMP. In: 2017 IEEE International Parallel and Distributed Processing Symposium (IPDPS), pp. 809–818 (2017)

25. Rothberg, E.E., Gupta, A.: An evaluation of left-looking, right-looking and multifrontal approaches to sparse Cholesky factorization on hierarchical-memory machines. Int. J. High Speed Comput. **5**, 537–593 (1991)

26. Scogland, T.R.W., Sunderland, D., Olivier, S.L., Hollman, D.S., Evans, N., de Supinski, B.R.: Making openmp ready for C++ executors. In: Fan, X., de Supinski, B.R., Sinnen, O., Giacaman, N. (eds.) IWOMP 2019. LNCS, vol. 11718, pp. 320–332. Springer, Cham (2019). https://doi.org/10.1007/978-3-030-28596-8_22

27. Slaughter, E., et al.: Task bench: a parameterized benchmark for evaluating parallel runtime performance. In: SC20: International Conference for High Performance Computing, Networking, Storage and Analysis, pp. 1–15. IEEE (2020)

28. Somasundaram, S.D.: Wideband robust capon beamforming for passive sonar. IEEE J. Oceanic Eng. **38**(2), 308–322 (2012)

29. Sun, H., Elghazi, R., Gainaru, A., Aupy, G., Raghavan, P.: Scheduling parallel tasks under multiple resources: list scheduling vs. pack scheduling. In: 2018 IEEE International Parallel and Distributed Processing Symposium, pp. 194–203 (2018)

30. Tchiboukdjian, M., Gast, N., Trystram, D.: Decentralized list scheduling. Ann. Oper. Res. **207**(1), 237–259 (2013)

31. Teruel, X., Klemm, M., Li, K., Martorell, X., Olivier, S.L., Terboven, C.: A proposal for task-generating loops in OpenMP*. In: Rendell, A.P., Chapman, B.M., Müller, M.S. (eds.) IWOMP 2013. LNCS, vol. 8122, pp. 1–14. Springer, Heidelberg (2013). https://doi.org/10.1007/978-3-642-40698-0_1

32. Thoman, P., Dichev, K., Heller, T., Iakymchuk, R., Aguilar, X., Hasanov, K., et al.: A taxonomy of task-based parallel programming technologies for high-performance computing. J. Supercomput. **74**(4), 1422–1434 (2018)

33. Yu, C., Royuela, S., Quiñones, E.: Enhancing openMP tasking model: performance and portability. In: McIntosh-Smith, S., de Supinski, B.R., Klinkenberg, J. (eds.) IWOMP 2021. LNCS, vol. 12870, pp. 35–49. Springer, Cham (2021). https://doi.org/10.1007/978-3-030-85262-7_3

Suspending OpenMP Tasks on Asynchronous Events: Extending the Taskwait Construct

Romain Pereira[1,3]([✉]), Maël Martin[1,2], Adrien Roussel[1,2], Patrick Carribault[1,2], and Thierry Gautier[3]

[1] CEA, DAM, DIF, 91297 Arpajon, France
{romain.pereira,manuel.ferat,mael.martin,adrien.roussel,
patrick.carribault}@cea.fr
[2] Université Paris-Saclay, CEA, Laboratoire en Informatique Haute Performance pour le Calcul et la simulation, 91680 Bruyères-le-Châtel, France
[3] Project Team AVALON INRIA, LIP, ENS-Lyon, Lyon, France
thierry.gautier@inrialpes.fr

Abstract. Many-core and heterogeneous architectures now require programmers to compose multiple asynchronous programming model to fully exploit hardware capabilities. As a shared-memory parallel programming model, OpenMP has the responsibility of orchestrating the suspension and progression of asynchronous operations occurring on a compute node, such as MPI communications or CUDA/HIP streams. Yet, specifications only come with the `task detach(event)` API to suspend tasks until an asynchronous operation is completed, which presents a few drawbacks. In this paper, we introduce the design and implementation of an extension on the `taskwait` construct to suspend a task until an asynchronous event completion. It aims to reduce runtime costs induced by the current solution, and to provide a standard API to automate portable task suspension solutions. The results show twice less overheads compared to the existing `task detach` clause.

Keywords: OpenMP · MPI · Asynchronous Programming · Dependent Task

1 Introduction

To increase computational power evermore, supercomputer nodes evolved towards many-cores and heterogeneous architectures. Currently, 2 out of the 3 most powerful supercomputers nodes are made of 64-core processors, 4 GPUs and NICs[1]. In the future, nodes may even become more complex with other accelerators such as FPGAs for their energy efficiency [25]. Programming portable and efficient scientific simulation on such architecture is challenging. Vendors, research laboratory and programmers built *programming models* such as OpenMP, MPI, CUDA, leading users to *compose* multiple programming models to fully exploit compute resources.

---

[1] https://www.top500.org/lists/top500.

S. McIntosh-Smith et al. (Eds.): IWOMP 2023, LNCS 14114, pp. 66–80, 2023.
https://doi.org/10.1007/978-3-031-40744-4_5

Recent work on interoperability with MPI [16,18,20,21] and multi-GPU offload through target tasks [3,6,23] shows that OpenMP dependent task model is promising to overlap computation using multiple heterogeneous and asynchronous programming model. However, porting existing applications to an asynchronous dependent task-based model creates more difficulties than historical MPI+OpenMP `parallel-for` programming.

The objective of this paper is to propose standard extensions to suspend tasks until the completion of an asynchronous event. Our contributions are

- (1) A proposal on extending the `taskwait` construct with the `detach(event)` clause, with a standard API, to wait until the completion of an external event,
- (2) Proof-of-concept implementations into LLVM and MPC-OMP available online[2],
- (3) Evaluations showing 2x less runtime overheads over existing solutions in case of low-concurrency (a synchronization followed by a continuation task).

The extension is further-motivated in Sect. 2. A definition is proposed in Sect. 3 and evaluations are conducted in Sect. 4. Related works are reviewed in Sect. 5 and we conclude this work in Sect. 6.

2   Motivations

OpenMP tasking model is a portable solution for composing multiple programming models and their asynchronous operations, such as MPI requests, CUDA streams, FPGAs offloads or even disk I/O. Yet, specifications mostly come with the `task detach(event)` clause and the `interop` construct for standard interoperability. We propose to extend the `taskwait` construct with the `detach` clause as an alternative interoperability building block to suspend a task until an asynchronous event completion.

Porting HPC Applications using OpenMP Tasks. Early porting of applications to task-based OpenMP showed difficulties in handling asynchronous operations synchronization within tasks. Using the `taskyield` construct in [14], programmers assumed that the thread necessarily switches to another task if one is ready: this is not the case, the standard only specifies it at a scheduling-point, and the implementation decides whether to actually switch tasks. In two other examples, the porting of a Cholesky factorization [22] and a plasma simulation [19] had to sequentialize MPI communications, potentially at the expense of performance, as the standard was not providing any guarantees on suspending tasks when synchronizing on MPI requests.

---

[2] https://gitlab.inria.fr/ropereir/iwomp23.

A Lack of Interoperability. These issues lead the community to develop interoperability interfaces between OpenMP and MPI. The Task-Aware MPI (TAMPI) [20] library was proposed as an extra layer above MPI, to overlap MPI request synchronization with useful computation through task-switches. This library must be used by programmers adapting their code to replace MPI with TAMPI calls. MPICH+BOLT [5,12] through Argobots, or MPC [16], proposed to automate this interoperability through the threading library, so that OpenMP tasks can perform blocking MPI calls and suspend seamlessly. While all these approaches enable working code, OpenMP and MPI standards provided no guarantees on it requiring programmers to manage an additional interoperability layer, and ensure its correct implementation from both runtimes.

Providing Guarantees. OpenMP specifications adopted the `detach` clause which provides guarantees to programmers, and enables the overlap of asynchronous operation progression with useful computation through task scheduling, as discussed in [1]. Though, the `detach` clause also impacted other asynchronous programming models. For instance, proposals were made to the MPI specifications to register a callback on request completion [18,21] which are being standardized[3][4]. This would be used in codes as depicted in Listing 1.1 which we retrieved from [18,20] as follows:

```
 1  omp_event_handle_t ev_handle;
 2  # pragma omp task detach(ev_handle) depend(out: data)
 3  {
 4      MPI_Request req;
 5      MPI_Irecv(data, ..., &req);
 6      MPIX_Detach(&req, omp_fulfill_event, ev_handle);
 7  }
 8  # pragma omp task depend(in: data)
 9  {
10      work_with(data);
11  }
```

Listing 1.1. task detach(event) approach retrieved from [18,20,21]

With the `task detach(event)` approach, application programmers express two dependent tasks for managing asynchronous operations: the launch (line 2) and its continuation after completion (line 8). `MPIX_Detach` (line 6) registers the `omp_fulfill_event(ev_handle)` callback on the MPI request completion, which raises an *allow-completion* event to the OpenMP runtime. This approach does provide guarantees for asynchronous operation overlapping expected by programmers, as opposed to the test-and-yield approach.

Limits of 'Task Detach'. Nevertheless, we argue the `task detach(event)` clause has three drawbacks on the minimal example presented: (a) it implies unneces-

---

[3] https://github.com/mpiwg-hybrid/hybrid-issues/issues/6.
[4] https://github.com/devreal/ompi/tree/mpi-continue-master.

sary costs on programming and execution, (b) it is error-prone and (c) it discards the interoperability responsibility to the programmer.

Regarding (a), creating two dependent tasks does not provide more parallelism in this case. Our evaluation Sect. 4.1 shows that our proposal can remove some task management costs by following the C sequential order of execution, and synchronizing at some point in the execution without spawning a new task.

On (b), OpenMP memory model does not mention anything specific on tasks with a `detach` clause. When a C variable is declared as such, we believe the memory model falls back to *"[...] the programmer must use synchronization that ensures that the lifetime of the variable does not end before completion of the explicit task region sharing it. Any other access by one task to the private variables of another task results in unspecified behavior"*. In practice, the code Listing 1.1 retrieved from [18, 20] will execute as follows: the variable `req` is pushed onto the executing thread stack (line 4), the asynchronous operation starts (line 5), a completion callback is registered into the MPI runtime (line 6) and the task returns (line 7). The thread may then schedule other tasks until the callback is raised, potentially erasing the `req` variable onto its stack that has been passed by address earlier. The `MPI_Detach` proposal [18] tackles this risk by dereferencing and copying the `MPI_Request` pointer[5]. Note that `MPI_Request` copy is not standardized, even though Open MPI, MPICH or MPC-MPI represents `MPI_Request` as integers so copies are achieved seamlessly. The `MPI_Continue` proposal [21] tackles this risk by consuming the `MPI_Request` setting it to `MPI_REQUEST_NULL` on return.

Finally, for (c), the programmer has to create a continuation task explicitly and remove the synchronization call (`MPI_Wait`). On the other hand, runtime interoperability requiring no user code modification is possible and has been proposed in [12, 16]: as illustrated on Listing 1.2, the MPI runtime will automatically suspend the current OpenMP task so the OpenMP task scheduler can overlap the synchronization line 4 with other tasks.

```
1  # pragma omp task untied
2  {
3      MPI_Recv(&req, ...);
4      work_with(data);
5  }
```

Listing 1.2. MPI and OpenMP runtime interoperability approach

3   Extending Taskwait to Asynchronous Events

We propose to extend the `taskwait` construct with the existing `detach(event)` clause and to provide an `omp_taskwait_detach(event)` routine. It is depicted on Listing 1.3 and fixes drawbacks (a) and (b): only one task and no dependency are needed, and variables pushed to the thread stack may not be erased. The

---

[5] https://github.com/RWTH-HPC/mpi-detach/blob/master/detach.cpp#L66.

routine is also a first step towards fixing the issue (c) and *standardizing run-time interoperability*, which is further discussed in Sect. 4.2. We introduce new elements to the standard specifications.

```
1  # pragma omp task
2  {
3      MPI_Request req;
4      MPI_Irecv(data, ..., &req);
5      omp_event_handle_t ev_handle = omp_task_continuation_event();
6      MPIX_Detach(&req, omp_fulfill_event, ev_handle);
7      # pragma omp taskwait detach(ev_handle)
8      work_with(data);
9  }
```

Listing 1.3. taskwait detach(event) proposal

3.1 Definitions

Taskwait Construct. The `taskwait` construct is extended as follows:

- **Semantics** - if a `detach` clause is present on a `taskwait` construct, the current task region is suspended until the current task continuation event is fulfilled.
- **Restrictions** - The `detach` clause may only appear on a `taskwait` if no `depend` or `nowait` clauses are present.

Combined-clauses restrictions were motivated by the lack of practical examples. If practical use-cases were to be found, we propose to follow the current specifications that replicates empty tasks behaviors:

If the **detach** clause is present on the **taskwait** construct, one or more depend clauses are present and the **nowait** clause is not present, the behavior is as if these clauses were applied to a **task** construct with an empty associated structured block that generates a *mergeable* and *included task*. Thus, the current task region is suspended until the *predecessor tasks* of this task complete execution and its `allow-continuation` event is fulfilled.

If the **detach** clause is present, one or more **depend** clauses are present, and the **nowait** clause is present on the **taskwait** construct, the behavior is as if these clauses were applied to a **task** construct with an empty associated structured block that generates a task for which execution may be deferred, converting the *allow-continuation* event to an *allow-completion* event. Thus, all *predecessor tasks* of this task must complete execution, and its `allow-completion` event must be fulfilled, before any subsequently generated task that depends on this task starts its execution.

Omp_taskwait_detach(event). The `omp_taskwait_detach(event)` routine behave as if a # `pragma omp taskwait detach(event)` had been specified.

Task Continuation (Tasking Terminology) is a condition on a task that is satisfied when its *allow-continuation event* is fulfilled.

Allow-Continuation Event. The *allow-continuation event* into the standard specifications. Each task is attached an implicit *allow-continuation event* that is initially fulfilled.

Omp_task_continuation_event.   The `omp_task_continuation_event` routine unfulfills and returns the *allow-continuation event* of the current task.

Omp_fulfill_event(event). The `omp_fulfill_event(event)` routine can be extended as follows:

– **Constraints on Arguments** A program that calls this routine on an event that was already fulfilled is non-conforming. A program that calls this routine with an event handle that was not created by the detach clause, or not returned by the `omp_task_continuation_event` routine, is non-conforming.

The constraint on argument now also allows the task implicit continuation event to be passed to the routine. If the multiple clauses restriction on the `taskwait` construct were to be relieved as proposed, the `omp_fulfill_event(event)` could also be extended as follows:

– **Execution Model Events** The *task-fulfill* event occurs in a thread that executes an `omp_fulfill_event` region before the event is fulfilled if the OpenMP event object was created by a detach clause on a task or returned by the `omp_task_continuation_event` routine.

3.2   Implementation

We implemented the OpenMP extension in the Clang compiler, LLVM runtime and MPC runtime. First, we added a new ABI `__omp_taskwait_detach`, which fallbacks to the `omp_taskwait_detach` runtimes implementation. In both implementations the thread blocking schedule any other ready tasks until the passed event argument is fulfilled.

Then, we added support for the `detach(event)` clause to the `taskwait` construct in the Clang compiler: the `pragma omp taskwait detach(event)` directive will result in the new ABI being called.

4   Evaluation

We characterized three drawbacks on the `task detach(event)` approach and motivated how the `taskwait detach(event)` proposal mitigates these when suspending tasks during an asynchronous operation progression. This section provides additional evaluations on drawbacks (a) and (c).

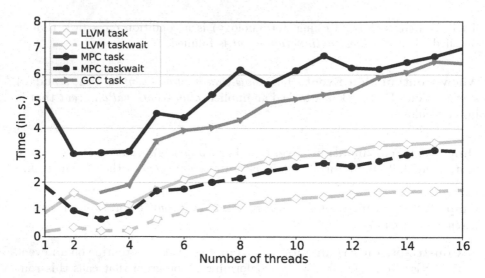

Fig. 1. Evaluation of the `task/taskwait detach` in LLVM, MPC and GCC with $N = 1,000,000$ in a NUMA region of an AMD EPYC CPU

4.1 Task Management Overheads

On (a), we made a microbenchmark to evaluate the tasking overheads of explicitly creating the continuation `task detach` against managing it implicitly using the `taskwait detach` proposal[6]. The microbenchmark has three-steps, it (1) warms up the runtime, (2) concurrently creates and schedules 2.N independent empty tasks with N empty dependent continuation tasks declared through the `task detach(event)` construct, and (3) concurrently creates and schedules 2.N independent empty tasks with an implicit sequential continuation task declared through the `taskwait detach(event)` construct we proposed. We tested on an AMD EPYC 7H12 CPU on a single NUMA region with $N = 1,000,000$ as a parameter, varying the number of threads to observe the impact of runtime contention. Figure 1 presents the execution time of steps (2) and (3) for our patched LLVM 16.x and MPC implementations, and the execution time of step (2) for GCC 12.2.0 (median of 5 executions). The x-axis is the number of threads, and the y-axis is the execution time. No performances could be recorded for 1 and 2 threads on GCC as the runtime was deadlocking.

First, it seems LLVM runtime manages fine-grain tasks more efficiently than MPC and GCC. Though, we observe that both the LLVM and MPC `taskwait detach` implementation always outperforms the `task detach` implementation. As predicted in the mentioned in the motivations: the runtime manages twice as fewer tasks and no dependencies as opposed to the `task detach(event)` approach in this minimal example. We also observe that using more than 3

---

[6] https://gitlab.inria.fr/ropereir/iwomp23/-/blob/main/bench/taskwait-detach.c.

threads deteriorates performances on every configuration as runtime contention on internal task data structure increases (tasks are empty).

In the LLVM implementation, using `taskwait detach` over `task detach` reduces per-task overheads for about $100ns$ depending on the number of threads. In applications such as Cholesky or LULESH, few tasks are suspended, so there is little performance gain to expect from using our proposal over the `task detach(event)` solution. For instance on LULESH, tasks suspending could be those performing MPI communications. It only represents ~20 tasks per iteration that may suspend, over ~10,000 computational tasks that may not suspend. However, our proposal could also ease application porting, which is the object of the two following sections.

4.2   Standardizing OpenMP Task Suspension on an Asynchronous Event

Currently, automatic task suspension when synchronizing on an external asynchronous event could be achieved as shown on Listing 1.4, using **pragmas** directly into the library implementation. However, OpenMP does not provide a standard ABI, and the (CUDA) runtime installation would be hardly dependant of a specific OpenMP runtime implementation.

```
1  int cuStreamSynchronize(CUstream hStream) {
2      if (/* within an OpenMP execution context */) {
3          omp_event_handle_t hdl;
4          # pragma omp task detach(hdl) depend(out: hdl)
5          {}
6          [...] /* differ stream synchronization to a progression engine */
7          # pragma omp taskwait depend(in: hdl)
8      } else {
9          [...] /* default implementation */
10     }
11 }
```

Listing 1.4. Runtime interoperability using task detach(event) approach

Our proposals provide a *standard* task suspension API/ABI. Using the proposed routines `omp_task_continuation_event` and `omp_taskwait_detach`, other asynchronous programming model runtimes (such as Cuda, MPI, libomptarget) could suspend OpenMP tasks and allow their continuation on an asynchronous event completion through a standard and portable interfaces across OpenMP implementations. This is depicted on Listing 1.5 on the CUDA and MPI runtime implementations; but could be extended to any other asynchronous programming model.

```
1  int cuStreamSynchronize(CUstream hStream) {
2      if (/* within an OpenMP execution context */) {
3          omp_event_handle_t hdl = omp_task_continuation_event();
4          [...] /* differ stream synchronization to a progression engine */
5          omp_taskwait_detach(hdl);
6      } else {
```

```
 7            [...] /* default implementation */
 8        }
 9        [...]
10   }
11
12   int MPI_Send(...) {
13       if (/* within an OpenMP execution context */) {
14           omp_event_handle_t hdl = omp_task_continuation_event();
15           [...] /* differ request synchronization to a progression engine */
16           omp_taskwait_detach(hdl);
17       } else {
18           [...] /* default implementation */
19       }
20       [...]
21   }
22
23   # pragma omp task untied
24   {
25       [...]
26       cuStreamSynchronize(...);
27       [...]
28       MPI_Send(...);
29       [...]
30   }
```

Listing 1.5. Runtime interoperability using taskwait detach(event) API

4.3   Effort on Porting Existing MPI Applications

Scientific simulation codes are complex, and synchronizations (MPI, CUDA, I/O) may be hidden deep into libraries, as in the Arcane framework [4]. Automatic and standard interoperability would ease the porting of existing scientific applications to a task-based model, relieving programmers from the task suspension interoperability burden in such cases.

```
1   void CalcForceForNodes(Domain & domain) {
2       MPI_Irecv(comBuf, ..., recvRequest) ;
3       [...]     /* computation */
4       MPI_Wait(recvRequest, ...) ;
5       for (Index_t i = 0; i < opCount; ++i)
6           (domain.*dest)(dx*dy*(dz - 1) + i) += comBuf[i] ;
7   }
```

Listing 1.6. LULESH point-to-point communication pattern

The code Listing 1.6 corresponds to a simplified view of the MPI receive communications occurring in the LULESH [7] proxy-application. The function CalcForceForNodes function initiates non-blocking reception to temporary buffers (comBuf) on line 2. Then, it overlaps the reception with some computation on mesh line 3. Finally, it waits for the reception completion line 4, and unpacks the temporary buffer to the mesh domain. A similar communication pattern can be found in most of the Collaboration of Oak Ridge, Argonne and Livermore (CORAL) proxy-applications. The continuation (line 4–7) is already explicit, and porting them with the `task detach` can be achieved by adding two tasks (line 2 and 4) as shown on Listing 1.7. Listing 1.8 shows a task-based version relying on runtime interoperability, that could be achieved using our proposal as discussed in the previous section. We move the continuation (message unpacking) right after a blocking `MPI_Recv` that shall suspend the task until the message is received, overlapping communication with other computational tasks. In such applications, our proposal reduces the runtime overheads (1 less task and dependency), and, likely, makes the code slightly more comprehensible: the continuation follows the predecessor sequentially, and synchronizations/overlap are managed implicitly by the task scheduler.

```
1   void CalcForceForNodes(Domain & domain) {
2       omp_event_handle_t event;
3       # pragma omp task detach(event) depend(out: recvRequest)
4       {
5           MPI_Irecv(comBuf, ..., recvRequest) ;
6           MPIX_Detach(&req, omp_fulfill_event, ev_handle);
7       }
8       [...] /* computation */
9       # pragma omp task depend(in: recvRequest)
10      {
11          for (Index_t i = 0; i < opCount; ++i)
12              (domain.*dest)(dx*dy*(dz - 1) + i) += comBuf[i] ;
13      }
14  }
```

Listing 1.7. LULESH task-based porting using task detach

```
1   void CalcForceForNodes(Domain & domain) {
2       # pragma omp task untied
3       {
4           MPI_Recv(comBuf, ...) ;
5           for (Index_t i = 0; i < opCount; ++i)
6               (domain.*dest)(dx*dy*(dz - 1) + i) += comBuf[i] ;
7       }
8       [...] /* computation */
9   }
```

Listing 1.8. LULESH task-based porting using runtime interfaces

5   Related Works

Weak Dependencies. In cases presenting more concurrency than our minimal example, the `taskwait detach` proposal is not sufficient compared to the `task detach`. In the example Listing 1.9, T3 depends on T1/T2, and T3/T4 cannot start until T2 executed and the event is fulfilled.

```
1  # pragma omp task depend(out: x) // T1
2      [...]
3
4  # pragma omp task depend(out: y) detach(hdl) // T2
5      [...]
6
7  # pragma omp task depend(in: x, y) // T3
8      [...]
9
10 # pragma omp task depend(in: y) // T4
11     [...]
```

Listing 1.9. Weak dependencies motivating example

In [17], authors introduce *weak* dependencies for OpenMP tasking. Weak dependencies could preserve both the concurrency and the task management costs saving from our proposal, as depicted on Listing 1.10. This code presents the same concurrency as the previous one, but T4 is executed as part of T2 following the C sequential order of execution, without the need of explicitly creating the continuation task T4 as previously.

```
1  # pragma omp task depend(out: x) // T1
2      [...]
3
4  # pragma omp task depend(weakin: x) // T2
5  {
6      [...]
7      # pragma omp taskwait detach(hdl)
8
9      # pragma omp task depend(in: x) // T3
10         [...]
11
12     [...] // T4
13 }
```

Listing 1.10. Weak dependencies example

Suspending OpenMP Tasks. The current OpenMP specifications on `taskyield` construct, and `untied` clause are fully implementation-dependent. For instance, in GCC `untied` tasks will never change threads, and `taskyield` is implemented as a no-op but is yet fully standard-compliant. In LLVM, the compiler generates multiple *continuations* on each scheduling point appearing in the outermost scope of the task, which are then sent at run-time to the task scheduler in a continuation-passing style (CPS). It privatizes `untied` tasks outermost scope variables to ensure that the continuations restart in a coherent state. The `taskyield` construct is implemented as a continuation task if appearing in the outermost scope of the task; else, a new task is stacked on the current thread (stack-algorithm presented in [22]). In the MPC-OMP runtime (implementing both GCC and LLVM ABI), the LLVM task continuations can be supported. In addition, tasks can be annotated to run on their own execution context (fixed-size stack + registers set). If suspending deep into the task call-stack, the task can be preempted for later resume on any thread without blocking onto its current thread. Every approach has its own limits. With GCC, scheduling flexibility is poor and may even lead to deadlocks when composing with other asynchronous programming models such as MPI, with threads spinning onto the same blocking task. With LLVM, scheduling points and variables must be fully known when compiling the task routine, which cannot be achieved for C Variable-Length Array (VLA) or Linux `alloca` routine leading to undefined behaviors[7]. With MPC-OMP, annotated tasks execution context may be created unnecessarily if the task never actually suspends; and statically fixing the stack size is an issue: too small, execution may stack-overflow; too big, unnecessary memory usage could impact performances. In [2], authors explore automated verification of stack size requirements for C programs at compile-time, that could complement MPC-OMP fixed-size stacks.

As a `taskwait` extension, our proposal integrates well into LLVM CPS tasking: the compiler could generate a continuation upon detecting a `taskwait detach(event)` construct on a task' outter-most scope. In other cases, stacking tasks frame on top of each other as done currently by LLVM/MPC restrict scheduling decision possibilities.

OpenMP as a Low-Level Parallel Runtime. OpenMP is used as a low-level back-end runtime for intra-node parallelization of higher-level programming models such as Kokkos [24], PGAS (XcalableMP [15]), or Domain Specific Languages/Abstraction (DSL/DSA) (Devito [11,13], Nablab [10]). They provide a higher abstraction that enables the user to write its code relieving programmers from low-level parallel implementation details. In the specific case of DSL using MLIR [9] compilers, OpenMP is easily targetable, and merging/suspending tasks can be achieved. Our contribution could be used by these programming models whenever a task must suspend.

Suspending Tasks in Rust. The Rust programming language [8] supports asynchronous programming which, much like OpenMP, allows sequential-looking code to be run concurrently. A report of the Rust programming language in 2017 showed interest in CPS tasking as it is a lightweight solution that does not require per-tasks stack[8]. An experimental implementation was made the same year[9] to suspend tasks using `async/await` syntax. The authors mention that *"[Rust] coroutines are translated to state machines internally by the compiler"* which is similar to the LLVM `untied` tasks implementation. In addition, Rust is currently implementing a `Generator` type that is not yet in release builds of the language, to suspend tasks with the same continuation-passing style[10].

---

[7] https://github.com/llvm/llvm-project/issues/61499.

[8] https://github.com/rust-lang/rfcs/blob/master/text/0230-remove-runtime.md.

[9] https://github.com/rust-lang/rfcs/blob/master/text/2033-experimental-coroutin es.md.

[10] https://doc.rust-lang.org/std/ops/trait.Generator.html.

6 Conclusion

Many-core and heterogeneous architectures impose on users to compose multiple asynchronous programming models. OpenMP managing CPUs resources is responsible for orchestrating the suspension and progression of each asynchronous operation. In this paper, we proposed to extend the specifications by adding the `detach(event)` clause on the `taskwait` construct and defining the `omp_taskwait_detach(event)` API with a standard ABI. These extensions reduce programming and runtime overhead and are a step towards automating synchronizations overlap by OpenMP task scheduler when mixing asynchronous programming models.

In the future, we would like to evaluate OpenMP as an *asynchronous progression operation engine*: as depicted on Listing 1.5 line 4, remains the question of asynchronous progression responsibility. CUDA stream or MPI requests, asynchronous operations need CPU cycles at some point to progress. Most runtimes currently come with dedicated (p)threads blocking at the kernel level; another way is possible through cooperative task scheduling via OpenMP.

Acknowledgments. This preprint has not undergone peer review (when applicable) or any post-submission improvements or correction. The Version of Record of this contribution is published in IWOMP 2023 and is available online at https://doi.org/<DOI>

References

1. Bak, S., et al.: OpenMP application experiences: porting to accelerated nodes. Parallel Comput. **109**, 102856 (2022). https://doi.org/10.1016/j.parco.2021.102856
2. Carbonneaux, Q., Hoffmann, J., Ramananandro, T., Shao, Z.: End-to-End Verification of Stack-Space Bounds for C Programs. In: Proceedings of the 35th ACM SIGPLAN Conference on Programming Language Design and Implementation. PLDI 2014, New York, NY, USA, pp. 270–281. Association for Computing Machinery (2014). https://doi.org/10.1145/2594291.2594301
3. Ferat, M., Pereira, R., Roussel, A., Carribault, P., Steffenel, L.A., Gautier, T.: Enhancing MPI+OpenMP task based applications for heterogeneous architectures with GPU Support. In: Klemm, M., de Supinski, B.R., Klinkenberg, J., Neth, B. (eds.) OpenMP in a Modern World: From Multi-device Support to Meta Programming, pp. 3–16. Springer, Cham (2022). https://doi.org/10.1007/978-3-031-15922-0_1
4. Grospellier, G., Lelandais, B.: The Arcane Development Framework. In: Proceedings of the 8th Workshop on Parallel/High-Performance Object-Oriented Scientific Computing. POOSC 2009, New York, NY, USA. Association for Computing Machinery (2009). https://doi.org/10.1145/1595655.1595659
5. Iwasaki, S., Amer, A., Taura, K., Seo, S., Balaji, P.: BOLT: optimizing OpenMP parallel regions with user-level threads. In: 2019 28th International Conference on Parallel Architectures and Compilation Techniques (PACT), pp. 29–42 (2019). https://doi.org/10.1109/PACT.2019.00011

6. Kale, V., Lu, W., Curtis, A., Malik, A.M., Chapman, B., Hernandez, O.: Toward supporting multi-GPU targets via taskloop and user-defined schedules. In: Milfeld, K., de Supinski, B.R., Koesterke, L., Klinkenberg, J. (eds.) IWOMP 2020. LNCS, vol. 12295, pp. 295–309. Springer, Cham (2020). https://doi.org/10.1007/978-3-030-58144-2_19

7. Karlin, I.: LULESH programming model and performance ports overview. Technical report, December 2012. https://doi.org/10.2172/1059462

8. Klabnik, S., Nichols, C.: The Rust Programming Language. No Starch Press, USA (2018)

9. Lattner, C., et al.: MLIR: Scaling compiler infrastructure for domain specific computation. In: 2021 IEEE/ACM International Symposium on Code Generation and Optimization (CGO), pp. 2–14 (2021). https://doi.org/10.1109/CGO51591.2021.9370308

10. Lelandais, B., Oudot, M.P., Combemale, B.: Fostering metamodels and grammars within a dedicated environment for HPC: the NabLab environment (Tool Demo). In: Proceedings of the 11th ACM SIGPLAN International Conference on Software Language Engineering. SLE 2018, New York, NY, USA, pp. 200–204. Association for Computing Machinery (2018). https://doi.org/10.1145/3276604.3276620

11. Louboutin, M., et al.: Devito (v3.1.0): an embedded domain-specific language for finite differences and geophysical exploration. Geosci. Model Dev. **12**(3), 1165–1187 (2019). https://doi.org/10.5194/gmd-12-1165-2019

12. Lu, H., Seo, S., Balaji, P.: MPI+ULT: overlapping communication and computation with user-level threads. In: 2015 IEEE 17th International Conference on High Performance Computing and Communications, 2015 IEEE 7th International Symposium on Cyberspace Safety and Security, and 2015 IEEE 12th International Conference on Embedded Software and Systems, pp. 444–454 (2015). https://doi.org/10.1109/HPCC-CSS-ICESS.2015.82

13. Luporini, F., et al.: Architecture and performance of devito, a system for automated stencil computation. ACM Trans. Math. Softw. **46**(1) (2020). https://doi.org/10.1145/3374916

14. Meadows, L., Ishikawa, K.: OpenMP tasking and MPI in a Lattice QCD benchmark. In: de Supinski, B.R., Olivier, S.L., Terboven, C., Chapman, B.M., Müller, M.S. (eds.) IWOMP 2017. LNCS, vol. 10468, pp. 77–91. Springer, Cham (2017). https://doi.org/10.1007/978-3-319-65578-9_6

15. Murai, H., Nakao, M., Sato, M.: XcalableMP programming model and language. In: Sato, M. (ed.) XcalableMP PGAS Programming Language, pp. 1–71. Springer, Singapore (2021). https://doi.org/10.1007/978-981-15-7683-6_1

16. Pereira, R., Roussel, A., Carribault, P., Gautier, T.: Communication-aware task scheduling strategy in hybrid MPI+OpenMP applications. In: McIntosh-Smith, S., de Supinski, B.R., Klinkenberg, J. (eds.) IWOMP 2021. LNCS, vol. 12870, pp. 197–210. Springer, Cham (2021). https://doi.org/10.1007/978-3-030-85262-7_14

17. Perez, J.M., Beltran, V., Labarta, J., Ayguadé, E.: Improving the integration of task nesting and dependencies in OpenMP. In: 2017 IEEE International Parallel and Distributed Processing Symposium (IPDPS), pp. 809–818 (2017). https://doi.org/10.1109/IPDPS.2017.69

18. Protze, J., Hermanns, M.A., Demiralp, A., Müller, M.S., Kuhlen, T.: MPI detach - asynchronous local completion. In: Proceedings of the 27th European MPI Users' Group Meeting. EuroMPI/USA 2020, New York, NY, USA, pp. 71–80. Association for Computing Machinery (2020). https://doi.org/10.1145/3416315.3416323

19. Richard, J., Latu, G., Bigot, J., Gautier, T.: Fine-Grained MPI+OpenMP plasma simulations: communication overlap with dependent tasks. In: Yahyapour, R. (ed.) Euro-Par 2019. LNCS, vol. 11725, pp. 419–433. Springer, Cham (2019). https://doi.org/10.1007/978-3-030-29400-7_30
20. Sala, K., Teruel, X., Perez, J.M., Peña, A.J., Beltran, V., Labarta, J.: Integrating blocking and non-blocking MPI primitives with task-based programming models. Parallel Comput. **85**, 153–166 (2019). https://doi.org/10.1016/j.parco.2018.12.008
21. Schuchart, J., Samfass, P., Niethammer, C., Gracia, J., Bosilca, G.: Callback-based completion notification using MPI Continuations. Parallel Comput. **106**, 102793 (2021). https://doi.org/10.1016/j.parco.2021.102793
22. Schuchart, J., Tsugane, K., Gracia, J., Sato, M.: The impact of taskyield on the design of tasks communicating through MPI. In: de Supinski, B.R., Valero-Lara, P., Martorell, X., Mateo Bellido, S., Labarta, J. (eds.) IWOMP 2018. LNCS, vol. 11128, pp. 3–17. Springer, Cham (2018). https://doi.org/10.1007/978-3-319-98521-3_1
23. Tian, S., Doerfert, J., Chapman, B.: Concurrent execution of deferred OpenMP target tasks with hidden helper threads. In: Chapman, B., Moreira, J. (eds.) Languages and Compilers for Parallel Computing, pp. 41–56. Springer, Cham (2022). https://doi.org/10.1007/978-3-030-95953-1_4
24. Trott, C.R., et al.: Kokkos 3: programming model extensions for the exascale era. IEEE Trans. Parallel Distrib. Syst. **33**(4), 805–817 (2022). https://doi.org/10.1109/TPDS.2021.3097283
25. Véstias, M., Neto, H.: Trends of CPU, GPU and FPGA for high-performance computing. In: 2014 24th International Conference on Field Programmable Logic and Applications (FPL), pp. 1–6 (2014). https://doi.org/10.1109/FPL.2014.6927483

How to Efficiently Parallelize Irregular DOACROSS Loops Using Fine Granularity and OpenMP Tasks: The SPEC mcf Case

Juan Salamanca$^{(\boxtimes)}$ (ID) and Alexandro Baldassin (ID)

DEMAC/IGCE – Sao Paulo State University (Unesp), Rio Claro, SP, Brazil
{juan,alex}@rc.unesp.br

Abstract. There are certain loops that are considered hard to parallelize. Examples of this type of loops are those that have loop-carried dependencies (DOACROSS loops) and that are also irregular, that is, the dependencies between iterations vary depending on the context. Many techniques have been studied before to be able to parallelize this type of loops, however in OpenMP standard there is no efficient way to parallelize them. From the literature, it is known that many of these loops can be efficiently parallelized using fine-grained techniques (identifying strongly connected components). On the other hand, the most efficient way to parallelize this type of loops using OpenMP tasks has not been explored. Thus, this paper discusses the various forms of parallelization of this type of loops using SPEC 429.mcf as a case study; particularly, how to parallelize mcf using fine granularity in tasks. For that, this paper proposes new constructs (`ste_for` and `ste`) and speculative dependency-types (`spec_in`, `spec_out`, and `spec_inout`). An initial evaluation using different implementations to parallelize the mcf hottest loop shows that it is possible to achieve speed-ups of up to 2.44× with respect to the **task-depend** version using Speculative Task Execution.

Keywords: DOACROSS Parallelization · Speculative Tasks · OpenMP

1 Introduction

Some loops are hard to parallelize because they can have dependencies between iterations that are irregular. Many techniques have been studied to parallelize them such as DOACROSS [3], DSWP [13], HELIX [2,9], and Thread-Level Speculation (TLS) [14,20]. As a conclusion, it can be stated that a fine-grained parallelization technique using the strongly connected components of a data dependency graph (DDG) of the loop is often the best option when the dependencies and components can be identified (generally this is also complicated). For instance, a very famous representative of such loops is the SPECint 2006

This work is supported by the Sao Paulo Research Foundation (grants 18/07446-8, 20/01665-0, and 18/15519-5).

```
    arc = arcs + group_pos;
    for(; arc<stop_arcs; arc+=nr_group){
1)    if (arc->ident>BASIC)){ //cond1
2)      red_cost = arc->cost - arc->tail->potential + arc->head->potential;
3)      if (bea_is_dual_infeasible(arc,red_cost)){ //cond2
4)        basket_size++;
5)        basket_aux=basket_size;
6)        perm[basket_aux]->a=arc;
7)        perm[basket_aux]->cost=red_cost;
8)        perm[basket_aux]->abs_cost=ABS(red_cost);
      }
    }
  }
```

Fig. 1. mcf's hottest loop

429.mcf benchmark [6] hottest loop (shown in Fig. 1) for which speed-ups can be obtained using fine-grained TLS [14]. There are other loops of this type such as the hottest loops of susan_c and bitcount benchmarks from cBench [4].

An important question is how to bring that lesson learned to an implementation of this type of parallelization with the current OpenMP specification. The first option that may come to mind is to use the DOACROSS mechanisms that are part of OpenMP such as the ordered clause of the construct for and the ordered doacross sink/source construct to surround the serial component [12]. Figure 2 shows the mcf code parallelized using this technique. Unfortunately, this implementation offers us very large slowdowns which may be improved by changing the schedule clause of the for construct to auto, but still the performance is very poor (7.14× of loop slowdown respect to serial execution).

A second lesson that previous works offer us is that strip mining should be used in order to improve the locality of data in memory, avoid false sharing, and reduce synchronization or speculation overhead. However, when carrying out the transformation, obtaining a single serial component as the body of the loop, then, as learned, other transformations are necessary, such as loop fission to separate the components and scalar expansion to communicate them. Then the OpenMP DOACROSS technique can be applied again as shown in Fig. 3. The performance of this new implementation improves the performance with respect to the previous one but still no speed-ups are obtained (0.92 of loop speed-up).

Another lesson learned is that the serial component or stage of a loop does not always have to be synchronized, since the dependency can be *may* loop-carried, that is, it does not exist or is transient for certain contexts (those loops are called *may* DOACROSS loops); in those cases the dependency can be speculated. STL [17] and FOR-TLS [14] were proposed for speculative parallelization in OpenMP. However, both STL and FOR-TLS were designed to be coarse grained, that is, they speculate entire iterations. So they could not be used for our purpose, that is, to achieve a fine-grained parallelization using strongly connected components, strip mining and only speculating the serial stage[1].

---

[1] A stage represents a component of DDG after strip mining, loop fission and scalar expansion.

```
                                          #pragma omp parallel for shared(basket_size)...
                                          for(i=0; i<iterations; i++){
                                            char cond_arr[S_SIZE]; /*local buffers*/
                                            ...
   arc2  = arcs + group_pos;              for (j=0, arc=arc_strip; j<S_SIZE &&
   #pragma omp parallel for ordered(1)           arc<stop_arcs; j++, arc+=nr_group){
        shared(basket_size)           A)    cond1=arc->ident->BASIC;
        schedule(auto)..                    if (cond1)){
   for(i=0; i<iterations; i++){       B)      red_cost_arr[j]=...;
     ...                              C)      cond2=bea_is_dual_infeasible(...);
A) cond1=arc->ident->BASIC;                  }
   if (cond1)){                             cond_arr[j]=cond1&&cond2;
B)   red_cost=...;                        }
C)   cond2=bea_is_dual_infeasible(...);   #pragma omp ordered doacross(sink:i-1)
   }                                      for (...){
   #pragma omp ordered                      if (cond_arr[j]){
        doacross(sink:i-1)            D)      basket_size++;
   if (cond1 && cond2){                      basket_arr[j]=basket_size;
D)   basket_size++;                        }
D)   basket_aux=basket_size;              }
   }                                      #pragma omp ordered doacross(source)
   #pragma omp ordered doacross(source)   for (...){
   if (cond1 && cond2){                     if (cond_arr[j]){
E)   perm[basket_aux]->a=arc;         E)      perm[basket_arr[j]]->a=arc;
F)   perm[basket_aux]->cost=red_cost; F)      perm[basket_arr[j]]->cost=red_cost_arr[j];
G)   perm[basket_aux]->abs_cost =     G)      perm[basket_arr[j]]->abs_cost= ...;
     ABS(red_cost);                        }
   }                                      }
 }                                      }
```

Fig. 2. Restructured mcf's hottest loop using ordered (DOACROSS-FINE)

Fig. 3. mcf's loop fine-grained parallelization using transformations and ordered doacross (DOACROSS-TILING)

On the other hand, OpenMP provides tasks as an extremely powerful tool due to its level of expressiveness [1]. So, one could try to parallelize mcf with fine granularity using a task for each stage and synchronizing only the serial one using task dependencies as shown in Fig. 4. However, this implementation is not efficient because the stages of the same iteration have communication and must be executed serially since one depends on the other. So, using a task for each stage increases the communication overhead between threads. For the mcf case, it would be better to use a single task with all the components of an iteration inside it. However, the performance is not much better with respect to the previous implementation since we are synchronizing the entire iteration with task depend and not as we did using ordered doacross in only the serial stage.

Due to this limitation, this paper proposes the specification of speculative type-dependencies in tasks, as seen in Fig. 5, where it is also shown the use of a new construct ste, allowing the stage that will be speculated to be indicated. Thus, tasks can be used to parallelize DOACROSS loops with fine granularity and fulfilling all the lessons learned mentioned above. These types of dependencies generate the *Speculative Task Execution* (STE) mechanism [15]. The key use of STE is to speculate a *task* with data or control dependencies but that is expected to be free of data dependencies at runtime or with a control dependency whose value is probably invariant for many iterations in a while loop.

```
1  for(i=0; i<iterations; i++){
2    char cond_arr[S_SIZE]; ...
3    #pragma omp task
            depend(out:cond_arr[0:S_SIZE])...
4    {
5      for (...){
6        cond1=arc->ident->BASIC;
7        if (cond1)){
8          ...
9        }
10       cond_arr[j]=cond1&&cond2;
11     }
12   }
13   #pragma omp task
            depend(inout:basket_size)
            depend(in:cond_arr[0:S_SIZE])
            depend(out:basket_arr[0:S_SIZE])
14   {
15     for (...){
16       if (cond_arr[j]){
17         basket_size++;
18         basket_arr[j]=basket_size;
19       }
20     }
21   }
22   #pragma omp task
            depend(in:basket_arr[0:S_SIZE]))
23   {
24     for (...){
25       if (cond_arr[j]){
26         basket_aux=basket_arr[j];
27         perm[basket_aux]->a=arc;
28         ...
29       }
30     }
31   }
32 }
```

```
1  #pragma omp ste_for iterator(i)
2  for(i=0; i<iterations; i++){
3    #pragma omp task
            depend(spec_inout:basket_size)
4    {
5      char cond_arr[S_SIZE];
6      ...
7      for (...){
8        cond1=arc->ident->BASIC;
9        if (cond1)){
10         ...
11       }
12       cond_arr[j]=cond1&&cond2;
13     }
14     #pragma omp ste spec_private(basket_size)
15     {
16       for (...){
17         if (cond_arr[j]){
18           #pragma omp tls if_read(basket_size)
19           basket_size++;
20           #pragma omp tls if_write(basket_size)
21           basket_arr[j]=basket_size;
22         }
23       }
24     }
25     for (...){
26       if (cond_arr[j]){
27         basket_aux=basket_arr[j];
28         perm[basket_aux]->a=arc;
29         ...
30       }
31     }
32   }
33 }
```

Fig. 4. mcf parallelization using loop transformations and a task for each stage (TASK-FULL)

Fig. 5. mcf fine-grained parallelization using STE and a task for each strip-mined iteration (STE-FINE)

STE needs mechanisms that support conflict detection, speculative storage, roll-back of transactions, and ordered transactions. Current commodity off-the-shelf microprocessors provide support for speculation by means of hardware transactions [7,8][2]. Thus, HTM has been used for implementing other speculative algorithms different from what it was originally created for [14,18]. In the same spirit, this work proposes a novel utility for HTM enabling the implementation of three key features required by STE: (a) conflict detection; (b) speculative storage; and (c) transaction roll-back.

Speculative tasks of hot-code regions can be generated by the taskloop construct or by the OpenMP task construct in three ways: (a) speculative tasks generated in a loop parallelized with taskloop where there are possible dependencies between iterations (*Speculative Taskloop* [17]); (b) speculative tasks generated within a while where the value of the stop condition depends on the result

---

[2] Intel recently included support for TSX and new instructions for suspend/resume in its Sapphire Rapids processors.

of the tasks of the current iteration (*Speculative While* [18]); and (c) speculative tasks generated by specifying speculative dependencies in OpenMP tasks (the `spec_in`, `spec_out`, and `spec_inout` dependency-types). In this work we will focus on the third way to generate speculative tasks: speculative dependencies in tasks.

In this paper we make the following contributions:

- We propose *Speculative Task Execution* in OpenMP — the novel `ste_for` and `ste` constructs and the `spec_in`, `spec_out`, `spec_inout` speculative dependency-types — to parallelize iterations speculating data dependencies between tasks through HTM's speculative support in hard-to-parallelize *may* DOACROSS loops, such as the `mcf` hottest loop;
- We describe an algorithm to implement speculative task dependencies using hardware transactional memory and code transformations, enabling the speculative execution of tasks from multiple `for`-loop iterations (Sect. 3.2);
- We evaluate the performance of this technique using the `mcf` benchmark. We further compare against the fine-grained parallelization of this benchmark using the `task depend` and the `depend doacross` constructs from standard OpenMP. The experimental results are promising with an average increase in the speed-up of 2.44× when compared to the non-speculative version using OpenMP tasks with dependencies (Sect. 5).

This paper is organized as follows. Section 2 describes the background material. Section 3 details the design and implementation of Speculative Task Execution on HTM. Benchmarks, methodology and settings are described in Sect. 4. Section 5 presents the experimental evaluation for the implementation of STE over HTM along with an analysis of the preliminary results. Finally, Sect. 6 concludes the work.

2   Background

This work is in the intersection of four different subjects: Transactional Memory, DOACROSS Parallelization, Thread-Level Speculation, and Task-based Parallelism. In the rest of this section we provide a background of each of these topics.

2.1   Transactional Memory

Transactional Memory (TM) uses the concept of transactions, borrowed from the Database community, to provide atomic and isolated updates to volatile memory (DRAM) [5]. Implementing transactions requires devising a version management and a conflict detection scheme. Conflict detection determines whether two operations executed in separate transactions cause a conflict, *i.e.*, if they access a common memory location and at least one of the operations is a write. A conflict causes at least one of the transactions involved in the conflict to abort and it may re-execute.

2.2 DOACROSS Parallelization

DOACROSS (proposed by Cytron et al. [3]) is a parallelizing algorithm for loops with loop-carried dependencies. The main idea is to distribute the iterations cyclically among the threads trying to simultaneously execute many iterations. As the algorithm makes an effort to parallelize loops with loop-carried dependencies, inter-thread communication is required to forward dependencies and synchronize shared resources.

DOACROSS in OpenMP. DOACROSS support in OpenMP is a variation of the DOACROSS algorithm [3] and was proposed by Shirako *et al.* [19] as an OpenMP construct, which was implemented in OpenMP 4.5 [10]. This construct, `ordered`, is used to annotate sequential loop components so as to enable fine-grained parallelism.

In this paper, we compare the performance of Speculative Task Execution with DOACROSS in OpenMP because is the main method available in OpenMP to parallelize loops with loop-carried dependencies of production codes. Nowadays, speculation is still not commonly employed for parallelization of loops in this kind of code.

2.3 Thread-Level Speculation

Thread-Level Speculation is a technique that allows for effectively parallelizing *may* DOACROSS loops that have a low probability of materializing their loop-carried dependencies at runtime. The lower this probability the more likely it is to achieve a performant parallelization. In the case that the loop is effectively DOACROSS at runtime, if the fraction of iterations with loop-carried dependencies is low with respect to the total number of iterations, TLS can still be performant; however, it also depends on the pattern of distribution of these loop-carried dependencies throughout loop iterations at runtime [14]. For performance, TLS requires hardware mechanisms that support four primary features: conflict detection, speculative storage, in-order commit of transactions, and transaction roll-back. HTM implements three out of the four key features required by TLS: conflict detection, speculative storage, and transaction roll-back. Therefore, these architectures have the potential to be used to implement TLS [14]. Our work is based on this approach but it differs in that we use Task-based Parallelism and fine-grained speculation instead of using the OpenMP's `for`-loop worksharing construct and coarse-grained speculation.

2.4 Fine-Grained Parallelization

Murphy *et al.* proposed fine-grained TLS and described an implementation on emulated hardware for speculative execution [9]. The goal of their fine-grained approach is to create transactions that surround only segments of a loop iteration instead of a whole iteration. To accomplish that, they use sequential segments

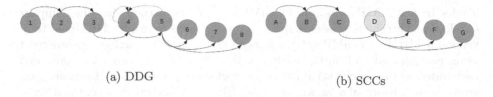

(a) DDG

(b) SCCs

Fig. 6. DDG and SCCs of mcf's hottest loop.

of HELIX [2] to define the beginning and the end of transactions. Fine-grained TLS decreases the overhead of speculating a whole iteration in comparison with coarse-grained speculation and avoids capacity aborts because not all reads and writes of an iteration are performed within the same transaction. Besides, in the case of a conflict only a sequential segment is rolled-back and retried (not the whole iteration). However, the HTM overhead may increase because, with multiple transactions per iteration, more transactions are started and finished.

Murphy *et al.*'s implementation of this approach surrounds sequential segments within transactions and distributes iterations to cores in a round-robin fashion. Hence they do not use techniques — such as strip mining or loop-unrolling — to group iterations. Salamanca *et al.* showed that strip mining is a code transformation that allows decreasing overhead of starting/finishing transactions, aborts, and false sharing when fine-grained TLS is used with off-the-shelf speculative support [14].

Figure 1 shows the serial code for the hottest loop of mcf. As explained earlier, to implement fine-grained parallelization, it is necessary to build the data dependence graph (DDG) of the code and to find the strongly connected components (SCCs) of the graph (Fig. 6). Each SCC with (*may*) loop-carried dependencies is considered a sequential segment, whereas each SCC without loop-carried dependencies is considered a parallel segment. Only sequential segments are speculated using TLS. In the case of fine-grained DOACROSS, sequential segments are synchronized. Figure 2 shows the SCCs (A, B, etc.) using `ordered` parallelization. For the mcf hottest loop, the component D is a sequential segment.

To implement fine-grained TLS with strip mining successfully, it is necessary to restructure the loop using well-known code-transformation techniques such as loop fission and scalar expansion [21]. Loop fission is used to separate each SCC in a loop iterating `S_SIZE` times. Each one of these loops can be considered a *stage*. If scalar variables need be communicated between stages, scalar expansion is used. Thus, thread-local buffers are created to store dependency variables for each iteration of a producer stage. The analogous OpenMP implementation for fine-grained DOACROSS of the mcf's hottest loop is shown in Fig. 3.

2.5 Task-Based Parallelism

Using tasks, the execution can be modeled as a directed acyclic graph, where nodes are tasks and edges define data dependencies between tasks. A runtime system schedules tasks whose dependencies are resolved over available worker threads, thus enabling load balancing and work stealing [1].

Tasks in OpenMP. Tasks in OpenMP are blocks of code that the compiler envelops and arranges to be executed in parallel. Tasks were added to OpenMP in version 3.0 [1]. In OpenMP 4.0, the depend clause and the taskgroup construct were incorporated and, in OpenMP 4.5, the taskloop construct was proposed and added to the specification [10]. Like worksharing constructs, tasks are generally created inside of a parallel region. To spawn each task once, the single or master constructs are used. The ordering of tasks is not defined, but there are ways to express it: (a) with directives such as taskgroup or taskwait; or (b) with task dependencies (depend clause). Variables that are used in tasks can be specified with data-sharing attribute clauses (private, firstprivate, shared, etc.) or, by default, data accessed by a task is shared. The depend clause takes a type (in, out, or inout) followed by a variable or a list of variables. These types establish an order between sibling tasks. The taskwait clause waits for the child tasks of the current task. taskgroup is similar to taskwait but it waits for all descendant tasks created in the block. Moreover, task reduction was introduced in OpenMP 5.0 [11].

3   Speculative Task Execution

Speculative Task Execution can be used to speculate data dependencies when a taskloop parallelization takes place (Speculative Taskloop), but the idea can be generalized to OpenMP tasks with data dependencies where these rarely exist. Consider the loop of Fig. 7 which shows a code parallelized using OpenMP tasks with the depend clause. STE can take advantage of the rare execution of B (the programmer knows that success is true only in 1% of the total executions) re-specifying the input dependency of the first task (depend(in: state)) as a speculative input dependency (depend(spec_in:state)). It indicates that the first task of the example turns into a speculative task but it also implies that spec_out dependencies on state may be ignored. Thus, some instances of the first task are not dependent of prior instances of the second task as shown in Fig. 8b. However, when success is true, it aborts all speculative tasks that are dependent on the current value of state, being re-executed.

3.1   The ste_for Construct and the Speculative Dependency Types

Speculative Task Execution is implemented over OpenMP using HTM through the ste_for construct and the spec_in, spec_out, and spec_inout dependency-types. The design of the ste_for construct is as follows:

```
#pragma omp ste_for iterator(ind_var)
   for-loop
```

where:

– *ind_var* is the induction variable of the for loop;

```
1   #pragma omp ste_for iterator(i)
2   for(int i = 0; i < n; i++) {
3     #pragma omp task depend(spec_in:state) depend (out:success,changes) ...
4       #pragma omp ste spec_private(state)
5       {
6         #pragma omp tls read(state)
7         A(state,success,changes);
8       }
9     #pragma omp task depend(in:success,changes) depend(spec_out:state) // task T
10      if (success)
11        B(state,changes);
12  }
```

Fig. 7. Loop with a loop-carried dependency parallelized using OpenMP tasks and speculative dependencies

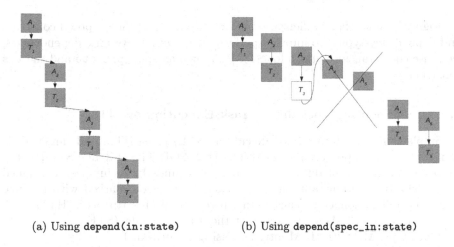

(a) Using **depend(in:state)**   (b) Using **depend(spec_in:state)**

Fig. 8. Possible execution flows of Fig. 7's loop

The task-construct specification allows the use of the **depend** clause, which enforces additional constraints on the scheduling of tasks. These constraints establish dependencies only between sibling tasks. Using STE, the constraints are relaxed because the dependencies are speculated, for that, new dependency types are specified in the **depend** clause:

depend(*dependency-type : list*))

where:

- *dependency-type* is one of the following: in, out, inout, spec_in, spec_out, and spec_inout;
- *list* consists of a collection of one or more *list-items* separated by commas;
- *list-item* is a scalar variable.

The ste Construct. For the speculative execution of tasks, a new construct called **ste** is also added. This construct allows us to specify the code region of the task that we want to be speculative thus enabling fine-grained parallelization by speculating only the serial stages and not the entire iteration. This construct can only be used inside a `task` that has some `spec_in` dependency specified. The design of the construct is as follows:

```
#pragma omp ste spec_private(list)
    structured-block
```

where:

- *list* consists of a collection of one or more *list-items* separated by commas;
- *list-item* is a scalar variable.

Figure 5 shows the parallelization of `mcf`'s loop using the proposed construct and dependency-types. To improve performance and remove false dependencies, we reuse code transformations for STL [15], such as `spec_private` and the `tls` construct.

3.2   Implementing Speculative Task Execution on HTM

We implement Speculative Task Execution (STE) using HTM and similar code transformations as proposed in HTM-TLS [14], FOR-TLS [14], and STL [15,17]. However, an important difference between STE and the techniques mentioned is that the transactions are started by each task region marked with the `ste` construct and no longer by each iteration (or iteration strip) as in HTM-TLS. For instance, Fig. 9 shows a sketch of the Fig. 5's code (STE) converted to standard OpenMP with HTM intrinsics using Algorithm 1.

Each speculative region in a task (marked with the `ste` construct) has a BEGIN function inserted at the beginning and an END function inserted at the end in Fig. 9. The task marked with `spec_out` or `spec_inout` updates the variable `next_basket` (Line 35 of Fig. 9), which is used to implement **ordered transactions** at the END function. The variable `next_basket` will be used by all speculative tasks marked with `spec_in(basket_size)` to validate whether they have to commit or abort. The method `Spec_Private_Scalar_Algorithm` (Line 16 of Algorithm 1) is explained in a previous work [15].

4   Benchmarks, Methodology and Experimental Setup

The performance assessment in this work reports speed-ups and abort/commit ratios (transaction outcome) for the STL [17] and STE parallelizations (two versions: (a) using a task for each iteration (STE-FINE); and (b) using a task for each iteration stage (STE-FULL)), and speed-ups for the `task-depend` (two versions like STE) and `doacrosss` (two versions: using loop transformations and not) parallelizations of the hottest loop from the `429.mcf` application from the SPEC CPU 2006 [6] benchmark suite running on Intel Core. For all experiments, the reference input for `mcf` is used. The baseline for speed-up comparisons is the

```
1   int next_basket=0;
2   #pragma omp parallel
        num_threads(N_CORES)
3   #pragma omp master
4   for(i=0; i<iterations; i++){
5     arc_strip=arc2+i*nr_group*S_SIZE;
6     #pragma omp task
          firstprivate(i,...)
          shared(next_basket,...)...
7     {
8       char cond_arr[S_SIZE];
9       ...
10      char flag_r_basket=0,
11      char flag_w_basket=0;
12      for (...){
13        cond1=arc->ident->BASIC;
14        if (cond1)){
15          ...
16        }
17        cond_arr[j]=cond1&&cond2;
18      }
19
20      char spec=BEGIN(next_basket,i)
21      for (...){
22        if (cond_arr[j]){
23          if (!flag_r_basket){
24            flag_r_basket=1;
25            basket_sizeL=basket_size;
26          }
27          basket_sizeL++;
28          flag_w_basket=1;
29          basket_arr[j]=basket_sizeL;
30        }
31      }
32      END(spec,&next_basket,i)
33      if (flag_w_basket)
34        basket_size=basket_sizeL;
35      next_basket++;
36
37      for (...){
38        if (cond_arr[j]){
39          basket_aux=basket_arr[j];
40          perm[basket_aux]->a=arc;...
41        }
42      }
43    }
44  }
```

Fig. 9. Fig. 5's code converted to standard OpenMP

Algorithm 1: Mechanism for STE with Speculative Dependencies

Data: ste_for construct (directive D and for-loop L), and induction_var
Result: Transformed code to be parallelized with STE on HTM

1 Create BEGIN and END functions;
2 Create hashmap map_next ;
3 **foreach** task $\in$ ($L.spec\_in\_list \cup$ $L.spec\_inout\_list$) **do**
4   Set induction_var as firstprivate in task;
5   **foreach** ste_task $\in$ task.ste_list **do**
6   Outside of the construct, create a new variable next whose identifier is "next" plus "<ste_task.spec_variable.id>" of the same type of the induction variable;
7   Insert next into map_next;
8   Initialize the value of next with the initial value of induction_var;
9   Set next as shared in task;
10   Create a new variable spec whose identifier is spec of type char;
11   Create a statement st_begin to attribute to spec the value returned by the call to the BEGIN function;
12   Insert st_begin before ste_task.body;
13   Insert a call to the END function after ste_task.body;
14   **if** ste_task.spec_private_list $\neq$ NULL **then**
15   **foreach** scalar var $\in$ ste_task.spec_private_list **do**
16   Run Spec_Private_Scalar_Algorithm;
17   **if** (task $\in$ L.spec_inout_list) **then**
18   Create a statement st_next to increment the value of next by L.step.value;
19   At the end of ste_task.body, insert st_next;
20 **foreach** task $\in$ L.spec_out_list **do**
21   **foreach** var $\in$ task.spec_out_list **do**
22   next $\leftarrow$ map_next[var.id];
23   Create a statement st_next to increment the value of next by L.step.value;
24   At the end of task.body, insert st_next;

serial execution of the same benchmark program compiled at the same optimization level. Loop and whole-program times are used to calculate speed-ups. Each software thread is bound to a unique core. Each benchmark was run twenty times and the average time is used. Runtime variations were negligible and are not presented. We made manual code transformations to the evaluated loops following the algorithms described in Sect. 3.2, thus obtaining the STE parallelization of the benchmarks.

429.mcf is a benchmark which is derived from MCF (Minimum-Cost Flow Problem), a program used for single-depot vehicle scheduling in public mass

Table 1. SPEC mcf Characterization

Loop ID	Benchmark	Location	Invocations	%Cov	N	%lc	AIS	Spec. Priv.	S_SIZE
mcf	429.mcf	pbeampp.c,165	21854886	40%	300	3.1%	300 B	yes, if_read, if_write	75

transportation. The benchmark version uses almost exclusively integer arithmetic [6]. The first part of the Table 1 lists some features of the 429.mcf hottest loop: (1) the ID of the loop in this study; (2) the benchmark of the loop; (3) the file/line of the target loop in the source code; and (4) the number of invocations of the loop in the entire program.

The programs using tasks were compiled at optimization level -O3 and with the set of flags specified in each benchmark program. Code compiled with clang -fopenmp was linked against the modified OpenMP runtime (libomp12) to enable monotonic scheduling [17]. doacross parallelization was compiled with Clang 12.0 and linked against libomp12. To guarantee that each software thread is bound to a unique core, the environment variable KMP_AFFINITY was set to granularity = fine, balanced. This experimental evaluation was carried out on an Intel Core i7-6700HQ processor with 4 cores with 2-way SMT, running at 2.6 GHz, with 16 GB of memory on Ubuntu 18.04.5 LTS (GNU/Linux 4.15.0-139-generic x86_64).[3] The cache-line prefetcher is enabled by default. Each core has a 32 KB L1 data cache and a 256 KB L2 unified cache. The four cores share an 6144KB L3 cache.

The implementations of mcf are the following:

- **DOACROSS-FINE** uses the OpenMP ordered doacross construct and fine-grained parallelization as in Fig. 2's code.
- **DOACROS-TILING** uses the ordered construct and loop transformations to implement fine-grained parallelization as in Fig. 3's code.
- **TASK-FINE** uses the task depend construct and loop transformations. A task is used to execute an iteration with three stages.
- **TASK-FULL** uses the task depend construct and loop transformations as in Fig. 4's code. A task is used for each stage.
- **STE-FINE** uses the proposed ste_for construct, speculative dependencies, and loop transformations to implement a parallelization with fine granularity. A task is created for each strip-mined iteration as in Fig. 5
- **STE-FULL** is similar to STE-FINE but a task is created for each stage.
- **STL** uses the taskloop construct and speculative execution to parallelize entire strip-mined iterations as explained in previous works [15, 17].

---

[3] It is important to mention that in June 2021 Intel disabled Intel TSX-NI from all its processors. Kernels newer than the one used in this experimentation disabled HTM support or allowed it but aborting all transactions, for this reason the used workstation has not yet been updated and is the only available off-the-shelf hardware option we have to test our ideas at the moment. Recent Intel processors, such as the Sapphire Rapids (launched in January 2023), bring back support for hardware transactional memory.

Table 2. Speed-ups of `mcf` Parallelizations

Speed-up	DOACROSS-FINE	DOACROSS-TILING	TASK-FINE	TASK-FULL	STE-FINE	STE-FULL	STL
Loop	0.14	0.92	0.50	0.49	1.22	0.54	1.15
Whole-program	0.34	1.09	0.80	0.80	1.20	0.83	1.17

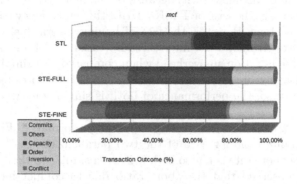

Fig. 10. Commit/Abort ratios (4 threads) for STE-FINE, STE-FULL, and STL parallelizations of `mcf` on Intel Core

5   Experimental Results

This section presents results and analysis. The features used to characterize the `mcf` hottest loops are shown in the second part of Table 1: (1) $\%Cov$, the fraction of the total execution time spent in the loop; (2) N, the average number of loop iterations; (3) $\%lc$, the percentage of iterations that have actual RAW loop-carried dependencies for the reference input of `mcf`; and (4) AIS, the average size in bytes read/written by an iteration. The parameters in the third part of Table 2 describe: (1) if speculative privatization is used (and the clause of `tls` directive) used in STE-FINE, STE-FULL, and STL; and (2) `S_SIZE`, the *strip size* used for the experimental evaluation of STE-FINE, STE-FULL, and STL parallelizations. We assess the STE and STL performance on `mcf` benchmark using an Intel Core machine with HTM support. Table 2 shows the average loop and whole-program speed-ups (four threads) with respect to serial execution for the seven parallel implementations described in Sect. 4. Analysis of `mcf` performance using STL is described in previous works [16,17].

The results show, as mentioned above, that the DOACROSS-FINE parallelization has the worst results since the synchronization cost is very high. This cost could be reduced using tiling, which would also improve cache and main memory usage between cores. Thus, this DOACROSS technique improves using tiling or strip mining (DOACROSS-TILING), in addition to the other transformations to produce stages. However, even with this improvement, loop speed-ups cannot be obtained since the cost of synchronization outweighs the gain of the parallelization.

Regarding the parallelizations using `task depend`, both have drawbacks. The main problem with TASK-FINE is that the dependency on `basket_size` is specified for the whole task and not only for the stage that actually has the dependency. So, in the presence of a actual dependency, the tasks are completely serialized obtaining only slowdowns because of the high cost of synchronization. On the other hand, in the case of TASK-FULL, the dependency can be specified for the indicated stage. However, the fact of having several tasks for each iteration (one per stage) makes the inter-threads (tasks) synchronization between stages of the same iteration an overhead when compared to a simple serial execution of these tasks by the same thread (task). TASK-FINE uses local buffers for each thread. Even so, the performance of both is similar and worse than serial execution.

Both STE versions have completely different performance. Figure 10 shows the aborts/commits ratio for each of the two parallelizations. With respect to STE-FULL, the abort rate is not so bad, it is even similar to that of STE-FINE. It can also be observed that the abort ratio due to conflict increases, which can be explained by the use of shared buffers between the cores. However, the main problem with this type of parallelization is the one explained for TASK-FULL: inter-thread synchronization is very high. Regarding STE-FINE, the use of the speculative dependencies allows to ignore the constraint of having to wait to execute each `task`. The buffers created for communication between threads are local, and the speculation is only done in the region marked by the `ste` construct. In this way, it has the best speed-ups and even up to 2.44× compared to TASK-FINE.

Finally, STE-FINE has even better performance than STL because since the entire strip-mined iteration is not speculated, but rather the segment marked by the `ste` construct, this significantly reduces aborts due to capacity overflow and other causes (mainly traps caused by the end of the OS quantum). The abort rate due to conflicts also decreases considerably, since reducing the code region to be speculated reduces the probability of false conflicts or false sharing. However, one of the main problems with STE is the high ratio of order-inversion aborts due to the lack of better mechanisms to implement ordered transactions using this TSX version.

6   Conclusions

This paper presents Speculative Task Execution (STE), a technique that speculates data dependencies in tasks of different iterations, in this way, constraints that most likely will never be carried out and are only placed to be conservative can be removed, allowing many tasks to be executed in parallel and thus accelerating the execution of the loop. The implementation of STE using HTM is proposed through new constructs and task dependency-types in OpenMP. A first evaluation using various parallelizations of the `429.mcf` benchmark shows promising results for STE, even getting speed-ups of 2.44× over the version using standard OpenMP tasks and of 1.22× over the serial version.

Acknowledgements. The authors would like to thank Prof. Eduard Ayguade and the anonymous reviewers for the insightful comments.

References

1. Ayguade, E., Copty, N., Duran, A., Hoeflinger, J., Lin, Y., Massaioli, F., Teruel, X., Unnikrishnan, P., Zhang, G.: The design of OpenMP tasks. IEEE Trans. Parallel Distributed Syst. (TPDS) **20**(3), 404–418 (2009)
2. Campanoni, S., Jones, T., Holloway, G., Reddi, V.J., Wei, G.Y., Brooks, D.: Helix: automatic parallelization of irregular programs for chip multiprocessing. In: Code Generation and Optimization (CGO), pp. 84–93. San Jose, USA (2012)
3. Cytron, R.: Doacross: beyond vectorization for multiprocessors. In: International Conference on Parallel Processing (ICPP), pp. 836–844 (1986)
4. cTuning, F.: cBench: Collective benchmarks (2016). http://ctuning.org/cbench
5. Harris, T., Larus, J., Rajwar, R.: Transactional memory. Synthesis Lectures Comput. Architecture **5**(1), 1–263 (2010)
6. Henning, J.L.: Spec cpu2006 benchmark descriptions. ACM SIGARCH Computer Architecture News **34**(4), 1–17 (2006)
7. Intel Corporation: Intel architecture instruction set extensions programming reference. Chapter 8: Intel transactional synchronization extensions (2015)
8. Le, H., et al.: Transactional memory support in the IBM POWER8 processor. IBM J. Res. Dev. **59**(1), 8:1–8:14 (2015)
9. Murphy, N., Jones, T., Mullins, R., Campanoni, S.: Performance implications of transient loop-carried data dependences in automatically parallelized loops. In: International Conference on Compiler Construction (CC), pp. 23–33, Barcelona, Spain (2016)
10. OpenMP-ARB: OpenMP application program interface version 4.5 (2015)
11. OpenMP-ARB: OpenMP application program interface version 5.0 (2018)
12. OpenMP-ARB: OpenMP application program interface version 5.2 (2021)
13. Rangan, R., Vachharajani, N., Vachharajani, M., August, D.I.: Decoupled software pipelining with the synchronization array. In: Parallel Architecture and Compilation Techniques (PACT) (2004)
14. Salamanca, J., Amaral, J.N., Araujo, G.: Using hardware-transactional-memory support to implement thread-level speculation. IEEE Trans. Parallel Distrib. Syst. **29**(2), 466–480 (2018)
15. Salamanca, J., Baldassin, A.: Evaluating the performance of speculative doacross loop parallelization with taskloop. In: International Conference on High Performance Computing and Simulation (HPCS), Barcelona, Spain (2020)
16. Salamanca, J.: Performance comparison of speculative taskloop and openmp-for-loop thread-level speculation on hardware transactional memory. In: International Symposium on Parallel and Distributed Computing (ISPDC), Basel, Switzerland, pp. 83–90 (2022)
17. Salamanca, J., Baldassin, A.: Improving speculative taskloop in hardware transactional memory. In: International Workshop on OpenMP, Bristol, UK, pp. 3–17 (2021)
18. Salamanca, J., Baldassin, A.: Using off-the-shelf hardware transactional memory to implement speculative while in openmp. In: International Workshop on OpenMP, Chattanooga, USA, pp. 50–64 (2022)

19. Shirako, J., Unnikrishnan, P., Chatterjee, S., Li, K., Sarkar, V.: Expressing doacross loop dependences in OpenMP. In: International Workshop on OpenMP, Camberra, Australia, pp. 30–44 (2013)
20. Steffan, J., Mowry, T.: The potential for using thread-level data speculation to facilitate automatic parallelization. In: High-Perform. Computer Architecture (HPCA), Washington, USA, pp. 2–13 (1998)
21. Wolfe, M.: High Performance Compilers for Parallel Computing. Addison-Wesley (1996)

OpenMP Offload Experiences

The Kokkos OpenMPTarget Backend: Implementation and Lessons Learned

Rahulkumar Gayatri[1]([✉]), Stephen L. Olivier[2], Christian R. Trott[2], Johannes Doerfert[3], Jan Ciesko[2], and Damien Lebrun-Grandie[4]

[1] Lawrence Berkeley National Laboratory, Berkeley, CA, USA
rgayatri@lbl.gov
[2] Sandia National Laboratories, Albuquerque, NM, USA
{slolivi,crtrott,jciesko}@sandia.gov
[3] Lawrence Livermore National Laboratory, Livermore, CA, USA
jdoerfert@llnl.gov
[4] Oak Ridge National Laboratory, Oak Ridge, TN, USA
lebrungrandt@ornl.gov

Abstract. As the supercomputing landscape diversifies, solutions such as Kokkos to write vendor agnostic applications and libraries have risen in popularity. Kokkos provides a programming model designed for performance portability, which allows developers to write a single source implementation that can run efficiently on various architectures. At its heart, Kokkos maps parallel algorithms to architecture and vendor specific backends written in lower level programming models such as CUDA and HIP. Another approach to writing vendor agnostic parallel code is using OpenMP's directives based approach, which lets developers annotate code to express parallelism. It is implemented at the compiler level and is supported by all major high performance computing vendors, as well as the primary Open Source toolchains GNU and LLVM. Since its inception, Kokkos has used OpenMP to parallelize on CPU architectures. In this paper, we explore leveraging OpenMP for a GPU backend and discuss the challenges we encountered when mapping the Kokkos APIs and semantics to OpenMP target constructs. As an exemplar workload we chose a simple conjugate gradient solver for sparse matrices. We find that performance on NVIDIA and AMD GPUs varies widely based on details of the implementation strategy and the chosen compiler. Furthermore, the performance of the OpenMP implementations decreases with increasing complexity of the investigated algorithms.

Keywords: Kokkos · OpenMP · GPUs · parallel programming · performance portability

1 Introduction

As high performance computing enters the exascale computing era, the largest supercomputers are dominated by GPU accelerated system designs. For almost a decade, these platforms, including the latest NERSC system, Perlmutter, exclusively deployed GPUs from NVIDIA. This single vendor trend is changing with the first deployed exascale machines. The recently launched Frontier system at Oak Ridge National Laboratory and the upcoming El Capitan platform at Lawrence Livermore National Laboratory use AMD GPUs, while Argonne National Laboratory's Aurora supercomputer will use Intel GPUs.

A challenge arising from this architectural diversity is that each vendor has their own preferred programming model. NVIDIA provides CUDA, first introduced in 2007. AMD developed the HIP programming model, which is closely modelled after CUDA. Data Parallel C++ (DPC++), an extension of the Khronos SYCL standard [7], is Intel's preferred choice for implementing code on their GPUs. Writing applications and libraries directly in each vendor's preferred programming model thus requires the implementation of four versions, assuming one would want to support multicore CPU execution as well. To eliminate this unmanageable software development and maintenance overhead, vendor independent higher-level frameworks such as Kokkos [2,11,12] and RAJA [1] were developed. These frameworks promise performance portability by providing a common interface for expressing parallelism and data management, which is then mapped to the vendor specific programming models.

There are also efforts to make the vendor specific models portable across architectures. SYCL itself is designed as a hardware agnostic programming model, and Intel's DPC++ compiler has the ability to target NVIDIA GPUs and to a lesser degree AMD GPUs. AMD's HIP model can be mapped to CUDA by coupling AMD's toolchain to NVIDIA's. Community research efforts in LLVM are also working to compile CUDA to other architectures [3]. However, in practice there are very few projects relying on these portability efforts of the vendor models, due to concerns over full support on all architectures. In particular, support contracts which are part of the large supercomputing procurements generally only cover the vendor's own toolchain. The portability frameworks do not have the same issue, since they leverage the native toolchains on each architecture.

OpenMP [10] is the one vendor independent node-level programming model standard which all the vendors support to varying degrees, and which is generally part of the contractual requirements in the large supercomputing procurements. Furthermore, it is not only supported by vendor specific compilers, but also by the two primary open source toolchains, LLVM and GCC. OpenMP uses a directive based approach, which allows developers to annotate existing code to express parallelism. This approach has been used to good effect on CPU based systems for two decades. Since version 4.0 [9], OpenMP has also supported directives for accelerators such as GPUs, and those directives have evolved significantly with subsequent versions. However, the available subset of the specification, the quality of implementation of those subsets, and even the interpretation of intended behavior of some features are different in each toolchain, causing challenges when using OpenMP for performance portability.

In this paper we explore these challenges using the effort of porting Kokkos to use OpenMP as a hardware independent backend implementation. That effort was conceived as a means to provide for Kokkos a second toolchain path on each platform, in addition to the vendor specific programming models. Having multiple toolchains, and specifically compilers, available on each system allows for redundancy and more overall robustness of the software stack. It also prepares Kokkos for a situation where a new hardware vendor may not develop a unique programming model, leveraging the OpenMP specification instead. Additionally, other performance portability frameworks have explored the use of OpenMP offloading in their backend implementations [6,8].

In this paper we use the conjugate gradient solver (CG-Solve) described in [12] as an exemplar to discuss various concepts in Kokkos, how they are mapped to OpenMP, and the challenges which arise. The results demonstrate the performance achieved by the CG-Solve example and its individual kernels on NVIDIA A100 GPUs available on Perlmutter and AMD MI250x available on Crusher (testbed for Frontier). We use the latest clang compiler from the main branch of llvm (dated 5/15/2023) and vendor specific compilers for each of the GPUs, i.e., NVHPC/22.7 on A100 and amdclang available with rocm/5.4.3 on MI250x. We will refer to these as LLVM, NVHPC and ROCM respectively.

Our CG-solve exemplar is not an attempt to present the very best implementation of CG-Solve, nor to improve upon the existing math algorithms. Specifically we are not exploring the use of different sparse matrix storage formats or various possible parallelization schemes for the algorithms. This paper is primarily concerned with the question of how Kokkos usage of OpenMP compares to the native OpenMP implementations and how the OpenMP offload implementation compares to the use of native CUDA and HIP backends in Kokkos, given a specific algorithm and parallelization strategy. Also, note that while we have used CG-solve as vehicle to present issues arising when mapping Kokkos to OpenMP, the actual Kokkos backend must be robust and applicable to a wide variety of applications built upon Kokkos. Therefore, optimizations, e.g., OpenMP settings, that may benefit CG-solve but are not be universally appropriate would not be considered for inclusion in the Kokkos OpenMPTarget backend.

2   CG-Solve

The conjugate gradient solver (CG-Solve) [5] is a simple iterative linear solver, which use three primary linear algebra functions: a vector addition (axpby), an inner product (dot) and a sparse matrix vector multiply (spmv). In each iteration the axpby is called four times, the dot twice and the spmv once. Listing 1.1 shows the pseudo code for the solver. The three operations exhibit three common patterns found in data parallel programming: simple data parallel loops, reductions, and nested loops. The overall algorithm is largely bandwidth limited. However the pure vector operations are often latency sensitive on GPU systems, since at typically observed vector lengths of 100,000 to 1,000,000 entries per device the vector operations can execute in under 20us there. Furthermore, axpby, dot and spmv are not just important for CG-Solve, but are also the fundamental building blocks in many other linear solvers.

Listing 1.1. CGSolve

```
for (int64_t k = 1; k <= max_iter && normr > tolerance; ++k) {
  if (k == 1) {
    axpby(p, one, r, zero, r);            // AXPBY
  } else {
    oldrtrans = rtrans;
    rtrans = dot(r, r);                   // DOT
    double beta = rtrans / oldrtrans;
    axpby(p, one, r, beta, p);            // AXPBY
  }
  normr = std::sqrt(rtrans);
  double alpha     = 0;
  double p_ap_dot = 0;
  spmv(Ap, A, p);                         // SPMV
  p_ap_dot = dot(Ap, p);                  // DOT
  if (p_ap_dot < brkdown_tol) {
    if (p_ap_dot < 0) {
      std::cerr << "miniFE::cg_solve␣ERROR,␣numerical␣breakdown!"
                << std::endl;
      return num_iters;
    } else
      brkdown_tol = 0.1 * p_ap_dot;
  }
  alpha = rtrans / p_ap_dot;
  axpby(x, one, x, alpha, p);             // AXPBY
  axpby(r, one, r, -alpha, Ap);           // AXPBY
  num_iters = k;
}
```

The remainder of this section discusses the Kokkos implementation of axpby, dot and spmv, mapping them to OpenMP, and the challenges we encountered.

2.1   AXPBY

The vector addition (axpby) function in CG-Solve is a simple data parallel loop, with no dependencies between iterations. It is straightforward to express in most programming models, including Kokkos.

Listing 1.2. Kokkos Vector Addition (axpby)

```
void axpby (double a, Kokkos::View<double*> x,
            double b, Kokkos::View<double*> y) {
  Kokkos::parallel_for("AXPBY", x.extent(0), KOKKOS_LAMBDA(const int i) {
      y(i) = a*x(i) + b*y(i);
  });
}
```

A Kokkos View expresses a possibly multi-dimensional array. This function only uses its simplest version representing a plain one-dimensional contiguous vector. The Kokkos parallel_for execution pattern expresses a parallelizable loop. It takes as arguments a label (for debugging and profiling purposes), an iteration range, and the loop body expressed through a C++ lambda. Kokkos is a descriptive programming model, which does not guarantee any specific implementation strategy on architectures. Its parallel loops do not imply order nor concurrency, and thus can be mapped to thread, vector or pipeline parallelism.

An equivalent OpenMP implementation of axpby for GPUs (assuming manual data management) is given in Listing 1.3.

Listing 1.3. OpenMP Vector Addition (`axpby`)

```
void axpby (int N, double a, double* x,
                   double b, double* y) {
  #pragma omp target teams distribute parallel for simd nowait is_device_ptr(
    x,y)
  for(int i=0; i< N; i++) {
    y[i] = a*x[i] + b*y[i];
  }
}
```

In its implementation of `parallel_for`, Kokkos uses a partial specialization approach, where the lambda is handed to a backend specific implementation of the parallel loop. Simplified, this strategy looks like the code in Listing 1.4.

Listing 1.4. `parallel_for` OpenMPTarget backend

```
template<Functor>
struct ParallelFor<Functor, OpenMPTarget> {
  int N; Functor f;
  void execute() {
    #pragma omp target teams distribute parallel for simd nowait
    for(int i=0; i< N; i++) { f(i); }
  }
};

template<class Functor>
void parallel_for(string label, int N, Functor f) {
  ParallelFor<Functor, OpenMPTarget> closure{N,f};
  closure.execute();
}
```

Note that the only fundamental difference between the direct OpenMP implementation and the Kokkos backend implementation is the expression of the loop body via a C++ lambda. However, we have observed that the OpenMP compilers are very sensitive to the use of seemingly unrelated C++ patterns. Specifically, significant performance difference can be observed when writing algorithms in two different – but from the C++ perspective equivalent – ways. One such instance is the use of C++ lambdas. To illustrate that difference, we measured performance also for versions of the algorithms written directly in OpenMP, but using lambdas, as shown in Listing 1.5.

Listing 1.5. OpenMP Vector Addition (`axpby`) as C++ lambda

```
void axpby (int N, double a, double* x,
                   double b, double* y) {
  auto f = [=](i) {y[i] = a*x[i] + b*y[i];};
#pragma omp target teams distribute parallel for simd nowait firstprivate(f)
  for(int i=0; i< N; i++) {
    f(i);
  }
}
```

A similar issue occurs with the use of OpenMP target regions inside class member functions. When the `axpby` is implemented as a class member function, where N is a class data member, performance drops even more than with the use of lambdas, compared to creating a local copy of N inside the member function.

Figure 1 shows the performance of the different versions of `axpby` discussed above. The figure shows 5 versions AXPBY, where the labels on the legends represent the following:

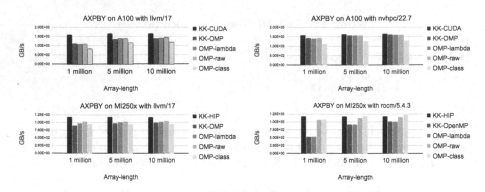

Fig. 1. AXPBY on NVIDIA A100 with LLVM and NVHPC compilers and on AMD MI250x with LLVM and ROCM compilers. Y axis is in GB/s, so higher is better.

1. *KK-CUDA* : Kokkos version with the CUDA backend
2. *KK-OMP* : Kokkos version with the OpenMPTarget backend
3. *OMP-lambda* : Direct OpenMP version using lambda inside a `target` region
4. *OMP-raw* : Direct OpenMP version not using lambda inside a `target` region
5. *OMP-class* : Variant of *OMP-raw* version using a class member inside the `target` region, instead of its equivalent local copy.

For this kernel, we see that the direct OpenMP code when compiled with the vendor compilers can achieve almost the same performance as Kokkos with the native CUDA/HIP backends. At larger vector lengths, the Kokkos OpenMP-Target backend approaches the raw OpenMP performance, and most of the difference can be explained by the previously noted issues around the use of Lambdas. However, NVHPC does not exhibit the lambda specific performance penalty, and the Kokkos OpenMPTarget backend in each case achieves the same performance as the lambda OpenMP implementation. Comparing the relative performance of the different implementations on the two different architectures, they appear to be a function of the compiler rather than the hardware.

2.2   DOT

The dot product (`dot`) function performs a single reduction on a given data type. In Kokkos this operation is expressed using the `parallel_reduce` pattern as shown in Listing 1.6. The equivalent direct OpenMP code is shown in Listing 1.7.

Listing 1.6. Kokkos Reduction (`dot`)

```
double dot(Kokkos::View<double*> x, Kokkos::View<double*> y) {
    double result = 0.;
    Kokkos::parallel_reduce("DOT", x.extent(0), KOKKOS_LAMBDA(const int i,
        double &lsum) {
        lsum += x(i) * y(i);
    }, result);
    return result;
}
```

Listing 1.7. OpenMP Reduction (`dot`)

```
void dot (int N, double* x, double* y) {
  double result = 0.;
  #pragma omp target teams distribute parallel for simd reduction(+:result)
    is_device_ptr(x,y)
  for(int i=0; i< N; i++) {
    result += x[i] * y[i];
  }
  return result;
}
```

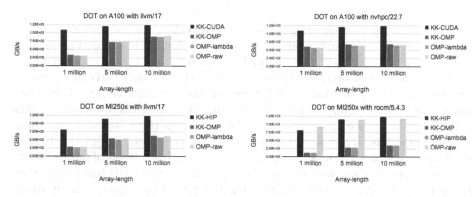

Fig. 2. DOT on NVIDIA A100 with LLVM and NVHPC compilers and on AMD MI250x with LLVM and ROCM compilers. Y axis is GB/s, so higher is better.

Figure 2 shows the bandwidth achieved by the `dot` kernel, with legend labels following the naming in Fig. 1. Only ROCM achieves the same performance as the native backends of Kokkos, and only in the absence of lambdas which otherwise reduce performance by 4-8x depending on the vector length. Here LLVM and NVHPC are not sensitive to the use of Lambdas. Still, with OpenMP, they only achieve between 30% and 70% of the performance of the native backends. Unlike the `axpby` results, NVHPC with OpenMP only reaches about 50% of the CUDA backend performance. A 2022 paper documenting the current design of the LLVM OpenMP runtime [4] remarks that recent improvements of that runtime have not included any work on better implementations of GPU reductions, but our understanding is that some vendors are working on this topic.

2.3 SPMV

The third algorithm needed for CG-Solve is a sparse-matrix vector multiply. Numerous sparse matrices representations exist. Here we employ the common compressed sparse row (CSR) representation, which comprises an array storing the non-zero values of the matrix, an array with the associated column indicies, and a vector storing the row offsets into the value and column index arrays.

At its simplest the spmv can then be implemented as loop over rows, with a nested reduction to compute the dot product of each row. Listing 1.8 provides a simple implementation of the spmv algorithm.

Listing 1.8. Sparse matrix vector multiply (spmv) sequential algorithm

```
for(row = 0; row < num_rows; row++) { // Loop over all rows
  row_start = row_offsets[row];
  row_end = row_offsets[row+1];
  // Reduction over non-zeros in each row
  for(idx = row_start; idx<row_end; idx++)
    y(row) += m_values[idx] * x[m_cold_idx[idx]];
}
```

This operation is more complex than either axpby or dot since for good performance on GPUs, nested parallelism must be exploited. The nested parallelism exposes more concurrency in the algorithm, which becomes more important with increasing number of non-zeros per row. Since the inner loop's trip count depends on the outer loop's iteration index, they can not be easily collapsed. Furthermore, the kernel exhibits a mix of streaming and irregular data access. The matrix data is accessed continuously, while accesses of the x vector are irregular.

While the basic spmv algorithm requires only two loops, In practice Kokkos implements a somewhat more complex version using three levels of parallelism to expose appropriate amounts of work for each level of the GPU hierarchy. Often the number of non-zeros per row, and thus the inner loop length, is fairly small. Thus it is beneficial to use only the third and innermost level of parallelism to perform the reduction, but to still group adjacent rows in threads sharing a common cache, to exploit data access locality of the vector x.

Both Kokkos and the OpenMP specification support three levels of parallelism using the concepts of teams, threads and vector parallelism. Kokkos provides special execution policies with the execution patterns, namely TeamPolicy, TeamThreadRange, and ThreadVectorRange. OpenMP expresses the same conceptual ideas with the teams distribute, parallel for, and simd constructs. Both Kokkos and many OpenMP compilers are consistent in mapping the first level of parallelism across streaming multiprocessors (SMs) or compute units (CUs) and the second level of parallelism within SMs or CUs.

Differences between Kokkos and many OpenMP compilers arise regarding the third level of parallelism (or lack thereof). While conceptually the single instruction multiple data (SIMD) model of lock-step execution exemplified by CPU vectorization is stricter than the single instruction multiple threads (SIMT) model of GPUs, SIMD can be profitably mapped onto SIMT and indeed lockstep execution at the lowest level of the GPU's hierarchy can be the most performant. However, the LLVM compiler, and many vendor compilers, including NVHPC and ROCM, treat OpenMP's simd as a hint, and do not map it to hardware parallelism. All threads in a GPU CUDA block or HIP group are instead activated together as part of the parallel for construct. This restriction, for now, limits the performance for any Kokkos application that uses the third parallel level explicitly. Moreover, the third level of parallelization enables efficient memory coalescing on GPU architectures that Kokkos works to exploit. When that third level of parallelism is not present, the memory references are not coalesced, resulting in inefficient access patterns. That said, a dedicated three level mapping honoring the `simd` construct is currently under development as part of LLVM.

Listing 1.9. Kokkos Hierarchical Parallelism for `spmv`

```
Kokkos::parallel_for(
 "SPMV", Kokkos::TeamPolicy<>(num_teams, team_size, vector_size),
 KOKKOS_LAMBDA(const Kokkos::TeamPolicy<>::member_type &team) {
    const int64_t first_row = team.league_rank() * rows_per_team;
    const int64_t last_row = first_row + rows_per_team < nrows
                              ? first_row + rows_per_team
                              : nrows;
    // iterate over rows owned by this team
    Kokkos::parallel_for(
        Kokkos::TeamThreadRange(team, first_row, last_row),
        [&](const int64_t row) {
            const int64_t row_start = A.row_ptr(row);
            const int64_t row_length =
                A.row_ptr(row + 1) - row_start;

            double y_row;
            // reduction over non-zeroes in the row
            Kokkos::parallel_reduce(
                Kokkos::ThreadVectorRange(team, row_length),
                [=](const int64_t i, double &sum) {
                    sum += A.values(i + row_start) *
                        x(A.col_idx(i + row_start));
                },
                y_row);
            y(row) = y_row;
        });
});
```

Listing 1.9 shows the implementation of SPMV using hierarchical execution patterns in Kokkos. The `Kokkos::TeamPolicy` is used to specify the number of teams, team size and the number of vector lanes used per thread. For this algorithm the team size and the vector length are optimization parameters that require tuning for each hardware platform. When using the CUDA or HIP backend, each team is mapped to a block, with the thread identifiers in each team mapped to `threadIdx.y` and vector lanes mapped to `threadIdx.x`. Vector lengths are limited by the warp or wavefront size respectively. In the `spmv` algorithm, each team is assigned a number of rows, which are then iterated over in parallel by the threads of the team. The nested reduction is performed by the vector lanes associated with each thread.

A direct mapping of the Kokkos semantics to OpenMP leads to an implementation as shown in Listing 1.10 In Kokkos, the loop body of the outer loop is executed by all threads within the team. This is achieved in OpenMP by a `parallel` region inside the outer loop. Now every thread computes redundantly `first_row` and `last_row`, avoiding an otherwise necessary broadcast upon entering the nested parallel loop. The nested reduction is annotated with the `simd` directive. As stated above, none of the compilers used for this work actually parallelize the `simd` loop for a GPU. In order to identify how much of a performance reductions is caused by that lack of parallelization we also ran the native CUDA/HIP Kokkos backend code with a vector-size of one.

There are other idioms of hierarchical parallelism where there is a mismatch of Kokkos and OpenMP semantics. Though not illustrated in CG-solve, Kokkos allows a team level reduction over a variable that is introduced within the team. The semantics are that each thread has copy of the variable that is initialized to the identity at the start of the reduction operation, and the final partial values of all copies are combined and the resulting value redistributed to all threads' copies at the end of the reduction operation. In contrast, OpenMP reduction semantics require that the reduction variable must be shared by the threads in a team and hence it must be known at the start of the **parallel** region. However, in some use cases, it may not be possible to identify such reductions at the start of the **parallel** region, since the nested reduction may occur in other functions.

Listing 1.10. OpenMP Hierarchical Parallelism **spmv** - Version A

```
int num_teams = (nrows + rows_per_team - 1)/rows_per_team;
#pragma omp target teams distribute is_device_ptr(x,y,A_row_ptr,A_values,
    A_col_idx)
for(int team = 0; team < num_teams; ++i)
#pragma omp parallel
{
    const int64_t first_row = omp_get_team_num() * rows_per_team;
    const int64_t last_row = first_row + rows_per_team < nrows ? first_row +
        rows_per_team : nrows;
    #pragma omp for
    for(int row = first_row; row < last_row; ++row)
    {
        const int64_t row_start = A_row_ptr[row];
        const int64_t row_length = A_row_ptr[row + 1] - row_start;

        double y_row;
        #pragma omp simd reduction(+:y_row)
        for(int i = 0; i < vector_size; ++i)
        {
            y_row += A_values[i + row_start] * x[A_col_idx[i + row_start]];
        }
        y[row] = y_row;
    }
}
```

Listing 1.11. OpenMP Hierarchical Parallelism **spmv** - Version B

```
#pragma omp target teams num_teams(leage_size) thread_limit(team_size)
    is_device_ptr(x,y,A_row_ptr,A_values,A_col_idx)
#pragma omp parallel
    {
    const int blockIdx = omp_get_team_num();
    const int gridDim  = omp_get_num_teams();

    for (int league_id = blockIdx; league_id < num_teams; league_id +=
        gridDim) {
    #pragma omp for
    for(int row = first_row; row < last_row; ++row)
    {
        // similar to above
    }
    }
    }
```

The native Kokkos backends implement the team level reduction using a memory buffer in device memory. Due to the mismatch in Kokkos and OpenMP semantics, this approach is also currently used for the OpenMPTarget backend. This workaround requires explicit control of the number of active teams using the **num_teams** clause to ensure that the correct amount of buffer space is allocated. Unfortunately adding that clause reduces the performance of Kokkos hierarchical parallelism on some compilers, even in the cases, such as **spmv**, where team level reductions are not present. We measured the impact of adding the num_teams clause for spmv in our experiments.

We also considered an alternative implementation strategy of Kokkos' hierarchical parallelism without the distribute construct that performs better in many cases. This strategy requires the loop over worksets to be a nested loop inside the target region as shown in Listing 1.11. Currently this approach is the default implementation strategy for the Kokkos OpenMPTarget backend on NVIDIA and AMD GPUs. However, different combinations of architecture and compiler can vary in their preference for implementations similar to Listing 1.10 or Listing 1.11, as our experiments will illustrate.

Figure 3 shows the performance of spmv on NVIDIA A100 and AMD MI250x GPUs. The labels for the legends of Fig. 3 represent the following:

1. *KK-CUDA 3 levels* - Kokkos version with CUDA backend, using all 3 levels of hierarchical parallelism
2. *KK-CUDA 2 levels* - Kokkos version with CUDA backend, using only 2 levels of hierarchical parallelism. (Set vector_size=1 for ThreadVector level.)
3. *KK-OMP-a* - Kokkos version with OpenMPTarget backend, implementing hierarchical parallelism similar to Listing 1.10
4. *KK-OMP-b* - Kokkos version with OpenMPTarget backend, implementing hierarchical parallelism similar to Listing 1.11.
5. *w/o num_teams* - allow the compiler to choose the number of teams
6. *OMP* - direct (non-Kokkos) OpenMP implementation

As with the previous algorithms, KK-CUDA/KK-HIP performance is significantly greater than any of the OpenMP variants. How, much however depends on the compiler, the hardware, and the specific variant of the OpenMP code. The experiment highlights the sensitivity of the OpenMP performance to specific implementation choices, with different choices resulting in better performance on different hardware and compiler combinations.

For example, consider the two compiler versions on NVIDIA's A100. Using LLVM compiler the native OpenMP version and the KK-OMP-B version without the num_teams clause come closest to the performance of the native backends, achieving approximately 70% of the KK-CUDA-3-level bandwidth. These optimized OpenMP versions using LLVM on A100 achieve performance similar to their equivalent native KK-CUDA-2-level version. In comparison, the KK-OMP-A version using LLVM shows a 25% performance gap, and this regression has been observed in other applications as well. The NVHPC compiler also prefers the KK-OMP-B style of parallel decomposition, and unlike LLVM it benefits immensely from the use of num_teams clause. Additionally in this combination of architecture and compiler versions, all OpenMP versions underperform compared to the equivalent native KK-CUDA-2-level version.

On AMD GPUs, even the 2-level native version significantly underperforms compared to the 3-level native version, highlighting the performance benefits that can be achieved by exploiting all 3 levels of hierarchical parallelism. Among the OpenMP versions, KK-OMP-A outperforms KK-OMP-B on both compilers.

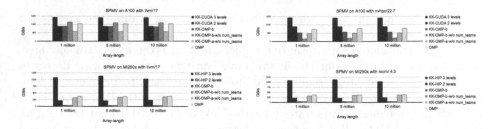

Fig. 3. SPMV on NVIDIA A100 with LLVM and NVHPC compilers and on AMD MI250x with LLVM and ROCM compilers. Y axis is GB/s, so higher is better.

The performance differences observed in this study make it difficult to maintain OpenMP code with consistent performance across different platforms.

The performance of the CG-Solve application as a whole is dominated by the performance of the SPMV kernel. Running the CG-Solve example with the OpenMPTarget backend of Kokkos without making any optimizations specific to CG-solve itself brings the performance close to 50% of the native backends.

3   Beyond the Basics

Besides the initial issues mapping Kokkos to OpenMP already discussed above, there are a number of other challenges that we outline briefly in this section. These challenges did not impact the CG-Solve example, but are of great concern when implementing more complex applications.

3.1   Scratch Memory

Kokkos' hierarchical parallelism provides the ability to allocate team and thread private scratch pads, which act as fast user-managed cache. These scratch pads can be mapped to CUDA and HIP shared memory, and generally are useful for cooperative work within a thread team. In principle the OpenMP specification has the concept of allocators which conceivably would be able to address part of the problem. However, currently this is not implemented by most compilers. Furthermore, in order to leverage aforementioned CUDA and HIP shared memory, the allocation size needs to be specified upon entry into a target region, something for which the OpenMP specification does not provide a mechanism.

3.2   Concurrency

Another capability in Kokkos which is difficult to reliably implement is querying available device concurrency. As mentioned in Sect. 2.3, there is a need to have tight control over the number of teams generated in order to support `TeamThread` level reductions in Kokkos. However we also do not want to restrict the parallelism that can be exploited by a compiler. A trade-off between the two constraints is to calculate the maximum number of in-flight teams possible on a given architecture based on the team size requested. This approach requires information about the number of execution resources available. Currently the backend uses a mix of hardware knowledge, OpenMP routines when applicable and an educated guess to determine this number since there is no single solution that reliably works on every applicable architecture-compiler combination.

One candidate solution is the `omp_get_num_procs()` routine. Because the routine returns the number of processors available on the current device, when called from the host it cannot provide information about concurrency on other devices. We suggest extending its functionality to take a device number as an argument and return the number of available processors on the device identified by that device number. A potential workaround is to open an empty target region at the start of the program only to call `omp_get_num_procs()` within it. Unfortunately, we have observed that the number returned by the routine when called from an accelerator device is not a consistent representation of the underlying hardware concurrency across implementations. Some implementations even return just 1 if the target region body contains only the call to that routine, because they try to optimize the amount of execution resources to match the computation in the target region.

Another use of device concurrency information in Kokkos is to support its `UniqueToken` feature, a locking mechanism that allows a caller to acquire a unique index. Ideally the number of unique index entries should match the number of execution resources. Otherwise, an arbitrarily large number of such unique indices must be created, which may not be practically useful.

Currently extensions to query device concurrency exist that are specific to some vendors, but we are not aware of a portable solution. We hope to converge onto a single cohesive and portable solution on this issue through collaboration with vendors and the community.

4   Conclusion

In this paper we have described mapping the Kokkos Performance Portability model to OpenMP for GPUs. Using a simple linear solver we have explored the state of the Kokkos OpenMPTarget backend on NVIDIA and AMD GPUs with multiple compilers. We find that the OpenMPTarget backend provides significantly less performance than the architecture specific CUDA and HIP backends, due to a mix of compiler implementation issues and limitations in the specification. On average the OpenMP variants (including Kokkos OpenMPTarget backend and raw OpenMP code) provide 57% of the CUDA and HIP backend performance, but at its worst it is about 30x slower than the HIP backend. The performance of the OpenMP implementation is very sensitive to particular construct choices, but the effect of these choices depends on both hardware and compiler. It is thus difficult to write and maintain code which performs consistently across different platforms. Extending OpenMP testing and verification suites to include performance testing across different hardware and compilers could help improve this situation, identify regressions in implementations and help develop best practices. We acknowledge that the current state of OpenMP offloading for GPUs represents an improvement from the past, when performance and even basic portability had been universally poor even for simple loops. We look forward to future enhancements in the specification and improvements in compiler/runtime implementations, which are becoming more commonplace as a result of collaborations between vendors and the community to address the challenge of performance portability.

Acknowledgments. Sandia National Laboratories is a multimission laboratory managed and operated by National Technology and Engineering Solutions of Sandia, LLC., a wholly owned subsidiary of Honeywell International, Inc., for the U.S. Department of Energy's National Nuclear Security Administration under contract DE-NA-0003525. This written work is authored by an employee of NTESS. The employee, not NTESS, owns the right, title and interest in and to the written work and is responsible for its contents. Any subjective views or opinions that might be expressed in the written work do not necessarily represent the views of the U.S. Government. The publisher acknowledges that the U.S. Government retains a non-exclusive, paid-up, irrevocable, world-wide license to publish or reproduce the published form of this written work or allow others to do so, for U.S. Government purposes. The DOE will provide public access to results of federally sponsored research in accordance with the DOE Public Access Plan. This work was supported by Exascale Computing Project 17-SC-20-SC, a joint project of the U.S. Department of Energy's Office of Science and National Nuclear Security Administration, responsible for delivering a capable exascale ecosystem, including software, applications, and hardware technology, to support the nation's exascale computing imperative. This research used resources of the National Energy Research Scientific Computing Center (NERSC), which is supported by the Office of Science of the U.S. Department of Energy under Contract No. DE-AC02-05CH11231, and the Oak Ridge Leadership Computing Facility at the Oak Ridge National Laboratory, which is supported by the Office of Science of the U.S. Department of Energy under Contract No. DE-AC05-00OR22725.

References

1. Beckingsale, D.A., et al.: RAJA: portable performance for large-scale scientific applications. In: 2019 IEEE/ACM International Workshop on Performance, Portability and Productivity in HPC (P3HPC), pp. 71–81. IEEE (2019)
2. Carter Edwards, H., Trott, C.R., Sunderland, D.: Kokkos: enabling manycore performance portability through polymorphic memory access patterns. J. Parall. Distrib. Comput. **74**(12), 3202–3216 (2014). https://doi.org/10.1016/j.jpdc.2014. 07.003. https://www.sciencedirect.com/science/article/pii/S0743731514001257. Domain-Specific Languages and High-Level Frameworks for High-Performance Computing
3. Doerfert, J., et al.: Breaking the vendor lock: performance portable programming through OpenMP as target independent runtime layer. In: Klöckner, A., Moreira, J. (eds.) Proceedings of the International Conference on Parallel Architectures and Compilation Techniques, PACT 2022, Chicago, Illinois, 8–12 October 2022, pp. 494–504. ACM (2022). https://doi.org/10.1145/3559009.3569687

4. Doerfert, J., et al.: Co-designing an OpenMP GPU runtime and optimizations for near-zero overhead execution. In: 2022 IEEE International Parallel and Distributed Processing Symposium (IPDPS), pp. 504–514 (2022). https://doi.org/10.1109/IPDPS53621.2022.00055
5. Hestenes, M.R., Stiefel, E., et al.: Methods of conjugate gradients for solving linear systems. J. Res. Natl. Bur. Stand. **49**(6), 409–436 (1952)
6. Kelling, J., et al.: Challenges porting a C++ template-metaprogramming abstraction layer to directive-based offloading. In: Bhalachandra, S., Daley, C., Melesse Vergara, V. (eds.) 2021 International Workshop on Accelerator Programming Using Directives. WACCPD 2021. Lecture Notes in Computer Science, vol. 13194. Springer, Cham (2022). https://doi.org/10.1007/978-3-030-97759-7_5
7. Khronos SYCL Working Group: SYCL specification (2020). https://www.khronos.org/registry/SYCL/specs/sycl-2020-provisional.pdf
8. Killian, W., Scogland, T., Kunen, A., Cavazos, J.: The design and implementation of openMP 4.5 and OpenACC backends for the RAJA C++ performance portability layer. In: Chandrasekaran, S., Juckeland, G. (eds.) WACCPD 2017. LNCS, vol. 10732, pp. 63–82. Springer, Cham (2018). https://doi.org/10.1007/978-3-319-74896-2_4
9. OpenMP Architecture Review Board: OpenMP Application Programming Interface, Version 4.0. https://www.openmp.org/wp-content/uploads/OpenMP4.0.0.pdf (2013)
10. OpenMP Architecture Review Board: OpenMP Application Programming Interface, Version 5.2. https://www.openmp.org/wp-content/uploads/OpenMP-API-Specification-5-2.pdf (2021)
11. Trott, C., et al.: The kokkos ecosystem: comprehensive performance portability for high performance computing. Comput. Sci. Eng. **23**(5), 10–18 (2021). https://doi.org/10.1109/MCSE.2021.3098509
12. Trott, C.R., et al.: Kokkos 3: Programming model extensions for the exascale era. IEEE Trans. Parallel Distrib. Syst. **33**(4), 805–817 (2021)

OpenMP Target Offload Utilizing GPU Shared Memory

Mathias Gammelmark[✉][iD], Anton Rydahl[iD], and Sven Karlsson[iD]

Technical University of Denmark, Anker Engelunds Vej 1, 2800 Kgs, Lyngby, Denmark
{magam,svea}@dtu.dk, rydahlanton@gmail.com

Abstract. Memory resources are an important aspect to consider when designing high performing programs. This is especially true for programs running on graphical processing units, GPUs, yet this is not something trivially done using current OpenMP target offloading. In this paper, we examine methods for implementing parallel programs running on GPUs, which rely on locally shared memory resources and intricate synchronization. Employing the methods, we show you can achieve between 1.5 to 9 relative speedup over a range of compilers. We evaluate portability by running experiments on two systems, utilizing different GPU technologies and vendors. We further investigate scheduling, synchronization and execution time of our experiments, to better understand the overhead associated with using OpenMP, compared to architecture specific languages. Lastly, we argue that improved GPU scheduling could yield a potential speedup of 3.

Keywords: GPGPU Programming · OpenMP Target Offloading · Shared Memory · Fine-Grained Parallelism

1 Introduction

As supercomputers advance towards exascale levels of performance, there is an increasing trend of incorporating accelerators such as Graphics Processing Units, *GPUs*, to enhance computational density and efficiency. However, the integration of GPUs into supercomputing systems introduces additional complexity for developers, necessitating the evolution of parallel programming models to keep pace with this trend. While architecture-specific languages and tools such as the Compute Unified Device Architecture, *CUDA* [17], provides lower-level control of the GPU hardware often allowing higher performing programs through hardware intrinsic functions, they also place a greater burden on developers, requiring them to invest more effort and time in development.

Open Multi-Processing, *OpenMP* [19], is an application programming interface, *API*, which has long been a popular choice for shared memory parallelism within the realm of High Performance Computing, *HPC*. OpenMP provides developers with a range of library routines and compiler directives that help

© The Author(s), under exclusive license to Springer Nature Switzerland AG 2023
S. McIntosh-Smith et al. (Eds.): IWOMP 2023, LNCS 14114, pp. 114–128, 2023.
https://doi.org/10.1007/978-3-031-40744-4_8

manage the low-level details of parallelization, allowing developers to focus on high-level logic. An important addition in OpenMP 4.0 [20] is the introduction of target offload, which allow developers to offload part of programs to GPUs using a similar syntax to traditional OpenMP parallelization, bringing the high portability of OpenMP to GPU programming.

Target offload in OpenMP is still in an early stage of development across many compilers, including different implementations of the standard. This can often lead to a significant difference in behavior and performance, for the same lines of code when using different compilers. Additionally, GPUs provide fast local memory resources, which is shared between groups of threads providing very fast access. This locally shared memory is important to consider for high performing GPU applications, as it enables fast data sharing and pre-fetching. Yet this area of controlling locally shared memory is not fully mature and can result in a high degree of variation in performance across compilers.

This paper aims to analyze the practical aspects of implementing portable programs with effective utilization of GPU shared memory with OpenMP, specifically focusing on block/chunk algorithms by conducting experiments on two different system, employing both NVIDIA and AMD hardware.

Furthermore, we compare the performance of compiler generated code and performance portability across different compilers. Lastly, we will profile the resulting GPU kernels, to further investigate the underlying scheduling and synchronization of the target regions.

The main contributions of this paper are as follows. We:

- examine the effectiveness of manual parallelization and automatic loop-based work-sharing constructs in OpenMP target offloading for fine-grained control of parallelization and evaluate their suitability for algorithms reliant on GPU shared memory and blocking.
- compare performance and usability of target offloading for blocking algorithms depending on local synchronization and memory resource sharing for the most common compilers on modern hardware.
- identify areas where OpenMP target offloading lags behind, compared to a equivalent program written in CUDA.

In Sect. 2, this paper provides an overview of OpenMP target offloading and introduces the two algorithms used for experimentation. Section 3 presents our experimental results, both considering methods of parallelization, compiler capabilities and in-depth profiling of GPU scheduling. Section 4 gives a brief summary of related works and Sect. 5 concludes the paper by summarizing key findings.

2   Background

GPUs are highly parallel processors, which excel especially at handling large workloads and processing where similar work is required for a large number of elements. They can typically run thousands of threads at the same time, spread across hundreds of cores, making it crucial to consider ways to maximize parallelization in one's programs.

GPUs are typically structured in many physical groups of tightly packed cores, utilizing a Single Instruction Multiple Data, *SIMD*, architecture, for maximizing the density of cores, allowing significantly higher core count compared to conventional CPUs. NVIDIA refer to these groups as Streaming Multiprocessors, *SMs*, containing 32 cores, while AMD designates them as Compute Units, *CUs*, containing 64 cores. Each of these SM/CU will process the same instruction across all cores and through smart hardware and software mapping enable execution of multiple threads at the same time, all executing the same instructions in lockstep. This results in great performance when the flow of execution is identical across all threads, but when a branch is encountered the efficiency will decrease as some cores will remain idle, while the neighbors are executing other branches.

The cores are not only densely clustered in groups, but is also tightly interconnected in the groups, sharing the same registers, L1 cache, and locally shared memory, enabling significantly faster data sharing and synchronization within a group compared to outside [16]. It is therefore important to structure programs in such a way, that most communication is happening within one group, to best utilize the local interconnection. This is already deeply embedded in the architecture-specific languages, such as CUDA and OpenCL, where GPU work is organized in *blocks* or *workgroups* respectively, representing a block/group of threads which work together within the same SM/CU. This organization enables efficient sharing and synchronization between the threads, as they all remain within the same group. Beyond the blocks/workgroup, synchronization becomes limited, although some data sharing can still be accomplished through the use of atomic operations and global memory access. If global synchronization is required, it becomes necessary to wait for all blocks/groups to complete before continuing.

There are several approaches to writing GPU programs using OpenMP target offloading. Section 2.1 discusses the available parallel constructs in OpenMP and Sect. 2.2 discusses the example applications being used for the experiments.

2.1 OpenMP Target Parallelism for GPUs

The analogous concept to *blocks* and *workgroups* in OpenMP is the `teams` construct, which similarly represents a group of threads working tightly together. We consider two main methods for organizing work into blocks. The first is manually defining the work-sharing and the number of teams in the `target teams` region, using the `num_teams` directive, with the intention of starting a team for each block. The number of teams created is a higher bound for OpenMP 5.0 and will be defined by the implementation, but both a lower and higher bound have later been introduced, making this methods more portable for newer versions of OpenMP. The second method is using the `distribute` work-sharing construct to parallelize a for-loop across all available teams, and then let the implementation decide how many actual teams are used, see Listing 1.1. This has the advantage of being independent of the actual number of teams created, making the methods much more portable. The negative side to this method is that it can introduce an additional overhead of managing an outer loop iterating over the blocks, depending on how the implementation decides to handle the distribution. This effect will be examined further in Sect. 3.3.

To fully utilize the hardware a second level of parallelism must be created using a parallel region. Similarly, to the **teams** construct, the parallel region can either be created by directly by specifying the number of threads, or by distributing a loop using the **parallel for** construct. The number of threads in a team can be specified using the **thread_limit** clause, but this also defines an upper limit in OpenMP 5.0, meaning that the actual number of threads in the team is implementation specific, but similarly this clause also received a lower bound in a later version of OpenMP, see Listing 1.2. Using the **parallel for** work-sharing construct is again the more portable solution but might add additional overhead from handling the loop logic and automatic work-sharing.

The main reason we have for separating the team and thread parallelization in OpenMP is to enable allocation of shared memory, which is done by handling array and variable initialization before starting the thread parallelization. A second reason is synchronization, which can be managed using either **barrier** constructs within parallel regions or by ending a loop parallelization for the work-sharing constructs. It is important to note that forking and joining of the loop parallelization can incur a significant overhead, depending on how the work-sharing is implemented.

In Listings 1.1 and 1.2 are code snippets illustrating the overall structure of both the manual work-sharing and the automatic **distribute** and **parallel for** based work-sharing. The outer most pragma is responsible for allocating all blocks and assigning them to the teams and initializing the shared memory, where the inner most pragma is responsible for distributing the blocks work across all available threads within the team.

```
1   #pragma omp target teams distribute thread_limit (BLOCK_SIZE ) nowait depend (...)
2   for  (int block_id  =  0;  block_id  <  n_blocks ;  ++block_id )  {
3       int temp [BLOCK_SIZE ];
4   #pragma omp parallel for num_threads (BLOCK_SZIE ) shared (tmp )
5       for  (int thid  =  0;  thid  <  BLOCK_SIZE ;  ++thid )  {
6           // Do Someting  ...
```

Listing 1.1. Worksharing constructs with distribute and parallel for

```
1   #pragma omp target teams num_teams (num_blocks ) thread_limit (BLOCK_SIZE ) nowait depend (...)
2   {
3       int temp [BLOCK_SIZE ];
4   #pragma omp parallel num_threads (BLOCK_SZIE ) shared (tmp )
5       {
6           // Do Someting  ...
```

Listing 1.2. Manual worksharing using num_teams and thread_limit

In OpenMP 5.0 the `loop` construct was introduced with higher restrictions, allowing potentially better static analysis and mapping to hardware [21]. The usage is very similar to the `distribute` and `parallel for` constructs, but allows mapping to either teams or parallel regions, based on the `bind` clause. However, the `loop` construct is still not widely supported across compilers and will only be examined using the NVC compiler.

2.2 Applications

The different parallel patterns are considered for two algorithms utilizing blocking and GPU shared memory. The first algorithm is the parallel scan based on the Blelloch algorithm [2], which computes the sum of all previous elements in an array. Scan, or also called prefix sums is widely used, eg. for binning and stream compaction in the AMReX framework [28], enabling large scale dynamic particle simulations on GPUs or for list compaction in tree construction algorithms as presented by Wu et al. [26]. Multiple variations of this algorithm exists, with current state of the art based on decoupled look-back [15]. However, for the context of this paper a more simplistic approach is taken, following the presented implementation by Harris et al. in *GPU gems 3* [11]. The overall idea of the algorithm is to calculate the prefix sum locally within a block using the Blelloch algorithm and writes out the total sums of the blocks to an auxiliary array, which then recursively have the prefix sum calculated, until the auxiliary array can fit into a single block. The prefix sum of the blocksums, then corresponds to the sum off all previous blocks, which then can be used to find the global prefix sum.

The second application considered is the parallel four-way LSB radix sorting algorithm, which additionally utilizes the parallel scan for iteratively sorting elements 2 bits at a time, from the lowest bit to the highest bits. A simplified version of the four-way radix sort as described by Linh Ha et al. [10] is used for the experiments, which is omitting the parallel order checking and is using a direct mapping instead of the coalesced block mapping presented. This is done to keep the complexity low, as the focus is held on how to best control the parallelism. Other versions of the parallel radix sort exist, such as 16-way radix sort, sorting by 4 bits at a time, or current state algorithms such as one-sweep radix sorting [1] using the previously mentioned single pass prefix sum, with decoupled look-back.

Both applications are heavily using blocking iteration, where data is processed in blocks and are heavily relying on shared memory. For this reason, we are forced to use separated teams and thread parallel regions, as described in Sect. 2.1.

3 Results

The applications are evaluated using multiple compilers, on two different HPC systems, using GPUs from both AMD and NVIDIA. Before reviewing the experimental results, we'll provide a short description of the two systems in Sect. 3.1 and the compilers in Sect. 3.2.

Table 1. Architecture information for the nodes used in the two systems. The information in 1a has been gathered from the A100 white-paper [16] for the GPU and CPU info have been reported with `lscpu` within the batch jobs. The information in 1b has been gathered from the LUMI documentation [4].

CPU Information	
Model name	Intel Xeon Gold G226G
GPU count	2
Sockets	2
Cores per socket	16
L1d cache	32KiB
L1i cache	32KiB
L2 cache	1024KiB
L3 cache	22528KiB

GPU Information	
Model name	Ampere A100
RAM	40 GiB
SM count	108
Shared mem / L1	192 KiB (*per SM*)
L2 cache	40 MiB

(a) Ampere Node

CPU Information	
Model name	AMD EPYC 7A53
GPU count	4 (*8 logical*)
Sockets	1
Cores per socket	64
L1d cache	32 KiB
L1i cache	32 KiB
L2 cache	512 KiB
L3 cache	256 MiB

GPU Information	
Model name	Instinct MI250X
RAM	128 GiB (*per module*)
CU count	110 (*per chip*)
Shared mem	64 KiB (*per CU*)
L1 cache	16 KiB (*per CU*)
L2 cache	8 MiB (*per chip*)

(b) LUMI Node

3.1 HPC System

The first system is a local cluster at the Technical University of Denmark, managed by DCC [9], which provides access to NVIDIA's A100 PCIE 40GB GPUs [16]. Only a single GPU is utilized for the experiments, with exclusive access to the node to minimize external contributors to noise and overhead.

The second system is the LUMI-G supercomputer [4], which is equipped with four AMD MI250X GPUs, each with a total of 128GB memory. The MI250X GPU is a multi-chip module containing two GPU dies, meaning that each node contain 8 logical GPU partitions where each pair, shares the 128GB memory. As we are using a single GPU for our experiments, this effectively means that only half of one MI250X is utilized.

A more detailed description of both systems is found in Table 1.

3.2 Compilers

The applications are developed using C++17 and are compiled with the -O3 flag for all experiments. The specific version of each compiler is listed in Table 2.

Table 2. Compilers used on the compute nodes from Tables 1a and b. No commit is present for the NVC compiler as it has not been installed from Git. Additionally, both clang and cray are mapping to HIP rocm version 5.2.21153.

Compiler	Version	Commit
clang DCC	16.0.0	710a834c4c822c5c444fc9715785d23959f5c645
clang LUMI	16.0.0	710a834c4c822c5c444fc9715785d23959f5c645
nvc	22.5	-
cray clang	15.0.0	324a8e7de6a18594c06a0ee5d8c0eda2109c6ac6
gcc	13.0.0	44baa34157cf81306be23eacece751aa020985d4

The first compiler is the C language family front-end for the LLVM project *Clang* [12], which we use across both systems. We have compiled Clang to support target offloading according to the LLVM compile guide for OpenMP [13]. The second compiler is the nvc++ compiler from NVIDIA, which is part of NVIDIA's HPC SDK [18] and is provided on the DCC system. We will refer to this compiler as *NVC*. The third compiler used is the cray clang++ compiler, which is provided by the LUMI system as part of their Cray Compiling Environment *CCE* [14], which we will refer to as *Cray*. The last compiler used is the GNU Compiler Collection *GCC* [24]. GCC is also compiled to support target offloading, where we followed the guide *Offloading Support in GCC* [3].

3.3 Parallel Scan

In this section we will compare the manual work-sharing with the automatic loop based work-sharing on the DCC system. The two methods will be compared using the parallel scan algorithm, presented in Sect. 2.2. Additionally, an equivalent CUDA implementation is used to compare similar levels of complexity with an explicit kernel definition. Figure 1 illustrates the execution time for both the manual work-sharing, automatic work-sharing with **parallel for** and the **loop** construct based work-sharing introduced in OpenMP 5.0.

Manual work-sharing demonstrates substantially better performance for both the Clang and NVC compilers, and we see that Clang deliverers comparable results to the pure CUDA implementation for large arrays. Additionally, it is noteworthy that NVC achieves a speedup of approximately 7 with manual work-sharing for large arrays compared to the **parallel for** constructs. For small arrays, Clang exhibits decreased performance, potentially attributed to overhead between kernels, which we will further investigate in Sect. 3.5.

We encountered difficulties with the GCC compiler, as it did not allocate more than 28-32 threads per team. To prevent errors, we had to reduce the block-size to 16 for GCC, alternative to 256 used for the remaining compilers. However, as mentioned in Sect. 2 this behavior is still compliant with the standard.

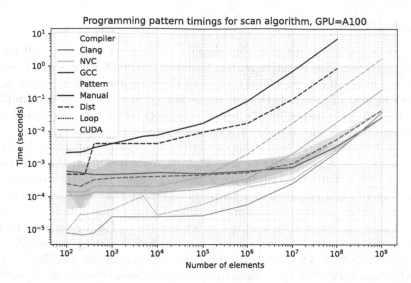

Fig. 1. Execution time for the 3 different parallelization methods across multiple compilers, including the equivalent CUDA implementation. All tests are performed on the DCC system, with A100 GPUs, and execution times include 95 percentile intervals for 200 runs.

The automatic work-sharing using `distribute` and `parallel for` yields lower performance across all array sizes for both NVC and Clang but demonstrates an improvement for GCC while also allowing the block-size to remain at 256. During the debugging process, it was found that GCC utilizes only 32 threads per team, deviating from the more ideal number of 128 threads used by both NVC and Clang. This clearly indicates improved performance stability when utilizing the work-sharing constructs, which further enables the use of much larger blocks which cannot be supported with the manual work-sharing or CUDA, without additional code complexity. However, the performance stability also comes with added overhead, which is indicated by the previously mentioned decreased performance for both NVC and Clang.

The OpenMP 5.0 `loop` construct demonstrates performance close to CUDA across all array sizes, and generally outperforms other patterns for NVC, with a speedup of almost 8 compared to the manual work-sharing. As earlier mentioned we only have support for this work-sharing construct in NVC, which limits further usage, but does show promise for future implementations of OpenMP target offloading.

In general, the manual work-sharing achieves better performance in our experiments, compared to the automatic based on the `distribute` and `parallel for` constructs. However, its effectiveness heavily relies on the implementation, leading to decreased portability across systems and compilers, as shown for the GCC compiler.

3.4 Radix Sort

Next, we examine the manual work-sharing using the four-way parallel radix sorting algorithm. The experiments will both run on the DCC and LUMI system. GCC is omitted due to problems related to the available number of threads in a teams region. The goal of the experiment is to give a better understanding of the expected performance for the tested compilers when using separated team and thread parallelism, to utilize the locally shared GPU memory.

The experiment consists of sorting an array of random numbers, with number of elements ranging from 100 to 10^8. Time is measured from the first target region is called, until the last target region completes and synchronizes. The sorting algorithm is run once as a warm-up to ensure that the run-time is fully initialized, before starting to measure the time. The resulting data is additionally verified after completion, to ensure correct behavior. Timings do not include allocation of data, as all allocations are handled before sorting is started.

Figure 2, illustrates the total execution time, using multiple compilers on both the A100 and MI250X GPUs. Similarly to the previous experiment we have an equivalent CUDA implementation measured on the same A100 GPUs, hinting to what execution time can ideally be expected from a very simple code without using any advanced features.

Clang still shows significant variation in performance for smaller arrays and shows an execution time that approaches the pure CUDA implementation for large arrays. Investigating the percentile interval of the Clang time, shows a relatively constant difference between the 0.01 percentile and 0.99 percentile, ranging from $0.010s$ to $0.012s$ over all sizes of the array larger than the block-size. The constant range of the variation indicates that it is not originating from the kernels themselves, but rather an overhead applied to each executed target region. We will investigate this further in the next section.

On LUMI, we see increased performance for Clang and similar performance for Cray. Clang show significantly reduced statistical variation between runs, compared to equivalent runs on the DCC system, with more than 30 times less variation for most array sizes. Whether the slightly better average performance for Clang on LUMI is due to the hardware, or due to a more efficient OpenMP run-time, is not possible to say from these experiments and is not examined further in this paper. However, it is still worth mentioning that Clang achieves better and clearer results on AMD, than on NVIDIA hardware.

NVC shows better performance with smaller arrays compared to Clang on A100, but falls behind around 10^5 elements, indicating a less efficient parallelization and mapping to the hardware. Similarly to the previous experiment, NVC does not show any large variation between runs and maintains a steady 10 times slowdown compared to the CUDA implementation across all array sizes. NVC could potentially achieve better performance using the `loop` construct, as observed in Fig. 1, where similar performance to CUDA is observed for some sizes.

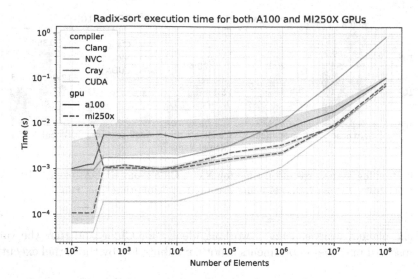

Fig. 2. Execution time of the radix sort implementation across a range of number of elements from 100 to 10^8 elements, with 95 percentile intervals for 200 runs. Experiments are conducted on both A100s from the DCC and MI250X on LUMI. The high variation for the Clang generated code is examined further in Sect. 3.5.

3.5   Profiling

In this section we perform a more in-depth examination of the kernel execution using profiling tools, to get a better understanding of the observed difference between NVC, Clang and CUDA on the DCC system.

The experiment have a similar setup as the previous experiment, where sorting of an array random numbers is performed, but here we fix the size to 10^6 elements for all tests. Profiling has been performed using `NVIDIA Nsight Systems` version `2021.3.3.2-b99c4d6`, which is shipped with `CUDA 11.5`[1] and is using `nsys profile --trace=cuda <program><args>` for all tests.

Figure 3 illustrates the average execution time for each kernel included in the radix sorting algorithm, which also includes all the kernels from the scan algorithm. A significant increase in kernel execution time is measured for NVC, across all kernels which utilize the separated team and thread parallelization for utilizing the shared memory, with slowdowns of between 5 to 10 compared to Clang and CUDA. However, we measure better performance for the `AddBlockSums` kernel, achieving similar results to Clang and CUDA, indicating that the lost performance is due to the separated team and thread parallelization. Clangs kernel execution achieves similar result to the CUDA implementation, indicating

---

[1] CUDA version 11.5 is the highest version still fully supported by the version of Clang used.

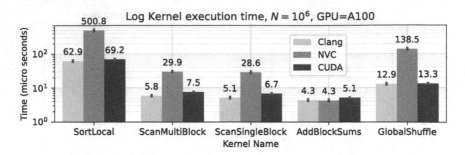

Fig. 3. Profiling kernel execution time for NVC, Clang and CUDA, using A100, with 5 runs per test, with each kernel being executed multiple times per run.

that the manual work-sharing is working ideally for Clang and that the variation observed in earlier experiments is not contributed to by the kernel execution itself.

By examining the profiling data further, we reveal that Clang utilizes synchronization with the host, resulting in additional latency from the communication between the host and device. This should not be necessary as the `nowait` and `depend` clauses are used to run the target regions asynchronously. This does correlate with the increase in time between kernels observed in Fig. 4, and could explain the large variation in execution time from earlier experiments. In contrast, both NVC and CUDA launch all kernels asynchronously and handles scheduling on the device, effectively removing the latency added by the communication.

Figure 4 illustrates this idle-time between kernels and show a significant amount for Clang with an average of $46.5\,\mu s$, compared to $9.2\,\mu s$ observed for NVC and $5.0\,\mu s$ observed for CUDA. As the overall kernel execution time is significantly better for Clang, compared to NVC, it is with high probability that the lost performance and large variation can be contributed to the scheduling and synchronization of the kernels.

We theorize that improving the scheduling in Clang has potential to yield a significant speedup for the overall run-time. To determine the potential, the combined execution time of all kernels is calculated while taking into account an estimated improved idle-time for each kernel. Realistic values for the estimated idle-time can be derived from the average values obtained for NVC or CUDA. Based on these specific experiments, it is found that Clang could achieve a speedup of 2.37 with an idle-time similar to NVC, and a 3.24 speedup with an idle-time similar to CUDA. It is important to note that these results are highly application-specific. Nonetheless, they highlight the potential for substantial performance enhancement in Clang, despite already achieving impressive performance without adding much complexity for the GPU target offloading.

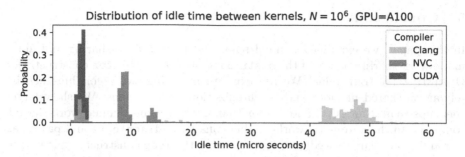

Fig. 4. Profiling idle time between kernels for code generated with NVC, Clang and CUDA, using A100. The idle time is found by the difference in start-time between the consecutive kernels, subtracted by the kernel execution time.

4 Related Work

Previous work by Chapman et al, [5,6] and Daley et al, [7] also report poor performance for `distribute` and `parallel for` constructs when using separate team and thread parallelization, similar to what we observe in Sect. 3.3. Davis et al. [8] further confirm this behavior and additionally show substantial performance improvement using manual team distribution compared to automatic distribution with the `distribute` construct. Chapman et al. [5,6], further show significant improvement using the OpenMP 5.0 `loop` directive, which was also observed in Sect. 3.3.

Rydahl et al. [22] investigated multi-GPU programming using target offloading for stencil operation, similarly performing asynchronous kernel execution using the `nowait` clause. Here multiple target regions were running in parallel allowing overlapping kernel execution, which could help reduce latency related to host-side synchronization.

Tian et al. [25], suggest extension to OpenMP allowing high performing target regions, including allocators for shared memory and synchronization intrinsic within teams. Talaashrafi et al. [23] suggest to automate utilization of shared memory for pre-fetching of read-only data, which could reduce the need for blocking in some algorithms.

Lastly, Zegarra et al. [27], propose a new scan clause for OpenMP, with similar performance as direct programming in OpenCL, but with much less design effort, essentially making it possible to implement our first application using a single OpenMP target construct. Introducing local scanning within teams would additionally help to significantly reduce the design effort for the radix sorting, as the majority of the complexity is related to a local Blelloch scan implementation. Having a local scan clause would additionally allow highly optimized OpenMP implementations taking full advantage of supported architecture features.

5 Conclusions

In this paper, we examined manual team and thread work-sharing and automatic work-sharing based on the `distribute` and `parallel for` constructs, for OpenMP target offloading. We ran experiments using two algorithms heavily relying on shared memory and synchronization within teams. We show larger speedups than 9 for NVC and 1.5 for Clang, when using manual work-sharing compared to the automatic work-sharing constructs `distribute` and `parallel for` and more than a speedup of 7, when using the `loop` construct, compared to the manual work-sharing for NVC.

For both parallel scan and radix sorting we found that Clang suffers from significant overhead for all target regions when running on A100 GPUs, which is revealed to most likely be caused by synchronization through the host, despite using the `nowait` and `depend` clauses, where applications compiled with NVC were able to launch all kernels from the host and handle execution asynchronously on the GPU. Through profiling we show that Clangs kernel execution is comparable to the simple pure CUDA implementation, but that a significant increase in idle-time between kernels is present compared to other compilers. This results in poor performance when applications consist of many smaller target regions, but have diminishing impact when the problem-size increase. Lastly, we estimate a potential speedup of 3 for the profiled applications compiled with Clang, if a scheduling similar to NVC and CUDA can be achieved.

Acknowledgement. This work was partially supported by DeiC National HPC (g.a. DeiC-DTU-N5-20230033) and by the "Compiler development" project (g.a. DeiC-DTU-N5-20230033).

We acknowledge Danish e-infrastructure Cooperation (DeiC), Denmark for awarding this project access to the LUMI supercomputer, owned by the EuroHPC Joint Undertaking, hosted by CSC (Finland) and the LUMI consortium through Danish e-infrastructure Cooperation (DeiC), Denmark, "Compiler development", DeiC-DTU-N5-20230033.

Lastly, we acknowledge DCC [9] for providing access to the A100 GPUs used for experiments as well as interactive environments used throughout development.

References

1. Adinets, A., Merrill, D.: Onesweep: a faster least significant digit radix sort for gpus. arXiv preprint arXiv:2206.01784 (2022). https://doi.org/10.48550/arXiv.2206.01784
2. Blelloch, G.E.: Prefix sums and their applications. Tech. Rep. CMU-CS-90-190, School of Computer Science, Carnegie Mellon University (1990)
3. Burnus, T.: Offloading support in GCC (2023). https://gcc.gnu.org/wiki/Offloading. Accessed 17 May 2023

4. Center for Science: LUMI-G documentation, GPU nodes. https://docs.lumi-supercomputer.eu/hardware/lumig/ (2023). Accessed 15 May 2023
5. Chapman, B., et al.: Outcomes of openMP hackathon: openMP application experiences with the offloading model (part I). In: McIntosh-Smith, S., de Supinski, B.R., Klinkenberg, J. (eds.) IWOMP 2021. LNCS, vol. 12870, pp. 67–80. Springer, Cham (2021). https://doi.org/10.1007/978-3-030-85262-7_5
6. Chapman, B., et al.: Outcomes of openMP hackathon: openMP application experiences with the offloading model (part II). In: McIntosh-Smith, S., de Supinski, B.R., Klinkenberg, J. (eds.) IWOMP 2021. LNCS, vol. 12870, pp. 81–95. Springer, Cham (2021). https://doi.org/10.1007/978-3-030-85262-7_6
7. Daley, C., Ahmed, H., Williams, S., Wright, N.: A case study of porting HPGMG from CUDA to openMP target offload. In: Milfeld, K., de Supinski, B.R., Koesterke, L., Klinkenberg, J. (eds.) IWOMP 2020. LNCS, vol. 12295, pp. 37–51. Springer, Cham (2020). https://doi.org/10.1007/978-3-030-58144-2_3
8. Davis, J.H., Daley, C., Pophale, S., Huber, T., Chandrasekaran, S., Wright, N.J.: Performance assessment of OpenMP compilers targeting NVIDIA V100 GPUs. In: Bhalachandra, S., Wienke, S., Chandrasekaran, S., Juckeland, G. (eds.) WACCPD 2020. LNCS, vol. 12655, pp. 25–44. Springer, Cham (2021). https://doi.org/10.1007/978-3-030-74224-9_2
9. DTU Computing Center: DTU Computing Center resources (2022). https://doi.org/10.48714/DTU.HPC.0001
10. Ha, L., Krüger, J., Silva, C.T.: Fast four-way parallel radix sorting on GPUs. Comput. Graph. Forum **28**(8), 2368–2378 (2009). https://doi.org/10.1111/j.1467-8659.2009.01542.x
11. Harris, M., Sengupta, S., Owens, J.D.: Parallel prefix sum (scan) with CUDA. In: GPU Gems 3, pp. 851–876. Addison-Wesley Professional (2007)
12. LLVM: Clang: a c language family frontend for LLVM (2023). https://clang.llvm.org/. Accessed 26 May 2023
13. LLVM: Support, getting involved, and FAQ (2023). https://openmp.llvm.org/SupportAndFAQ.html. Accessed 17 May 2023
14. LUMI: Cray compilers (2023). https://docs.lumi-supercomputer.eu/development/compiling/cce/. Accessed 26 May 2023
15. Merrill, D., Garland, M.: Single-pass parallel prefix scan with decoupled look-back. Tech. Rep. NVR-2016-002, NVIDIA (2016)
16. NVIDIA: Nvidia a100 tensor core gpu architecture, unprecedented acceleration at every scale (2020). https://images.nvidia.com/aem-dam/en-zz/Solutions/datacenter/nvidia-ampere-architecture-whitepaper.pdf. Accessed 15 May 2023
17. NVIDIA: CUDA toolkit documentation v11.5.0 (2023). https://docs.nvidia.com/cuda/archive/11.5.0/. Accessed 26 May 2023
18. NVIDIA: Nvidia HPC SDK documentation (2023). https://docs.nvidia.com/hpc-sdk/archive/22.7/. Accessed 26 May 2023
19. OpenMP Architecture Review Board: OpenMP (2023). https://www.openmp.org/. Accessed 15 May 2023
20. OpenMP Architecture Review Board: Openmp application programming interface version 4.0 (2023). https://www.openmp.org/wp-content/uploads/OpenMP4.0.0.pdf. Accessed 15 May 2023
21. OpenMP Architecture Review Board: OpenMP application programming interface version 5.0 (2023). https://www.openmp.org/wp-content/uploads/OpenMP-API-Specification-5.0.pdf. Accessed 15 May 2023

22. Rydahl, A., Gammelmark, M., Karlsson, S.: Feasibility studies in multi-GPU target offloading. In: Klemm, M., de Supinski, B.R., Klinkenberg, J., Neth, B. (eds.) OpenMP in a Modern World: From Multi-device Support to Meta Programming. IWOMP 2022. Lecture Notes in Computer Science, vol. 13527, pp. 81–93. Springer, Cham (2022). https://doi.org/10.1007/978-3-031-15922-0_6
23. Talaashrafi, D., Maza, M.M., Doerfert, J.: Towards automatic openMP-aware utilization of fast GPU memory. In: Klemm, M., de Supinski, B.R., Klinkenberg, J., Neth, B. (eds.) OpenMP in a Modern World: From Multi-device Support to Meta Programming. IWOMP 2022. Lecture Notes in Computer Science, vol. 13527, pp. 67–80. Springer, Cham (2022). https://doi.org/10.1007/978-3-031-15922-0_5
24. The GCC team: Offloading support in GCC (2023). https://gcc.gnu.org/. Accessed 26 May 2023
25. Tian, S., Chesterfield, J., Doerfert, J., Chapman, B.: Experience report: writing a portable GPU runtime with OpenMP 5.1. In: McIntosh-Smith, S., de Supinski, B.R., Klinkenberg, J. (eds.) IWOMP 2021. LNCS, vol. 12870, pp. 159–169. Springer, Cham (2021). https://doi.org/10.1007/978-3-030-85262-7_11
26. Wu, K., Truong, N., Yuksel, C., Hoetzlein, R.: Fast fluid simulations with sparse volumes on the GPU. Comput. Graph. Forum **37**(2), 157–167 (2018). https://doi.org/10.1111/cgf.13350
27. Zegarra, M., Pereira, M., Martorell, X., Araujo, G.: Automatic scan parallelization in openmp. In: 2017 International Symposium on Computer Architecture and High Performance Computing Workshops (SBAC-PADW), pp. 85–90. IEEE (2017). https://doi.org/10.1109/SBAC-PADW.2017.23
28. Zhang, W., Myers, A., Gott, K., Almgren, A., Bell, J.: AmReX: block-structured adaptive mesh refinement for multiphysics applications. Int. J. High Perform. Computing Applications **35**(6), 508–526 (2021). https://doi.org/10.1177/10943420211022811

Improving a Multigrid Poisson Solver with Peer-to-Peer Communication and Task Dependencies

Anton Rydahl$^{(\boxtimes)}$ (ID) and Sven Karlsson (ID)

Technical University of Denmark, Anker Engelunds Vej 1, 2800 Kgs, Lyngby, Denmark
rydahlanton@gmail.com, svea@dtu.dk

Abstract. Multigrid methods are a family of mathematical methods governing linear time and storage complexity for solving several elliptic partial differential equations. The logarithmically decaying resolution of the grids in the multigrid hierarchy poses a challenge to achieving high parallel efficiency on highly heterogeneous systems. At the same time, supercomputers have become increasingly heterogeneous with the advent of general-purpose graphics processing units.

This paper presents a highly optimized geometric multigrid Poisson solver that leverages multiple general-purpose graphics processing units with OpenMP target offloading and tasking.

We demonstrate that advanced OpenMP features, such as task dependencies and peer-to-peer data transfers, can decrease the amount of idle time on the accelerators and thereby increase the parallel efficiency for a multigrid application.

Weak scaling results are presented for two high-performance computing systems with NVIDIA and AMD accelerators. We use four NVIDIA Tesla GV100 general-purpose graphics processing units to achieve a parallel efficiency of 94 percent for a solver based on V-cycles with seven multigrid levels.

Keywords: Target Offloading · Multigrid methods · Task dependencies · Task reductions · Peer-to-peer communication

1 Introduction

Geometric multigrid methods are powerful mathematical models that solve several elliptic partial differential equation problems in linear serial time and space complexity [15, page 196]. The recursion consists of iteratively improving the solution estimate on a predefined hierarchy of discretizations.

The convergence rate depends highly on the number of grids; therefore, very low-resolution grids must be included in the grid hierarchy. The computations on fine-resolution grids can significantly benefit from leveraging the general-purpose graphics processing units, *GPGPUs*, found on modern supercomputers [13]. However, the computations on the coarsest grids are less suitable for

© The Author(s), under exclusive license to Springer Nature Switzerland AG 2023
S. McIntosh-Smith et al. (Eds.): IWOMP 2023, LNCS 14114, pp. 129–143, 2023.
https://doi.org/10.1007/978-3-031-40744-4_9

the GPGPUs as the level of parallelism needs to be higher to scale to highly heterogeneous hardware. Therefore, implementing multigrid methods that efficiently use the accelerators without limiting the number of levels is challenging.

By eliminating synchronization points with task dependencies and task reductions, we hide the communication overhead and minimize idle time on the accelerators. Further, by using the runtime function `omp_target_memcpy()` from the OpenMP 5.0 specification [12] rather than directives for mapping, we show how peer-to-peer communication between GPGPUs can improve the parallel efficiency of the geometric multigrid Poisson solver.

Large Unified Modern Infrastructure, *LUMI* [3], which at the time of writing is the third fastest computer in the world [14], comes with four AMD Instinct MI250X [1] GPGPUs per compute node in the GPU partition. As many of the largest systems have AMD GPGPUs, it is essential to understand behavior and potential bottlenecks.

It is found that the approach outlined in this paper weakly scales worse on LUMI than on another system with NVIDIA Tesla GV100 GPGPUs, primarily due to peer-to-peer data transfers, which are more than an order of magnitude slower than on the NVIDIA system.

Our primary contributions follow below:

- We present a single-node multi-GPU geometric multigrid Poisson solver for efficiently solving the Poisson equation in 3D with different combinations of inhomogeneous Dirichlet and Neumann boundary conditions.
- The solver has similar weak scaling properties to other GPU-accelerated geometric multigrid Poisson solvers based on MPI plus CUDA.
- We demonstrate how advanced OpenMP features can be used to improve the scalability of multigrid applications.

2   Mathematical Background

The Poisson equation is an elliptic partial differential equation arising in several science and engineering fields. It can be stated on the form

$$\Delta u(x, y, z) = f(x, y, z), \qquad\qquad (x, y, z) \in \Omega \qquad\qquad (1)$$

where $\Delta = \nabla^2$ is the Laplacian operator, and Ω is a hyperrectangle,

$$\Omega = \left\{ (x, y, z) : x_0 \leq x \leq x_0 + L_x, y_0 \leq y \leq y_0 + L_y, z_0 \leq z \leq z_0 + L_z \right\}.$$

The Poisson Eq. (1) will be considered together with two sets of boundary conditions. In the first case, inhomogeneous Dirichlet conditions are imposed on all surfaces of the hyperrectangular domain. The other set of boundary conditions consists of inhomogeneous Dirichlet conditions on horizontal surfaces of Ω,

$$u(x, y, z_0) = g_{min}(x, y), \qquad\qquad u(x, y, z_0 + L_z) = g_{max}(x, y) \qquad\qquad (2)$$

and inhomogeneous Neumann conditions on vertical surfaces of Ω,

$$\frac{\partial u}{\partial x}(x_0, y, z) = \eta_{min}(y, z) \qquad \frac{\partial u}{\partial x}(x_0 + L_x, y, z) = \eta_{max}(y, z)$$

$$\frac{\partial u}{\partial y}(x, y_0, z) = \xi_{min}(x, z) \qquad \frac{\partial u}{\partial y}(x, y_0 + L_y, z) = \xi_{max}(x, z). \qquad (3)$$

The first set of Boundary conditions is commonly called a *pure* Dirichlet problem. In contrast, the second set of boundary conditions will be called the mixed boundary problem. The numerical procedure described in this chapter works for all combinations of Dirichlet and Neumann conditions except for pure Neumann problems.

2.1 Finite Difference Discretization

In one dimension, the second-order central finite difference operator can be used to derive a second-order accurate finite difference scheme for the Poisson Eq. (1) with Dirichlet (2) and Neumann (3) boundary conditions. The separability of the Laplacian operator makes it sufficient to cover the one-dimensional discretization and boundary modifications. The second-order central finite difference operator on an equidistant grid $\mathcal{G}^h$ with a uniform grid spacing h is given by

$$u_i^{(2)} \simeq \frac{u_{i-1} - 2u_i + u_{i+1}}{h^2} \qquad (4)$$

which can be derived by considering a Taylor expansion in the points $\{u_{i-1}, u_i, u_{i+1}\}$, isolating $u_i^{(2)}$ and dropping higher-order terms [2]. Here, the superscript in parenthesis indicates the order of the derivative.

2.2 Geometric Multigrid Methods for the Discrete Poisson Equation

A geometric multigrid method consists of a prescribed hierarchy of grids $\mathcal{G}^h$ to $\mathcal{G}^{2^{l-1}h}$ together with a set of mathematical operators, namely a relaxation scheme, a restriction operator, and a prolongation operator. The superscripts indicate the grid spacing. The relaxation operator S is used to improve the approximation to the linear system $A^h u^h = f^h$ on grid $\mathcal{G}^h$. The restriction operator maps $\mathcal{I}_h^{2h} : \mathcal{G}^h \rightarrow \mathcal{G}^{2h}$, and the prolongation operator defines the inverse mapping $\mathcal{I}_{2h}^h : \mathcal{G}^{2h} \rightarrow \mathcal{G}^h$ from the coarser to the finer grid. This follows the notation from *Multilevel Projection Methods for Partial Differential Equations* [10]. The concept is to find the residual $r^h = f^h - A^h u^h$ on the fine grid $\mathcal{G}^h$. By computing the defect d^{2h} from $A^{2h} d^{2h} = r^{2h}$ on the coarser grid $\mathcal{G}^{2h}$, the solution estimate on the fine grid $\mathcal{G}^h$ can be improved by adding $d^h = I_{2h}^h d^{2h}$ to u^h. The residual defect can further be reduced by recursively leveraging several coarser grid levels.

2.3   Boundary Conditions

Eliminated Dirichlet boundary conditions can be imposed in points u_0 or u_{n-1}, when the one-dimensional grid $\mathcal{G}$ consists of n points.

Ghost points u_{-1} and u_n can be introduced to derive non-eliminated Neumann boundary conditions. We may consider the first-order central finite difference operator to ensure that the approximate derivative of u_0 and u_{n-1} equals the Neumann conditions. For the left boundary, this corresponds to the choice of u_{-1} given by

$$u_0^{(1)} \simeq \frac{u_1 - u_{-1}}{2h} \qquad \Leftrightarrow \qquad u_{-1} \simeq u_1 - 2hu_0^{(1)}. \tag{5}$$

2.4   Restricting Boundary Conditions

Because the defect equation is solved on all levels, except for the finest, new boundary conditions for the defect equation must be derived.

The analytic solution to the Poisson equation is known at the boundary points for Dirichlet conditions. Hence by definition, the residual of Dirichlet boundary points is zero.

In this work, Neumann conditions are imposed such that the first derivative of the defect must equal the difference between the prescribed derivative and the approximate derivative. Appropriate choices that have the same order of accuracy as the second-order central finite difference operator (4) are given by

$$u_0^{(1)^{2h}} \simeq u_0^{(1)^h} - h^{-1}\left(\frac{-3}{2}u_0^h + 2u_1^h - \frac{1}{2}u_2^h\right) \tag{6}$$

$$u_{n-1}^{(1)^{2h}} \simeq u_{n-1}^{(1)^h} - h^{-1}\left(\frac{1}{2}u_{n-3}^h - 2u_{n-2}^h + \frac{3}{2}u_{n-1}^h\right). \tag{7}$$

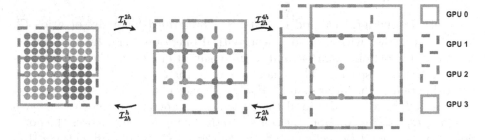

Fig. 1. This figure shows standard coarsening for a cube decomposition. The figure portrays a 2D slice of a cubic domain for easy understanding. The figure shows that four cells in 2D are collapsed into one cell by the restriction operator. For the ease of implementing appropriate boundary modifications, the restriction operator increases the size of the halo. In this example, three levels in the multigrid hierarchy have a uniform grid spacing h, $2h$, and $4h$, respectively. It should be emphasized that using more than three levels is desirable in practice.

2.5 Domain Decomposition

Domain decomposition introduces internal *boundaries*. They can be considered a Dirichlet condition that needs to be updated every time the estimate of u is updated on level 0 or the estimate of d is updated on level $l > 0$.

Figure 1 illustrates the concept of standard coarsening in two dimensions for two-dimensional domain decomposition. In standard coarsening, every point in the coarse grid $\mathcal{G}^{2h}$ corresponds to every second point in the fine grid $\mathcal{G}^h$. When using uniform grid spacing, the physical size of the domain increases when the domain is restricted to a coarser grid because the ghost points used for storing non-eliminated boundary corrections are now placed $2h$ from the boundary.

3 Implementation

The Poisson solver described in the previous section was implemented in C++ and can be used with any combination of Dirichlet and Neumann boundary conditions, except for a pure Neumann problem.

The implementation described in this section is available at https://github. com/AntonRydahl/multigrid-poisson.

```
template<class T>
T DeviceArray<T>::infinity_norm() const {
    T res = 0.0;
    const int _dev = this->device;
    const int * _shape = this->shape;
    const Halo & _halo = this->halo;
    const int (&_stride)[3] = this->stride;
    const T * _devptr = this->devptr;
#pragma omp target device(_dev) is_device_ptr(_devptr) map(always,tofrom:res)
    {
#pragma omp teams distribute parallel for reduction(max:res) collapse(3)
        for(int i = 0;i<_shape[0];i++)
        for(int j = 0;j<_shape[1];j++)
        for (int k_block = 0;k_block<_shape[2];k_block+=BLOCK){
            T tmp = 0.0;
#pragma omp simd reduction(max:tmp)
            for (int_t k = k_block;k<std::min(k_block+BLOCK,_shape[2]);k++){
                T abselem = std::abs(_devptr[idx(i,j,k,_halo,_stride)]);
                tmp = std::max(abselem,tmp);
            }
            res = std::max(res,tmp);
        }
    }
    return res;
}
```

Listing 1.1: Example kernel from the solver. This kernel computes the infinity norm of a subdomain. The **DeviceArray** class contains information about shape, stride, and halo, and the **idx** function is a constant expression that computes the index taking halo and stride into account. One-dimensional blocking is used in the least strided dimension.

3.1 Offloading

The solver contains multiple kernels for smoothing, restriction, prolongation, boundary transfers, norm calculations, and more. They are all implemented using blocking in the least strided dimension.

Listing 1.1 shows an example of how the infinity norm of a subdomain can be computed on the device. The `DeviceArray` class template stores information about host and device pointers, shape, halo size, and element stride. The index is computed based on halo and stride with a constant expression. The combined clause `omp target teams distribute parallel for collapse(3)` is used to distribute the loop iterations with two levels of parallelism across teams and threads on the device. Hardware parallelism is enabled with a single instruction, multiple data, *SIMD*, reduction.

The remaining GPU kernels are implemented similarly and consider three levels of parallelism across teams, threads, and SIMD lanes.

3.2 Task Dependencies

Due to the associated communication, the smoothing operation is the step in the multigrid algorithm that is hardest to get to run efficiently on multiple devices. Especially when considering three-dimensional domain partitioning and coarser levels, overlapping multiple data transfers and computations becomes challenging because the computational load is very small relative to the communication overhead.

```
#pragma omp parallel
#pragma omp single nowait
for (int s = 0; s < nsmooth; s++)
for (int i = 0; i < omp_get_num_devices(); i++){
#pragma omp task depend(inout:u[i],v[i])
    // Swap the solution estimates
#pragma omp task depend(in:u[i],v[i],east_neighbor[i]) depend(out:east[i])
    // Impose the east boundary conditions
#pragma omp task depend(in:u[i],v[i],west_neighbor[i]) depend(out:west[i])
    // Impose the west boundary condition
    ...
#pragma omp task depend(in:east[i]) depend(out:east_neighbor[i])
    // Compute and send the east boundary
#pragma omp task depend(in:west[i]) depend(out:west_neighbor[i])
    // Compute and send the west boundary
    ...
#pragma omp task depend(out:u[i],v[i]) \
depend(in:east[i],west[i],north[i],south[i],top[i],bottom[i])
    // Perform Jacobi relaxation
}
```

Listing 1.2: Simplified example of running the Jacobi relaxation. The aim is to show that multiple relaxations can be run without synchronization when using task dependencies.

A naïve approach to running multiple devices in parallel was first attempted by simply looping over the devices in a parallel-for region with the same number of threads as the number of available devices.

However, each smoothing must have at least two synchronization points with this approach. The first synchronization point is placed after the boundary conditions have been imposed. This enforces that the halo values are not sent before an adjacent device is finished using the halo values from the previous iteration. The second is ensuring that the data transfer between adjacent devices is finished before the next iteration.

To avoid synchronization points, the programming pattern from Listing 1.2 was applied. In the listing, *north, south, east, west, top,* and *bottom* refer to the six surfaces of each subdomain. With the task-based approach, several smoothing iterations can be run without synchronization points between iterations. Some of the tasks have been omitted to simplify the example. For example, there is a dependency between east and west boundaries. The west data transfer will need to specify `depend(out:...)` on the buffer, and the adjacent east internal boundary will specify `depend(in:...)` on the same buffer for imposing the boundary condition.

In Listing 1.2, both the boundary exchange and smoothing operation have **in** dependencies on the boundaries rather than **inout** dependencies. This requires duplicate computations of boundary points and storing halo values in separate buffers. This provides a higher level of parallelism, as boundary transfers can start immediately after the internal boundary conditions have been imposed.

The dependency on the send and receive buffers must not be **inout** as this would require that the tasks imposing, for instance, east and west boundary conditions, would be mutually exclusive, when **west_neighbor** is a reference to the adjacent east boundary and vice versa. The correct execution order is ensured by the **inout** dependencies on the solution estimates, denoted **u** and **v** in the first task in the example code.

```
double fnorm = 0.0;
#pragma omp parallel reduction(+:fnorm) reduction(+:rnorm)
#pragma omp single nowait
#pragma omp taskgroup task_reduction(+:fnorm)
for (int i = 0; i<omp_get_num_devices();i++){
#pragma omp task default(none) shared(u,...) firstprivate(i)\
    in_reduction(+:fnorm)
    {
        double fnorm_task = u[i].infinity_norm();
        fnorm += fnorm_task;
    }
}
```

Listing 1.3: Host parallelism for efficient reductions on multiple GPUs. The partial results are computed with Listing 1.1.

Task Reductions. A standard way of measuring whether a multigrid algorithm has converged is to compute the relative residual defined by

$$\frac{||Au - f||_\infty}{||f||_\infty} \tag{8}$$

and measure whether it has changed since the last cycle. The infinity norm can efficiently be computed using OpenMP task reductions. Listing 1.3 shows the host parallelism needed to compute reductions across multiple devices. The example does not convey the full potential of using task reductions. In reality, many kernels may need to be executed to compute the relative residual because of boundary corrections.

3.3   Direct Peer-to-Peer Communication

Many OpenMP applications rely on directive-based data mapping between host and devices with `omp target data enter()` and similar directives. So did this application, to begin with.

Many modern supercomputers have multiple devices per compute node, typically interconnected with fast direct links. The OpenMP standard does not define a directive to make direct transfers from one device to another. Thereby, directive-based data mapping does not leverage the fast links between GPUs.

While the OpenMP specification does not provide a directive for peer-to-peer communication, it introduced a runtime function for that purpose in the OpenMP 5.0 specification [12], namely `omp_target_memcpy()`. As per the specifications, this function supports data transfers between any combination of host and device pointers. However, most compiler vendors do not support peer-to-peer communication at the time of writing. It is supported in version 16 of the `clang++` compiler from the LLVM project [7], which will be used to illustrate the potential of using `omp_target_memcpy()`.

Listing 1.4 shows how data transfers can be sent directly from device-to-device with `omp_target_memcpy()` using host and device pointers.

```
template <class T>
void Array<T>::device_to_device(Array<T> & arr) {
    // Device-to-device
    int res = omp_target_memcpy(arr.devptr,this->devptr,this->size*sizeof(T)
        ,0,0,arr.device,this->device);
    if (res != 0){/* Handle errors */}
};
```

Listing 1.4: If a compiler, such as `clang` 16, supports any combination of host and device pointers, direct communication can be used.

Table 1. Sub-table 1a states the most crucial device information for the compute node from DCC. It has four NVIDIA Tesla GV100 GPUs interconnected with fast Infiniband links. The host on the node is a dual-socket Intel Xeon Gold 6142.
Sub-table 1b lists the equivalent information for a compute node from LUMI. It has four AMD MI250X GPUs, which contain two GPU dies each. The accelerator metrics are listed per GPU die. The host on the LUMI G node is a single socket AMD EPYC 7A53.

(a) DCC Node		(b) LUMI G Node	
Number of GPGPUs	4	Number of GPGPUs	4
Model name	NVIDIA Tesla GV100	Model name	AMD Instinct MI250X
RAM	32 GB	RAM	64 GB
FP64 Units	2560	FP64 Units	7040
L1 cache	10.2 MB	L1 cache	1.76 MB
L2 cache	6.1 MB	L2 cache	8 MB

4 HPC Systems

Experiments have been performed at two HPC systems; a compute node from Large Unified Modern Infrastructure, *LUMI* [3], and one from the DTU Computing Center, *DCC* [4]. Table 1 gives an overview of the accelerators on the two compute nodes.

The compute node from LUMI has four AMD Instinct MI250X GPGPUs, each consisting of two GPU dies. The two GPU dies within one MI250X are connected with four Infinity Fabric links, each with a theoretical bandwidth of 50 GB/s [16]. GPU dies that do not reside within the same GPU are connected with a single Infinity Fabric link with a bandwidth of 50 GB/s. Each GPU die is connected to the host with an Infinity Fabric link with a 36 GB/s theoretical bandwidth.

The compute node from DCC has four NVIDIA Tesla GV100 GPGPUs. All GPUs are interconnected with 25 GB/s NVLink connections. Furthermore, there is an additional NVLink connection between GPU 0 and 3, and between 1 and 2 such that these links have a bandwidth of 50 GB/s [5, topology A, page 63].

The `clang++` 16 compiler was installed according to the guide [8] from commit `bf82070ea465969e9ae86a31dfcbf94c2a7b4c4c` on DCC and `710a834c4c822c5c444fc9715785d23959f5c645` on LUMI.

5 Experimental Results

5.1 Convergence Experiment

Two test problems were used to verify the correctness of the implementation. The first one is given by

$$\Delta u(x,y,z) = -\,(k_x^2 + k_y^2 + k_z^2)\sin(k_x x)\sin(k_y y)\sin(k_z z) \tag{9}$$

which has the analytic solution $u(x,y,x) = \sin(k_x x)\sin(k_y y)\sin(k_z z)$. In the convergence experiment, frequencies $(k_x, k_y, k_z) = (3, 5.3, -7.8)$ were used. The second test problem has the analytic solution $u(x,y,z) = \cos(xz^2)\sin(y^3)$ and is given by

$$\Delta u(x,y,z) = \big(-\,(4x^2 z^2 + 9y^4 + z^4)\sin(y^3) + 6y\cos(y^3)\big)\cos(xz^2) \tag{10}$$
$$-\,2x\sin(xz^2)\sin(y^3).$$

It can be assumed that no errors were introduced during the implementation if the observed convergence rate matches the expected convergence rate of the discretization. Ordinary least squares estimates are one way to approximate the convergence rate of the solver. The normal equations are given by

$$X^\top X\theta = X^\top y, \quad X = \begin{bmatrix} 1 & \log h_1 \\ \vdots & \vdots \\ 1 & \log h_k \end{bmatrix}, \quad y = \begin{bmatrix} \log \tau_1 \\ \vdots \\ \log \tau_k \end{bmatrix}, \quad \theta = \begin{bmatrix} \alpha \\ \beta \end{bmatrix} \tag{11}$$

where k is the number of observations, $h_1, \ldots, h_k$ are the grid spacings, $\tau_1, \ldots, \tau_k$ are the observed errors, α is the intercept, and β is the slope [9].

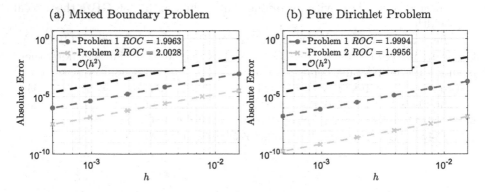

Fig. 2. The maximum absolute error has been plotted as a function of the grid spacing h for test problems (9) and (10). The convergence rate has been found as the slope of the least squares linear fit in logarithmic space. Eight GPUs were used to solve the three test problems and a $2 \times 2 \times 2 \times 2$ hyperrectangular 3D domain decomposition. The dashed black line shows the theoretical rate of convergence of the 7-point stencil.

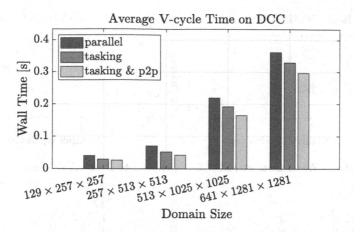

Fig. 3. Comparison of average runtime of a V-cycle on the DCC node when using all four devices in a pencil partitioning. Four pre- and post-smoothing were used in the experiment, and the results were averaged over 30 iterations, even though the method converges in less. The experiment used six, seven, eight, and eight levels.

Fig. 2 shows that the ordinary least squares estimate of the rate of convergence, ROC, the slope β from the normal equations (11), matches the expectation of a second-order accurate numerical method.

5.2   Evaluating Improvements

The compute node from DCC with four NVIDIA Tesla GV100 GPUs was used to evaluate the improvements made to the initial code, which were described in Sect. 3. Three versions were tested: A naïve approach where multiple devices were run in parallel using parallel for loops, and one where task dependencies and task reductions had been employed to remove synchronization points. Additionally, the task-based approach was extended with direct peer-to-peer communication.

Figure 3 shows the results of the experiments. Going from the naive approach to the tasking approach gave a 10 percent speedup. Improving the data transfers with peer-to-peer communication gave an additional improvement of 11 percent for the largest experiment size.

5.3   Weak Scaling Analysis

The weak scaling experiment was performed by considering a pencil decomposition on the DCC node and a hyperrectangle decomposition on the LUMI node. Due to the vastly different amounts of device memory, a domain consisting of $640 \times 1024 \times 640$ voxels was considered for the DCC node, while a domain of

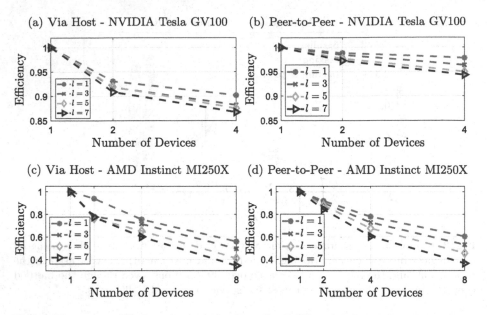

Fig. 4. Upper row: Weak scaling results from the DCC node when using peer-to-peer communication and redirecting data transfers via the host. The efficiency is given for different numbers of levels in the multigrid hierarchy. The lower row shows the same experiments on LUMI. Note the very different scales of the vertical axes for the compute node from DCC and the compute node from LUMI.

$1024 \times 1280 \times 1024$ voxels was used on the LUMI node. On the DCC node, it was scaled to dimensions $640 \times 2048 \times 1280$ and $2048 \times 2560 \times 2048$ on the LUMI node.

The efficiency was measured as $\frac{t(1)}{t(k)}$ where $t(1)$ is the average time per V-cycle and $t(k)$ is the average time for a k times larger domain when using k devices.

On the DCC node, the efficiency for one multigrid level, corresponding to the Jacobi relaxation and convergence estimates alone, is 99 and 98 percent for two and four devices, respectively. When using more levels, it gradually decreases to 94 percent for seven multigrid levels and four devices. When using four devices and seven multigrid levels, the finest domain has a size of $640 \times 2048 \times 1280$, meaning that the coarsest level has only $5 \times 16 \times 10$ cells distributed across the four devices.

However, on the compute node from LUMI G, the weak scaling results are very different. Using just one level has worse scaling than using all seven levels on the DCC node. Further, when using eight devices on LUMI and seven multigrid levels, the parallel efficiency drops as low as 38 percent, and peer-to-peer communication does not improve the results significantly.

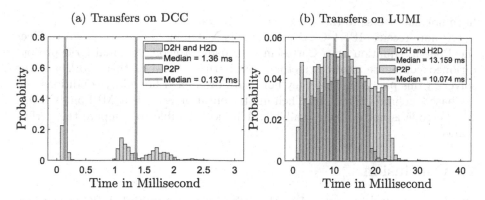

Fig. 5. Histograms of the data transfers using peer-to-peer and redirected communication. The timings are for sending interior boundaries of size 513×513 double precision floating-points corresponding to approximately 2.1 megabytes.

5.4 Boundary Transfers

The transfer times for peer-to-peer communication and communication redirected via the host were estimated to explain the difference in weak scaling results. The transfer times were estimated by measuring wall-clock time immediately before and after the transfers on the host.

As described in Sect. 4, the theoretical bandwidth of the Infinity Fabric connections between the devices on the compute node from LUMI is greater than or equal to the theoretical bandwidth of the NVLinks on the compute node from DCC. However, it was found that the direct GPU-to-GPU data transfers were many times slower on LUMI than on DCC. Figure 5 shows a probability histogram of the timings. It was found that the peer-to-peer transfers on LUMI were approximately 73.5 times slower than on the DCC compute node.

On LUMI, the median peer-to-peer transfer was approximately 31 percent faster than the median communication via the host. On the DCC compute node, using the peer-to-peer connections for halo exchange was ten times faster than redirecting the communication via the host.

6 Related Work

D. Jacobsen et al. [6] present a geometric multigrid solver based on finite differences. The implementation is conceptually similar to ours but is implemented in MPI + CUDA and is not publicly available. Due to the use of MPI, their solver scales to more GPUs. On the DCC node, our solver achieves better weak scaling than the results reported by D. Jacobsen et al. When using four pre- and post-smoothings and five multigrid levels, they report a parallel efficiency of 86 percent on two GPGPUs. In contrast, the solver from this paper achieves 95 percent efficiency on four NVIDIA Tesla GV100. However, on the LUMI node, we achieve similar results. Note that this comparison is approximate since we have not had access to the same computing systems.

A more recent MPI + CUDA example is N. Onodera et al. [11], which solves the Poisson equation on a Cartesian grid using a geometric multigrid precon-ditioned conjugate gradient method. Similarities between their work and the solver in this paper are that they both support mixed boundary conditions and are based on finite differences. Their implementation is made in MPI plus CUDA. As the code is not publicly available, it is not possible to compare the perfor-mance.

7 Conclusion

Developing multigrid applications that efficiently use multiple GPGPUs in par-allel is a design challenge. That is because the low-resolution grids do not nec-essarily benefit from leveraging multiple accelerators.

It has been demonstrated that direct communication between GPUs, intro-duced in version 5.0 of the OpenMP standard, can significantly improve the weak scaling of multigrid applications. While we observed significant improvements on a compute node with NVIDIA Tesla GV100 GPGPUs interconnected with fast NVLink connections, the optimization had little to no effect on a compute node from LUMI with AMD Instinct MI250X GPGPUs interconnected with Infinity Fabric. It was found that the peer-to-peer communication on the former system was, on the median, 73.5 times faster than on the latter system. Therefore, the potential of leveraging the direct GPU-to-GPU connections on LUMI was much smaller and did not provide a significant improvement.

Acknowledgment. This project has received funding from the European High-Performance Computing Joint Undertaking (JU) under grant agreement No 951732. We acknowledge the Danish e-Infrastructure Cooperation (DeiC), Denmark, for awarding this project access to the LUMI supercomputer, owned by the EuroHPC Joint Under-taking, hosted by CSC (Finland) and the LUMI consortium through DeiC, Denmark, *Compiler development* (DeiC-DTU-N5-20230033). Lastly, we acknowledge DCC [4] for providing access to compute resources.

References

1. AMD: Introducing AMD CDNA 2 Architecture. https://www.amd.com/system/files/documents/amd-cdna2-white-paper.pdf (2022). Accessed 23 Mar 2023
2. Bingham, H., Larsen, P., Barker, A.: Computational Fluid Dynamics. Technical University of Denmark, Kongens Lyngby, Denmark (2020)
3. Center for Science: GPU nodes - LUMI-G. https://docs.lumi-supercomputer.eu/hardware/lumig/ (2023). Accessed 16 May 2023
4. DTU Computing Center: DTU Computing Center resources (2022). https://doi.org/10.48714/DTU.HPC.0001
5. Hewlett Packard Enterprise: HPE Apollo 6500 Gen10 System/HPE Pro-LiantXL270d Gen10 Server User Guide. https://support.hpe.com/hpesc/public/docDisplay?docLocale=en_US&docId=a00045705en_us (2019). Accessed 16 May 2023

6. Jacobsen, D., Senocak, I.: A full-depth amalgamated parallel 3d geometric multi-grid solver for GPU clusters. In: Aerospace Sciences Meeting Including the New Horizons Forum and Aerospace Exposition (2011). https://doi.org/10.2514/6.2011-946

7. Lattner, C., Adve, V.: LLVM: a compilation framework for lifelong program analysis & transformation. In: International Symposium on Code Generation and Optimization, 2004. CGO 2004. CGO 2004, IEEE Computer Society, USA (2004)

8. LLVM: Support, Getting Involved, and FAQ. https://openmp.llvm.org/SupportAndFAQ.html#build-amdgpu-offload-capable-compiler (2023). Accessed 16 Feb 2023

9. Madsen, H.: Time Series Analysis. Chapman and Hall (2000)

10. McCormick, S.: Multilevel Projection Methods for Partial Differential Equations. SIAM, Denver, Colorado (1992)

11. Onodera, N., Idomura, Y., Hasegawa, Y., Yamashita, S., Shimokawabe, T., Aoki, T.: GPU Acceleration of multigrid preconditioned conjugate gradient solver on block-structured cartesian grid. In: The International Conference on High Performance Computing in Asia-Pacific Region, pp. 120–128. HPC Asia 2021, Association for Computing Machinery, New York, NY, USA (2021). https://doi.org/10.1145/3432261.3432273

12. OpenMP Architecture Review Board: OpenMP Application Programming Interface - Version 5.0 November 2018. https://www.openmp.org/wp-content/uploads/OpenMP-API-Specification-5.0.pdf (2018). Accessed 18 May 2023

13. Rydahl, A., Gammelmark, M., Karlsson, S.: Feasibility Studies in Multi-GPU Target Offloading. In: Klemm, M., de Supinski, B.R., Klinkenberg, J., Neth, B. (eds.) OpenMP in a Modern World: From Multi-device Support to Meta Programming. IWOMP 2022. Lecture Notes in Computer Science, vol. 13527, pp. 81–93. Springer, Cham (2022). https://doi.org/10.1007/978-3-031-15922-0_6

14. Top 500: November 2022. https://top500.org/lists/top500/2022/11/ (2022). Accessed 18 May 2023

15. Trottenberg, U., Oosterlee, C.W., Schüller, A.: Multigrid. London, 1 edn. (2001)

16. Vicherek, J.: Introduction of LUMI supercomputer. https://events.it4i.cz/event/160/attachments/457/1717/lumi-intro.pdf (2023). Accessed 16 May 2023

Beyond Explicit GPU Support

Multipurpose Cacheing to Accelerate OpenMP Target Regions on FPGAs

Julian Brandner$^{(\boxtimes)}$, Florian Mayer, and Michael Philippsen

Friedrich-Alexander Universität Erlangen-Nürnberg (FAU) Programming Systems
Group, Erlangen, Germany
{julian.brandner,florian.andrefranc.mayer,michael.philippsen}@fau.de

Abstract. While FPGAs can offer great throughput and energy efficiency, when offloading OpenMP target regions to them the memory
bandwidth often limits the ability to exploit their potential. As a rem-
edy, our OpenMP-to-FPGA compiler fully automatically inserts optimized multipurpose cache blocks into the generated FPGA hardware.
We exploit characteristics of OpenMP target regions to both avoid costly
bus snooping hardware and to achieve cache consistency. On a diverse
set of benchmarks with data reuse the caches reduce the runtime by 43%
on average, while only consuming slightly more FPGA resource.

Keywords: FPGA · OpenMP · target offloading · hardware cache

1 Introduction

FPGAs promise a huge potential for computational tasks. In the right domain
they can outperform CPUs as well as GPUs in terms of performance [3] and
energy efficiency [29]. However, many attempts to automatically offload OpenMP
target regions to FPGAs [12,18,20,24] still cannot unleash the potential of the
FPGA. One of their common problems is that large amounts of data can only be
stored in the DDR memory of the FPGA, and due to the limited clock frequency
of the FPGA, memory bandwidth poses a significant performance bottleneck.

We improve this by automatically inserting a highly optimized multipurpose
cache into the generated FPGA hardware and use it in the kernels that encode
offloaded OpenMP target regions on the FPGA. As we use a multipurpose cache
any target region that exhibits data reuse benefits form the cache, regardless of
its algorithm and without the need to statically determine the data reuse patterns. While the presence of a cache is transparent and can be ignored when
compiling for a standard processor, this is no longer the case for cache block on
the FPGA. Here the inserted cache needs to be actively controlled to guarantee cache consistency. And it can also only occupy a small fraction of FPGA
resources as it competes with the offloaded computation.

To the best of our knowledge we are the first to add a multipurpose cache
to the FPGA hardware generated for an offloaded OpenMP target region. We
exploit characteristics of the OpenMP target regions to avoid both resource-
hungry bus snooping hardware on the FPGA and cache consistency issues.

S. McIntosh-Smith et al. (Eds.): IWOMP 2023, LNCS 14114, pp. 147–162, 2023.
https://doi.org/10.1007/978-3-031-40744-4_10

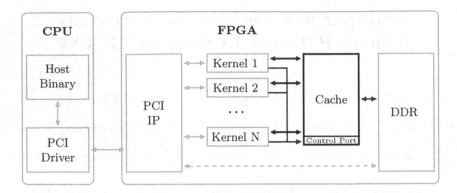

Fig. 1. A typical CPU-FPGA system with an added cache (bold).

Section 2 sketches the workflow of typical OpenMP-to-FPGA compilers and their resulting FPGA design. Section 3 explains how we to improve this design. Section 4 covers our implementation. Section 5 presents our evaluation and findings. In Sect. 6 we discuss related work before we conclude.

2   State of the Art

The various OpenMP-to-FPGA compilers generate both a host binary and FPGA hardware (see Fig. 1, but ignore the bold elements for now). For the host binary, they replace the OpenMP target regions with code that handles the necessary data transfers and starts and awaits the FPGA-side computations. For the FPGA hardware they use a so-called high level synthesis (HLS) to translate target regions into hardware blocks (kernels) and embed them into a low-level platform (LLP) that also holds pre-built blocks like a PCI controller, a DDR memory interface, etc. The latter serve as an interface between the kernels and the host. To execute the complete program, the FPGA is initialized with this bitstream (generated from the LLP and all kernels) and connected to the host system (e.g. by PCI Express).

On all the OpenMP-to-FPGA offloading systems there is the following flow of execution: Fist, the necessary data is passed to the FPGA, where a PCI controller stores the data into onboard DDR memory. Then the PCI controller passes the memory locations to the kernel, launches the kernel, and awaits its termination. The host binary is typically blocked during this process. Finally, when the host requests the results, the PCI controller directly loads them from the onboard DDR memory. Typical applications alternate between data shipment (in/out) phases and FPGA computation phases.

There is a need for a cache. In addition to the data shipment that the PCI controller performs, the kernels also frequently access the onboard memory. On the FPGA the gap between kernels and the onboard memory is even worse than the gap between processor and memory in standard computer architecture. The reason is that on an FPGA it in general requires multiple interconnecting hardware blocks between the kernels and the memory, i.e., long data paths with significant latencies that severely reduce the throughput, since FPGAs usually operate with relatively low clock frequencies ($< 200\,\mathrm{MHz}$). Therefore, to reduce these latencies, we suggest adding a cache between the kernels and the DDR memory, see the bold elements of Fig. 1.

However, cache consistency solutions from standard computer architecture are not applicable to caches on the FPGA. In standard computer architecture it is mainly the processor that accesses the memory. When DMA controllers seldomly accesses it, this is transparent for the processor as extra hardware detects and resolves potential inconsistencies. The situation is different in the flow of execution used for FPGA offloading. First, both the PCI controller and the kernel access the onboard memory frequently, which often causes memory consistency issues when a cache is present. Second, due to their complexity and the structure of buses in FPGA design, the inconsistency resolving techniques from standard computer architecture would consume a significant fraction of FPGA resources and restrict the space that the kernels have for computing. We address these technical issues below and demonstrate how we exploit characteristics of the offloaded OpenMP target regions to solve them.

3   Approach

For decades computer architects have used caches to grant processors fast access to data that reside in slow memory. Hence, it is promising to add an onboard multipurpose cache to the generated FPGA hardware to speedup memory access for the kernels, see Fig. 1. We use a readily available cache block that is designed at register transfer level, is highly resource-efficient, and scales well.

But adding a cache block to an FPGA is far from trivial. In addition to the inconsistency issues mentioned above, there are two more problems. First, the cache competes for FPGA resources that are needed for computing. We address this problem by picking a cache block that is known to have a small footprint. Second, HLS kernels need extra mechanisms that tell a cache block if a certain memory address can or cannot be cached, and they need to actively control the cache w.r.t. consistency issues.

3.1   Cache Integration

At first glance hardware caches appear to be transparent. They can be inserted into a communication bus (or other connections), to automatically store passing data for faster future requests and to defer write accesses in order to save time. But not every read or write request can be safely cached or deferred since for addresses of memory mapped peripherals (instead of memory regions) caching may lead to incorrect behavior. Therefore, typical bus protocols include an extra set of data lines to indicate what type of device is being addressed and what kinds of optimizations are safe.

During HLS however, the address space has yet to be determined and thus the HLS cannot determine how to set these lines. The HLS therefore settles with a safe option that either completely prevents caching, or does not cause any incorrect behavior. In practice the HLS often disables the allocation of new cache lines or leaves the cache empty. Simply adding a cache block to an HLS kernel does not improve performance.

Luckily we can solve this problem in the context of OpenMP-to-FPGA offloading by exploiting that the kernels do not directly interact with peripheral devices. They only use their outgoing ports to communicate with the onboard DDR memory. And since we handle consistency separately (see below in Sect. 3.2), it is safe to enable aggressive caching. We fully engage the cache by writing fixed values to the corresponding extra data lines that control the cache.

3.2   Cache Consistency

We place the cache between the kernels and the onboard memory. Due to architectural constraints it is impossible to route the direct memory lines from the PCI controller (dashed arrow in Fig. 1) through the cache. This causes consistency problems: The PCI can read data that is not yet updated, and the kernels may see outdated values from the cache and miss changes that the host previously made to the onboard memory. Standard computer architecture typically solves such problems by means of a snooping cache that has extra hardware circuits for monitoring the bus. If an address comes by that would lead to consistency issues the cache reacts. On a write request, it invalidates the affected cache line. On a read request it responds with the cached result, even though the cache was not the recipient of the request.

While conceptually it may be possible to add bus snooping circuits to an LLP, it is impractical for two reasons: First, bus snooping and its dynamic inconsistency detection and resolution require complex hardware circuits that would occupy valuable resources and take them away from computing. Second, FPGAs typically employ point-to-point bus system topologies, instead of, for instance, a daisy chain. Hence, a passing request does not physically reach the cache block at all. Workarounds would require additional snooping blocks in the bus network that not only introduce additional latencies but also occupy even more resources.

Luckily we are offloading OpenMP target regions. Due to their copy-in/copy-out semantics, we only have to synchronize cache and memory at the beginning and at the end of an offloaded region.

To solve the cache consistency issues, we add an additional outgoing port to every kernel and connect it to the control interface of the cache (bold lines to "control port" in Fig. 1). We also add explicit code to the kernel code that controls the cache via this interface. At the beginning of a target region the kernel issues a clearing of the cache, so that it sees any updates the PCI controller may have written to the DDR memory before. If we can statically determine that no two kernels ever run simultaneously in the OpenMP program we optimize and drop the checking for previously deferred writes. Otherwise, the cache is instructed to write this data to memory during cache invalidation to avoid interfering with other kernels that were either started concurrently or non-blocking. At the end of the target region the kernel issues a flush before it signals its completion to the platform. This way the PCI controller only accesses the DDR memory after the cache is flushed.

4   Implementation

We implemented our approach by extending the ORKA OpenMP-to-FPGA compiler [18] and the underlying TaPaSCo system composer [14]. We target the Xilinx FPGA ecosystem and used Vitis HLS and Vivado v2021.2 respectively for the hardware generation. We conducted our experiments on the AMD Virtex UltraScale+ FPGA VCU118 Evaluation Kit. For the host system we used an Intel Core i7-4770 CPU which was connected to the FPGA board via PCI Express.

We used the LogiCORE System Cache Version 5 provided by Xilinx. We chose this cache block as it is officially developed and optimized for Xilinx platforms. To the best of our knowledge it is the only publicly available implementation of a cache block for Xilinx FPGAS that natively supports the AMBA AXI4 interface used by Vitis HLS kernels and that offers extensive reconfigurability. The cache size, the cache line length, and the associativity can be chosen freely.

To fully engage the cache (see Sect. 3.1), we set the ARCACHE as well as the AWCACHE lines of the AXI4 bus interface protocol to all ones. To circumvent cache consistency problems (see Sect. 3.2), according to the LogiCORE documentation the kernel has to write certain fixed values to a specific address (0x1C000) of the cache control port. The value 0x200 issues an invalidation of the cache, the value 0x8000 a flush.

Even though we only implemented our ideas as part of the ORKA compiler and only targeted a single FPGA platform, our work is relevant to other OpenMP-to-FPGA offloading systems. As they all construct a similar LLP and compose kernels that access the onboard memory (see Fig. 1), they all can integrate a cache block in the way we suggest. Even works that employ domain specific analyses to generate kernel-local caches (see Sect. 6), can benefit from an additional multipurpose cache, as not every reuse can be determined statically.

5   Evaluation

5.1   Benchmarks

To evaluate the effect of the added cache blocks we use a benchmark set consisting of a 2D convolution (Filter), a Matrix Multiplication, the Levenshtein Distance, the Knapsack problem, two different sorting algorithms, the SHA256 hash, and the computation of the Mandelbrot set (see Table 1). We chose these 8 tasks because, first, the research on FPGA optimization frequently uses them for FPGA system benchmarking ("see also" column). Second, the 8 codes are diverse with respect to both memory access patterns and other properties. The Filter and the Matrix Multiplication access the memory in a regular reuse pattern that is independent of the input. The Levenshtein Distance and the Knapsack problem are examples of popular dynamic programming algorithms. For the

Table 1. Benchmark set.

Benchmark	See Also	Data Reuse	2D Data	SizeIndep. Reuse	Lines of Code	Memory Demand Range (KB)	
Filter	[4,8,22,26]	X	X	X	21	40	– 16000
Matrix Multiplication	[8,16,23,28]	X	X		12	30	– 7680
Levenshtein Distance	[5,34]	X	X	X	30	40	– 313
Knapsack	[9,25]	X	X		30	4	– 2200
OE-Transposition Sort	[4,11,15,30]	X			15	0.4	– 60
Bitonic Sort	[6,16,30]	X			25	0.4	– 60
SHA256	[4,21]				200	40	– 960
Mandelbrot	[4,10,13,32]				20	40	– 16000

Knapcksack problem the data access pattern cannot be statically determined but strongly depends on the input, while the Levenshtein Distance exhibits a static and highly local pattern. As sorting is a building block of many algorithms we included Odd-Even Transposition Sort and Bitonic Sort which are typical for use on FPGAs. Both sorts repeatedly iterate over the dataset, leading to large temporal gaps between reuses. Lastly, we included the SHA256 hash and the Mandelbrot set, since both do have many memory accesses but with hardly any data reuse (see column "data reuse").

The benchmarks also vary with respect to other properties. Four of the benchmarks (column "2D data") work with conceptual 2D data that the codes linearize into accesses to 1D arrays because of HLS limitations. This leads to a typical memory access pattern as two adjacent array elements in the 2D array after linearization are separated by a fixed offset. Our performance measurements, however, did not confirm the reasonable suspicion that this access pattern may affect cache performance. Two of the codes (column "size independent reuse") have – in contrast to the other six ones – a unique property in respect to the spatial locality of their memory accesses: Their data access pattern is not only static, but the number of memory accesses between the use and the reuse of an address is independent of the problem size. This property impacts performance as we discuss in Sect. 5.2.

We took the codes of all benchmarks from textbooks and open implementations and supplied them to the ORKA compiler as standard OpenMP codes with the algorithmic parts marked as target regions. Table 1 shows the number of lines of code of the target regions for each benchmark, including the sizes of the functions called from there. Every benchmark contains exactly one target region and thereby produces one hardware kernel. We generated the input data for the benchmarks randomly from fixed seeds. We tested every benchmark on a wide range of problem sizes, leading to a variation in their memory demand shown in the column "memory demand range". The ranges were chosen according to the complexity of the respective algorithm to achieve reasonable runtimes. For reproducibility the benchmark codes, including their input generation, as well as all the performance measurements discussed below are publicly available.[1]

---

[1] https://doi.org/10.5281/zenodo.8055888.

Table 2. Runtime reduction per benchmark. (Problem data size ca. 40 KB, 128 KiByte 2-way cache with 64 Byte lines).

Benchmark	Runtime w/o. Cache in μs	Runtime w. Cache in μs	Runtime Reduction
Filter	63219	36034	43%
Matrix Multiplication	74133	33956	54%
Levenshtein Distance	21827	13581	38%
Knapsack	5712	3427	40%
OE-Transposition Sort	145819750	88003888	40%
Bitonic Sort	90026	53280	41%
SHA256	52136	52174	0%
Mandelbrot	68062	67382	1%

We synthesized two FPGA versions (without a cache/with a cache) both with a clock frequency of 100 MHz, except for the Levenshtein Distance and the OE-Transposition Sort. Here the vendor tools failed to achieve timing closure, so we had to settle with 50 MHz for both versions. This deviation for two benchmarks does not falsify the results, as the interconnection between the kernels and the memory is always driven at the same frequency as the kernels and the cache, leading to the same runtime behavior across frequencies. We chose these frequencies as a trade-off. We consider them realistic and fast enough for real use cases. But they are also slow enough for the sythesis tools to sport high success rates.

5.2   Runtime Performance

To determine the runtime effects of our approach we synthesized FPGA hardware without and with a cache block. We measured only the time spent on the offloaded target regions on the FPGA since neither the host side of the generated code nor the data transfers to/from the FPGA vary between the two versions. In addition to the axis without/with there are 4 more axes that span the space of our measurements. a) Problem size: Table 2 picks from the measurement space a problem size that demands roughly 40 KB of memory and thus achieves comparability among the benchmarks. The reason for this choice is that this size causes a computational load on the less demanding benchmarks that is clearly above the resolution of the timers. And this size is also small enough for the more complex benchmarks to finish within minutes. For Table 2 we also selected from all our measurements fixed values for the three other axes that configure the cache. b) Cache size: We show measurements for a cache size of 128 KiBytes that is larger than the benchmarks' memory demands of 40 KB.

This is a sensible assumption as on an FPGA a large cache has a reasonable cost (see Sect. 5.4). Section 5.3 shows the effects of caches that are smaller than the problem data. c) Associativity: As the cache size is significantly larger than the problem size, the 4-way cache does shorten the runtimes. Hence, it suffices that Table 2 only shows the measurements for the 2-way cache. d) Cache line length: We only show measurements for 64 Byte lines – the smallest possible setting – because in our experiments the line length had little impact on the runtimes. Both the 4-way associativity and longer cache lines only increased the resource consumption of the cache (see Sect. 5.4).

With this reasoning we can boil down the huge space of measurements Table 2 that characterize the effect of the added cache block for average situations. The insights are, first, as excepted, benchmarks that do not exhibit any data reuse, cannot benefit from a cache (SHA256, Mandelbrot). But the good news is that the existence of the cache does slow them down either. Second, for the remaining six benchmarks we gain an average runtime reduction of 43% (fairly similar across the six benchmarks) for caches that are large enough to fit the entire problem data. We discuss below, how the kernels behave for smaller caches.

5.3   Expected Scaling of the Runtime Performance

The decisive factor for the performance of a hardware cache is its hit rate. If a requested address is still cached from a previous request, the cache can respond quickly without accessing the main memory (cache hit). However, if too many requests have occurred since the last use of a certain address, the corresponding cache line may have been replaced, leading to a cache miss when the address is used again. In general, the smaller the cache is in relation to the problem data of an application with a general reuse pattern, the more cache misses slow down the runtime. Above in Sect. 5.2 and Table 2 we discussed the runtime effects of adding a large enough cache as this is a frequent situation for on-FPGA caches.

Let us now demonstrate that our added cache behaves as expected for larger problem sizes. Let us first look at benchmarks that feature general reuse patterns. As an example, Fig. 2a shows the runtime reductions for the Matrix Multiplication. (Note that the problem data grows quadratically with the width/height of a square matrix.) Other benchmarks have similar graphs. We plot four different cache sizes for growing problem data. The two graphs show the runtime reduction for a 2-way and a 4-way associative cache. As known from Sect. 5.2, for small problem sizes, even the smallest caches can yield good results, regardless of the associativity. For large problem sizes and with more memory accesses between reuses, there are more cache misses. If the cache size is far too small the cache even slows down the runtime. In total, our inserted caches show textbook behavior. This is also true for the effect of associativity. The 4-way associative caches are less likely to replace an address early. Therefore, it needs a larger disproportion between the cache size and the problem data than with a 2-way associative cache before the cache looses its boosting effect.

The decrease in cache performance for larger problem sizes is typical for applications with a general reuse pattern, i.e., for which the number of addresses

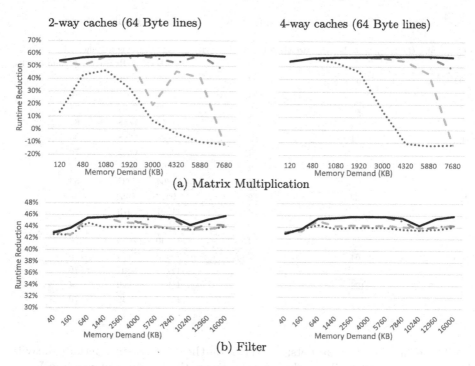

Fig. 2. Runtime reduction for growing problem sizes and various cache sizes:
······ 32 KiB ‒ ‒ 64 KiB ‒ · · 128 KiB ▬▬▬ 256 KiB

that have to be cached between reuses grows with the problem sizes. There are however also applications like the Filter and Levenshtein Distance benchmarks. As for them the number of memory accesses between a use and a reuse is independent of the problem size, the cache performance is (almost) independent as well, as Fig. 2b exemplary shows for the Filter benchmark. For them our inserted caches show the expected behavior, i.e., replacement is not an issue for small caches. And since there is no unwanted replacement, the cache associativity also does not have any impact on the runtime.

5.4 Resource Utilization

To determine the resource utilization of our approach, we synthesized bitstreams without and with a cache block and measured the consumption of the three main FPGA resources: lookup tables (LUTs), registers, and ram blocks (not to be confused with the onboard DDR memory). Our design does not use any digital signal processors, DSPs. The differences between the numbers with/without a cache given in Table 3 represent the cost of adding the cache and the control logic. The measured numbers were very similar for all 8 benchmarks. The bold numbers highlight the configuration used in Table 2.

Table 3. Resource consumption of the various cache configurations.

Cache Size (KiByte)	Cache Line Size (Byte)	Associativity	Cost of adding a cache		
			# LUTs	# Registers	# Ram Blocks
32	64	2	9225	5708	36
		4	11887	7059	66
	128	2	11439	7224	34
		4	13312	7858	65
64	64	2	9928	7298	36
		4	10941	6852	70
	128	2	11208	6916	36
		4	13864	7932	66
128	**64**	**2**	**9495**	**8061**	**36**
		4	11201	6473	70
	128	2	11065	6915	36
		4	13540	7656	70
256	64	2	10433	5734	6
		4	11759	6504	70
	128	2	11967	6929	4
		4	12555	7949	70

These are the key insights: a) Whereas the total costs fluctuate heavily between seemingly similar cache configurations, the numbers of required LUTs and registers stay in a similar range with only a slight upwards trend for more complex caches. There is a more pronounced fluctuation for the number of ram blocks. b) The total cost of the cache is marginal. The highest number of required LUTs for any cache is 13864, which for our target platform corresponds to about 1% of the available LUTs. For the registers, the maximal resource consumption was even lower with 9131, accounting for 0.4% of the available registers. The maximal consumption of ram blocks is 70, corresponding to only 3% of the available number of blocks. c) A 4-way cache occupies significantly more ram blocks than a 2-way cache. Effects, about which we can only speculate, led to the fact that the largest cache size for 2-way associative caches was reproducibly the cheapest in terms of ram blocks. d) Longer cache lines require more resources.

The pure LLP without any cache only consumed about 8%, 6%, and 5% of the FPGAs LUTs, registers, and ram blocks, respectively.

From these insights we derive the recommended and default cache configuration of our ORKA compiler extension uses (and that we also used for the runtime measurements in Table 2): As longer cache lines do not yield any performance benefits we use the smallest cache line length (64 Bytes). As the total resource consumption of the inserted cache is small we fill up the FPGA with the largest possible caches. For the associativity there is no suggested default value.

6   Related Work

The latency and bandwidth of the on-FPGA memory are known problems that the related work addresses in three general ways. (1) One area of research (ours) adds cache hardware to the FPGA. The other two areas are orthogonal to us: (2) optimize the latency and bandwidth of the kernel software or (3) improve cache circuits for FPGAs.

Hardware Cache Block on the FPGA. Our work is unique in this area as no other research group (a) addresses general OpenMP target regions, (b) uses a highly optimized off-the-shelf cache block, (c) relies on an established, productive toolchain (HLS, LLP), and (d) employs standard FPGA hardware for PCI slots.

By exploiting the copy-in/copy-out semantics of OpenMP target regions we are able to use a single cache without costly bus snooping hardware for achieving cache consistency. The related work does not exploit this and hence has to find other means to achieve cache consistency. In all the publications known to us, the researchers gave up on at least one of our unique strengths (a)-(d).

Cheng et al. [7] give up on (b) and (c). Their idea is to add hand-crafted cache blocks with resource-hungry consistency monitoring hardware that works with their special interconnection circuits. As this cannot (easily) be done with standard HLS tools, they use their custom research HLS. Instead of a single large cache, they add multiple smaller caches, one per segment of the offloaded code that works with a certain set of memory addresses. In a way, each of those smaller caches is closer to the computations than our large cache block. The authors' reasoning is that the total cost of the consistency control circuits of all the smaller caches is lower than the cost of the complexity of a single bus snooping cache. The authors find the code segments to which they add caches by monitoring an execution and identifying so-called access hot spots. We do not need such an analysis and get away with two simple cache flushes per target region, one at the beginning and one at the end. While we achieve our runtime improvements on codes that are typical for FPGAs, they only evaluate with some CPU codes from the SPEC2006 benchmark suite [31].

Putnam et al. [28] give up on (c) and (d). They use their custom HLS and only target a single custom host-sided ASIC hardware platform that provides a single shared address space for both the CPU and the FPGA. Their approach relies on this global shared address space. In contrast, we can accelerate kernels on any system with an FPGA on a PCIe interconnect. They also evaluate on Matrix Multiplication and Smith-Waterman (memory access pattern similar to our Levenshtein Distance). One of their other 3 benchmark codes is another matrix operation. We evaluate on a larger set of 6 other benchmarks.

Adler et al. [1] give up on (a) as their LEAP framework is not an OpenMP-to-FPGA compiler. It is an LLP-generator similar to TaPaSCo (which is our LLP generator) that can build cached FPGA designs around user-provided hardware written in a Bluespec register-transfer level (RTL) description [2]. As they work with any custom hardware, they need to connect all caches to an expensive ring network to enable bus snooping. In contrast, we build an FPGA from unmodified OpenMP code and use the properties of OpenMP target regions to allow for a cache with less expensive consistency circuitry.

Winterstein et al. [33] also give up on (a) as they cannot process OpenMP code, but instead use generic C code as input. Since they automatically build hardware cores that are compatible with the LEAP platform (see above) they inherit its costly consistency hardware. In contrast to our general OpenMP target regions, they only target pointer-chasing algorithms.

Latency and Bandwidth Improvement in Source Code. Instead of adding cache hardware, there are optimizations on the level of the programming language that improve the latency and the bandwidth of memory accesses by means of extra code. The HLS generates FPGAs with circuits for the extra code. The research in this area exploits specific features of the applications to achieve excellent performance. While the optimizations are not applicable to all memory access patterns, they are orthogonal to adding hardware caches.

Liang et al. [16] target codes that only read from or only write to each array (half of our benchmarks). Their runtime reductions (up to 88%) come from manually replacing the array access expressions in the C++ codes with calls into a library that mimics a cache-like behaviour per array. Mayer et al. [19] target regularly structured stencil codes with canonical loop nests with contiguous read and write accesses (half of our benchmarks). Their runtime reductions (up to 83%) come from added buffer arrays and HLS pragmas to access them with memory bursts. Pouchet et al. [27] also address stencil codes. They add FIFO buffers to exploit data reuse and perform standard loop transformations. They reduce the runtime by 50% to 95% on suitable benchmarks.

While for specific memory access patterns source-level only solutions can in general outperform general purpose cache hardware, the works in this area can benefit from additional cache blocks for other memory access patterns.

Better FPGA Cache Blocks. Finally, there is research on how to build good cache architectures on FPGAs. Choi et al. [8] work on general purpose caches for FPGA use. Matthews et al. [17] target a specific cache for FPGAs that serve a special multi-core soft-processor also built on the FPGA. They specifically tailor a cache block to the internals of that processor.

Such work is also orthogonal to ours as we could switch to and use improved cache blocks in our LLP.

7   Conclusion

We integrate a highly optimized multipurpose cache block in the hardware that an OpenMP-to-FPGA compiler fully automatically generates when offloading an OpenMP target region. This cache addresses the latency and bandwidth bottlenecks between the kernels and the on-FPGA memory. We exploit special properties of OpenMP target regions to fully engage these caches and to ensure cache consistency without resource-hungry bus snooping circuits. On a diverse benchmark set with data reuse the added caches on average save 43% of the runtime while only requiring less than 3% of the FPGA's resources.

Acknowledgments. The authors acknowledge the financial support by the Federal Ministry of Education and Research of Germany in the framework of ORKA-HPC (project number 01IH17003A).

References

1. Adler, M., Fleming, K.E., Parashar, A., Pellauer, M., Emer, J.: Leap scratchpads: automatic memory and cache management for reconfigurable logic. In: Proceedings of the International Symposium Field Programmable Gate Arrays (FPGA 2011), Monterey, CA, pp. 25–28, February 2011. https://doi.org/10.1145/1950413. 1950421. Accessed 11 May 2023
2. Arvind: Bluespec: a language for hardware design, simulation, synthesis and verification invited talk. In: Proceedings of the ACM and IEEE International Conference on Formal Methods and Models for Co-Design (MEMOCODE 2003), Mont Saint-Michel, France, pp. 249. IEEE Computer Society, June 2003
3. Asano, S., Maruyama, T., Yamaguchi, Y.: Performance comparison of FPGA, GPU and CPU in image processing. In: Proceedings of the International Conference on Field Programmable Logic and Applications (FPL 2009), Prague, Czech Republic, pp. 126–131, September 2009. https://doi.org/10.1109/FPL.2009. 5272532. Accessed 11 May 2023
4. Brandner, J., Mayer, F., Philippsen, M.: Reducing OpenMP to FPGA round-trip times with predictive modelling. In: Klemm, M., de Supinski, B.R., Klinkenberg, J., Neth, B. (eds.) IWOMP 2022. LNCS, vol. 13527, pp. 94–108. Springer, Cham (2022). https://doi.org/10.1007/978-3-031-15922-0_7. Accessed 11 May 2023
5. Castells-Rufas, D., et al.: Opencl-based FPGA accelerator for semi-global approximate string matching using diagonal bit-vectors. In: Proceedings of the International Conference on Field Programmable Logic and Applications (FPL 2021), Dresden, Germany, pp. 174–178, May 2021. https://doi.org/10.1109/FPL53798. 2021.00036. Accessed 11 May 2023
6. Chen, R., Siriyal, S., Prasanna, V.: Energy and memory efficient mapping of bitonic sorting on FPGA. In: Proceedings of the International Symposium Field Programmable Gate Arrays (FPGA 2015), Monterey, CA, pp. 240–249, February 2015. https://doi.org/10.1145/2684746.2689068. Accessed 11 May 2023
7. Cheng, S., Lin, M., Liu, H.J., Scott, S., Wawrzynek, J.: Exploiting memory-level parallelism in reconfigurable accelerators. In: Proceedings of the International Symposium Field-Programmable Custom Computing Machines (FCCM 2012), Toronto, Canada, pp. 157–160, April 2012. https://doi.org/10.1109/FCCM.2012. 35. Accessed 11 May 2023
8. Choi, J., Nam, K., Canis, A., Anderson, J., Brown, S., Czajkowski, T.: Impact of cache architecture and interface on performance and area of FPGA-based processor/parallel-accelerator systems. In: Proceedings of the International Symposium Field-Programmable Custom Computing Machines (FCCM 2012), Toronto, Canada, pp. 17–24, April 2012. https://doi.org/10.1109/FCCM.2012.13. Accessed 11 May 2023
9. Escobar, F.A., Kolar, A., Harb, N., Vinci Dos Santos, F., Valderrama, C.: Scalable shared-memory architecture to solve the knapsack 0/1 problem. Microprocessors Microsyst. **50**(3), 189–201 (2017). https://doi.org/10.1016/j.micpro.2017.04.001. Accessed 11 May 2023

10. Färber, C., Schwemmer, R., Machen, J., Neufeld, N.: Particle identification on an FPGA accelerated compute platform for the LHCb upgrade. IEEE Trans. Nuclear Sci. **64**(7), 1994–1999 (2017). https://doi.org/10.1109/TNS.2017.2715900. Accessed 11 May 2023

11. Hematian, A., Chuprat, S., Manaf, A.A., Parsazadeh, N.: Zero-delay FPGA-based odd-even sorting network. In: Proceedings of the IEEE Symposium Computers Informatics (ISCI 2013), Langkawi, Malaysia, pp. 128–131, April 2013. https://doi.org/10.1109/ISCI.2013.6612389. Accessed 11 May 2023

12. Huthmann, J., Sommer, L., Podobas, A., Koch, A., Sano, K.: OpenMP device offloading to FPGAs using the nymble infrastructure. In: Milfeld, K., de Supinski, B.R., Koesterke, L., Klinkenberg, J. (eds.) IWOMP 2020. LNCS, vol. 12295, pp. 265–279. Springer, Cham (2020). https://doi.org/10.1007/978-3-030-58144-2_17 Accessed 11 May 2023

13. Knaust, M., Mayer, F., Steinke, T.: OpenMP to FPGA offloading prototype using OpenCL SDK. In: Proceedings of the International Workshop High-Level Parallel Programing Models and Supportive Environment (HIPS 2019), Rio de Janeiro, Brazil, pp. 387–390, May 2019. https://doi.org/10.1109/IPDPSW.2019.00072 (Accessed on May 11, 2023)

14. Korinth, J., Hofmann, J., Heinz, C., Koch, A.: The TaPaSCo open-source toolflow for the automated composition of task-based parallel reconfigurable computing systems. In: Proceedings of the International Symposium Applied Reconfigurable Computing, (ARC 2019), Darmstadt, Germany, pp. 214–229, April 2019

15. Lipu, A.R., Amin, R., Islam Mondal, M.N., Mamun, M.A.: Exploiting parallelism for faster implementation of bubble sort algorithm using FPGA. In: Proceedings of the International Conference Electrical, Computer Telecommunication Engineering (ICECTE 2016), Rajshahi, Bangladesh, pp. 1–4, December 2016. https://doi.org/10.1109/ICECTE.2016.7879576. Accessed 11 May 2023

16. Ma, L., Lavagno, L., Lazarescu, M.T., Arif, A.: Acceleration by inline cache for memory-intensive algorithms on FPGA via high-level synthesis. IEEE Access **5**, 18953–18974 (2017). https://doi.org/10.1109/ACCESS.2017.2750923. Accessed 11 May 2023

17. Matthews, E., Doyle, N.C., Shannon, L.: Design space exploration of l1 data caches for FPGA-based multiprocessor systems. In: Proceedings of the International Symposium Field Programmable Gate Arrays (FPGA 2015), Monterey, CA, pp. 156–159, February 2015. https://doi.org/10.1145/2684746.2689083 (Accessed on May 11, 2023)

18. Mayer, F., Brandner, J., Hellmann, M., Schwarzer, J., Philippsen, M.: The ORKA-HPC compiler–practical OpenMP for FPGAs. In: Proceedings of the International Workshop Languages and Compilers for Parallel Computing (LCPC 2021). LNCS, Newark, DE, vol. 13181, pp. 83–97, October 2021. https://doi.org/10.1007/978-3-030-99372-6_6. Accessed 11 May 2023

19. Mayer, F., Brandner, J., Philippsen, M.: Employing polyhedral methods to reduce data movement in FPGA stencil codes. In: Mendis, C., Rauchwerger, L. (eds) LCPC 2022. LNCS, vol. 13829, pp. 47–63. Springer, Cham (2022). https://doi.org/10.1007/978-3-031-31445-2_4. Accessed 11 May 2023

20. Mayer, F., Knaust, M., Philippsen, M.: OpenMP on FPGAs-a survey. In: Proceedings of the International Workshop OpenMP (IWOMP 2019), Auckland, New Zealand, pp. 94–108, August 2019. https://doi.org/10.1007/978-3-030-28596-8_7. Accessed 11 May 2023

21. McEvoy, R.P., Crowe, F.M., Murphy, C.C., Marnane, W.P.: Optimisation of the SHA-2 family of hash functions on FPGAs. In: Proceedings of the IEEE Computer Society Annual Symposium Emerging VLSI Technologies and Architectures (ISVLSI 2006), Karlsruhe, Germany, pp. 317–322, March 2006. https://doi.org/10.1109/ISVLSI.2006.70, Accessed 11 May 2023
22. Meher, P.K., Chandrasekaran, S., Amira, A.: FPGA realization of FIR filters by efficient and flexible systolization using distributed arithmetic. IEEE Trans. Signal Processing **56**(7), 3009–3017 (2008). https://doi.org/10.1109/TSP.2007.914926. Accessed 11 May 2023
23. Moss, D.J., et al.: A customizable matrix multiplication framework for the Intel HARPv2 Xeon+FPGA platform: a deep learning case study. In: Proceedings of the International Symposium Field Programmable Gate Arrays (FPGA 2018), Monterey, CA, pp. 107–116, February 2018. https://doi.org/10.1145/3174243.3174258. Accessed 11 May 2023
24. Nepomuceno, R., Sterle, R., Valarini, G., Pereira, M., Yviquel, H., Araujo, G.: Enabling OpenMP task parallelism on multi-FPGAs. arXiv:2103.10573 [cs.DC], March 2021. https://doi.org/10.1109/FCCM51124.2021.00047. Accessed 11 May 2023
25. Nibbelink, K., Rajopadhye, S., McConnell, R.: 0/1 knapsack on hardware: a complete solution. In: Proceedings of the International Conference on Application-Specific Systems, Architectures and Processors (ASAP 2007), Montréal, Canada, pp. 160–167, July 2007. https://doi.org/10.1109/ASAP.2007.4429974. Accessed 11 May 2023
26. Park, S.Y., Meher, P.K.: Efficient FPGA and ASIC realizations of a DA-based reconfigurable FIR digital filter. IEEE Trans. Circuits and Systems II: Express Briefs **61**(7), 511–515 (2014). https://doi.org/10.1109/TCSII.2014.2324418. Accessed 11 May 2023
27. Pouchet, L.N., Zhang, P., Sadayappan, P., Cong, J.: Polyhedral-based data reuse optimization for configurable computing. In: Proceedings of the International Symposium Field Programmable Gate Arrays (FPGA 2013), Montery, CA, pp. 29–38, February 2013
28. Putnam, A., et al.: Performance and power of cache-based reconfigurable computing. SIGARCH Comput. Archit. News **37**(3), 395–405 (2009). https://doi.org/10.1145/1555815.1555804. Accessed 11 May 2023
29. Qasaimeh, M., Denolf, K., Lo, J., Vissers, K., Zambreno, J., Jones, P.H.: Comparing energy efficiency of CPU, GPU and FPGA implementations for vision kernels. In: Proceedings of the IEEE International Conference on Embedded Software and Systems (ICESS 2019), Las Vegas, NV, pp. 1–8, June 2019. https://doi.org/10.1109/ICESS.2019.8782524. Accessed 11 May 2023
30. Sklyarov, V., Skliarova, I.: High-performance implementation of regular and easily scalable sorting networks on an FPGA. Microprocessors and Microsystems **38**(5), 470–484 (2014). https://doi.org/10.1016/j.micpro.2014.03.003. Accessed 11 May 2023
31. SPEC: SPEC CPU 2006. https://www.spec.org/cpu2006/. Accessed 11 May 2023
32. Wang, K., Nurmi, J.: Using OpenCL to rapidly prototype FPGA designs. In: Proceedings of the IEEE Nordic Circuits and Systems Conference (NORCAS 2016), Copenhagen, Denmark, pp. 1–6, November 2016. https://doi.org/10.1109/NORCHIP.2016.7792907. Accessed 11 May 2023

33. Winterstein, F., Fleming, K., Yang, H.J., Wickerson, J., Constantinides, G.: Custom-sized caches in application-specific memory hierarchies. In: Proceedings of the International Conference on Field Programmable Technology (FPT 2015), pp. 144–151 (2015). https://doi.org/10.1109/FPT.2015.7393141. Accessed 11 May 2023
34. Yoshimi, M., Nishikawa, Y., Miki, M., Hiroyasu, T., Amano, H., Mencer, O.: A performance evaluation of CUBE: One-dimensional 512 FPGA cluster. In: Proceedings of the International Symposium Applied Reconfigurable Computing (ARC 2010), Bangkok, Thailand, pp. 372–381, March 2010

Generalizing Hierarchical Parallelism

Michael Kruse$^{(\boxtimes)}$ (iD)

Mathematics and Computer Science Division, Argonne National Laboratory,
9700 S S. Cass Avenue, Lemont, IL 60439, USA
`michael.kruse@anl.gov`

Abstract. Since the days of OpenMP 1.0 computer hardware has become more complex, typically by specializing compute units for coarse- and fine-grained parallelism in incrementally deeper hierarchies of parallelism. Newer versions of OpenMP reacted by introducing new mechanisms for querying or controlling its individual levels, each time adding another concept such as places, teams, and progress groups. In this paper we propose going back to the roots of OpenMP in the form of nested parallelism for a simpler model and more flexible handling of arbitrary deep hardware hierarchies.

Keywords: Parallelism Hierarchy · Nested Parallelism · OpenMP · Heterogeneity

1 Introduction

Contemporary hardware architecture has changed significantly since OpenMP was introduced. OpenMP 1.0 was designed for symmetric multiprocessing (SMP) systems, when processors could run at most one thread [16]. There was no hierarchy, as implied by *symmetric*: Everything was at the same level without differences in performance or communication between any two CPUs.

The programming model therefore was comparatively simple: one directive to start f(thread-)parallelism (`#pragma omp parallel`) and execute its associated region as a single program multiple data (SPMD) instance, two directives to distribute work between them (`#pragma omp for` and `#pragma omp sections`), and some directives such as barriers and memory fences. It was intended mainly to standardize proprietary compiler extensions that various companies introduced. It was possible to establish a logical hierarchy by executing a parallel directive inside another parallel-construct, but this has no performance advantage over using all threads in a single parallel construct and makes it difficult to not under- or oversubscribe the available hardware.

This model was not sufficient anymore after the hardware became more complex and introduced NUMA, multiple cores per CPU, SMT, and SIMD. While applications could just ignore these characteristics and continue to work correctly, these applications would not be able to reach the best possible performance. Therefore, shown in Table 1, OpenMP 3.1 introduced the `proc_bind`

S. McIntosh-Smith et al. (Eds.): IWOMP 2023, LNCS 14114, pp. 163–178, 2023.
https://doi.org/10.1007/978-3-031-40744-4_11

Table 1. Changes in compute architectures and how OpenMP addressed them.

Hardware Feature	OpenMP Feature	Version
Symmetric Multiprocessing (SMP)	`#pragma omp parallel for`	1.0
scheduling with dependencies	`#pragma omp task`	3.0
Non-Uniform Memory Access (NUMA)	`OMP_PROC_BIND, OMP_PLACES`	3.1, 4.0
Cores, shared caches	`OMP_PROC_BIND, OMP_PLACES`	3.1, 4.0
Symmetric Multithreading (SMT)	`OMP_PROC_BIND, OMP_PLACES`	3.1, 4.0
Single Instruction Multiple Data (SIMD)	`#pragma omp simd`	4.0
Heterogeneous Accelerators	`#pragma omp target`	4.0
GPGPU Multiprocessors	`#pragma omp teams distribute`	4.0
Single Instruction Multiple Threads (SIMT)	`#pragma omp parallel for, safesync`	1.0, 6.0

mechanism, affinity, and other features to account for work placement to hardware units.

The assumption that everything is an abstraction of SMP threads then was broken with the advent of GPGPUs. Nvidia GPUs split the execution into grid, block, and warp and introduced the CUDA programming language, which abstracted hardware blocks and warps into the single instruction multiple threads (SIMT) model, but the grid remained separate because of not supporting fundamental mechanisms across processing units such as barriers. OpenMP could no longer be used as a programming model; only Intel's Xeon Phi many-core accelerator held up the global cache coherency required by OpenMP. Consequently, OpenMP added two new layers: `target` for device memory and `teams` for computations with fewer synchronization guarantees than threads to match the CUDA model. Unlike traditional threads, SIMT threads are executed in lockstep which was a breaking change since older OpenMP applications may have assumed a fair scheduler. The current draft of OpenMP 6.0 takes this into accounting with a `safesync` clause.

The current hardware generation has many more levels that we explore in Appendix A. For instance, most vendors these days combine multiple chiplets into a single packaging, where communication between chiplets is necessarily slower than within a single die, i.e. NUMA but for `teams` [1]. We expect that future processors will be even more complex and its consequences in terms of performance even more noticeable.

Also, even today most high-performance computing platforms have multiple GPUs per node; but since OpenMP has no constructs to represent this level of parallelism, each GPU has to be targeted separately. One proposal is to another pair of constructs: `leagues` to start multiple sets of teams (one set per GPU) and `spread` for work distribution between them. The composite directive for embarrassingly parallel code using all available parallelism therefore would become[1]

```
#pragma omp target leagues spread teams distribute parallel for simd .
```

---

[1] Our proposal is `#pragma omp parallel for level(devices,teams,threads,lanes)`.

Another proposal is to make a league span over teams from different GPUs, either by the compiler treating them as such, or the runtime offering a 'superdevice' combining multiple GPUs. In addition to creating another NUMA problem when `OMP_PLACES` currently applies only to host code, GPUs may not support all the synchronization mechanisms across GPUs, such as atomics. This may actually change in the future, similar to most GPUs now support these mechanisms on the `teams`-level.

Since the term *thread* has many meanings that depend on context, in the following we avoid this term. We will use *task* to mean an execution of an SPMD region[2], *warp* to mean a collection of tasks that may execute in lockstep (even on non-Nvidia hardware), and *lane* to denote one of the tasks executed in a warp.

2   Algorithms for Using Multiple Levels

Beyond individual algorithms that are specifically optimized to make use of a specific level's feature—such as lookup-tables that fits a specific level's local memory—some classes of algorithms can be implemented recursively and profit from any number of levels. One of the most elementary is an implementation of a reduction: on each level, one of the tasks collects the results from all sibling tasks. The most efficient means of communication on each level is chosen, for example, shuffle instructions on the warp level, to reduce the amount of work on the slower parent levels. OpenMP has a reduction clause, but for user-defined operators, it does not permit non-commutativeness or making use of level-specific optimizations such as CUDA's `__shfl_xor_sync`.

Another class of algorithms is stencils. In addition to profiting from warp-level instructions [20], they can be tiled to an arbitrary level [8]. A region of stencil computations can be chosen such that their input region just fits into the local memory. This can be repeated on any level that has local memory.

Other algorithms making use of multiple levels are tensor comprehensions including matrix-matrix multiplications [10] and butterfly-access patterns such as exposed by fast Fourier transforms [3]. In both cases, optimized algorithms select a subset of computations with data reuse and for each level ensure that this data is in local memory.

3   Language Extensions for Hierarchical Parallelism

The idea we propose is to reuse the mechanism of nested parallelism from OpenMP 1.0 but allow the nested construct to choose where to get the new parallelism from. In this section we explore various aspects of controlling where a computation runs, and we continue in Sect. 4 on using levels with local memory.

---

[2] The meaning in OpenMP is "instance of executable code and its data environment", which also includes non-SPMD regions such as in the `task`-construct.

3.1   Explicitly Selecting a Level

The *level* clause selects the level of parallelism to use, as shown below.

```
#pragma omp parallel level(devices(0,1))
  #pragma omp parallel level(multiprocessors)
  {
    printf("Hello from multiprocessor %d\n", omp_get_thread_num());
    #pragma omp parallel level(warps)
    {
      #pragma omp parallel level(lanes)
      printf("Hello from lane %d of warp %d\n", omp_get_thread_num(), \
        omp_get_ancestor_thread_num(2));
  } }
```

One of the motivations of this proposal is allowing performance optimization of specific devices, hence the arguments of the clause can be implementation-specific. It is sensible to also specify a set of predefined levels for device-independent code that match the units of parallelism of the current OpenMP specification: `devices`, `teams`, `threads`, and `simd`. The example above shows that the clause argument may take options; in the case of `devices` it selects which devices participate in the SPMD region. These could also be filtered by a selector; for example, `device={isa("nvptx")}` would select all CUDA-based devices. The `teams` and `threads` arguments correspond to the definition of the current teams and parallel directives, respectively;

Levels can be collapsed to form a single, encompassing level. For instance,

```
#pragma omp parallel level(devices(0-3),teams,threads)
```

executes the tasks using all threads in all teams of the selected devices. Only synchronization guarantees that are common for all levels are also guaranteed for the collapsed levels. Implementations may use aliases for common combinations of levels. For instance, `level(teams)` could be considered an alias for `level(partitions,gpcs,tpcs,multiprocessors,tbps,ctas)` to hide the hardware-level details of Nvidia H100 GPUs.

In order to preserve compatibility with current OpenMP programs, the default level-clause argument has to be `threads`. There is the potential for `#pragma omp parallel level(teams)` to subsume the semantics of `#pragma omp teams` including its combined and composite directives.

3.2   Selecting Levels by Property

The level clause (and teams/parallel constructs) assumes the programmer already has an idea about how the algorithm should execute, but this should not be relevant for first designing an algorithm. Alternatively, the programmer could just define what features are needed for an algorithm, and then the compiler or runtime can select the appropriate hardware and levels to use. The following code indicates that it needs a working implementation of a barrier.

```
#pragma omp parallel sync(barrier)
{
  [...]
  #pragma omp barrier
  [...]
}
```

OpenMP's teams directive does support a barrier that works across team boundaries, so only parallelism within a team could be used. However, many targets support barriers on the hardware level that teams maps to and therefore use this level of parallelism. `barrier` is an example of a level property, but many other properties could be defined; more possible properties are listed in Table 2.

Table 2. Level properties.

Name	Description
`barrier, critical, atomic`	Whether this named synchronization directive is supported on this level
`shuffle`	Whether shuffle instructions are supported on this level; see Sect. 3.7
`oversubcribable`	Whether more tasks can be launched than the hardware can execute in parallel. In this case the operating system has to time-share the resource
`dynamic`	Whether nonstatic schedules are allowed; see Sect. 3.5
`lockstep, progress`	Whether the tasks execute in lockstep. If not, whether there is a forward progress guarantee
`globalmem`	Whether the level has access to the global address space. If not, explicit mapping using the `map` clause is required; see Sect. 4
`localmem`	Whether there is local memory on this level that can be accessed efficiently but only by task in this level
`groupmem`	Whether there is memory that has different contents for each sibling on this level, such as `threadprivate` and its generalization `groupprivate`
`cache`	Whether there is a transparent cache on this level
`num($c$)`	Number of tasks this level can run in parallel
`grainedness($r$)`	Measure of how long tasks on this levels should execute. The more nested the hardware level, the smaller the graininess should be, meaning fewer synchronizable tasks but also has less synchronization overhead

The properties as defined here are *positive* properties. This contradicts the current semantics of the parallel directive, which, for example, has to support barrier directives even without `sync(barrier)`. Hence, a `nobarrier` clause would be needed instead, to indicate the code does not need this feature. However, we think it would be preferable if users would specify the features they need, rather than having to specify for each directive the list of features that are not used. We propose to apply the default semantics of the parallel directive only if the sync clause is not present; that is, `sync()` has a different meaning from not specifying the clause at all.

3.3   Reserving Nested Parallelism

By default, *#pragma omp parallel sync()* would use all available parallelism, but with nested parallel constructs some of the hardware parallelism needs to be reserved for the inner levels. This can be done with a reserve clause.

```
#pragma omp parallel sync() reserve(sync(barrier))
  #pragma omp parallel sync(barrier)
  [...]
```

The outer directive uses all levels except the ones that match the reserve clause argument, but implementations should make at least some parallelism available to each level, if necessary by subdividing it (see Sect. 3.8). OpenMP's current teams and parallel constructs match this example. In addition to the sync argument, the level to be reserved could be selected explicitly by using the level-clause-style argument. Multiple levels can be reserved by using multiple arguments to the reserve clause.

Implementing this may not be trivial, however, since at compile time it may not be known what kind of parallelism has been reserved for the inner construct. In the example above, the threads level and the simd level provide support barriers but are compiled differently. It may just compile the region for both of them, which is then selected by the runtime. Some restrictions may be needed to limit the number of versions when selecting levels by property, especially for numeric variations such as by the simdlen clause.

3.4   Work Distribution

Currently, the worksharing loop and sections directives always bind to the innermost parallel construct, and the distribute directive always binds to the innermost teams construct. With parallel gaining the functionality of both and more levels, it needs to gain the ability to bind to any surrounding parallel construct. Our proposal suggests using a `bind_ancestor` clause, which is similar to the `bind` clause but takes an argument analogous to `omp_get_ancestor_thread_num(level)`. The shorter variant would be `bind(-1)`, which takes an argument relative to the current level.

```
#pragma omp parallel sync() reserve(sync())
  #pragma omp parallel sync()
    #pragma omp for bind_ancestor(0) // bind to outermost parallel
    for (int i = 0; i < 128; ++i)
      #pragma omp for // bind to innermost parallel
      for (int j = 0; j < 64; ++j)
        [...]
```

The reader may have noticed that the example first starts two levels of parallelism and then work-distributes both levels independently. This is contrary to how it currently needs to be written in OpenMP and to how OpenMP defines composite constructs.

```
#pragma omp teams
  #pragma omp distribute
  for (int i = 0; i < 128; ++i)
    #pragma omp parallel
    #pragma omp for
    for (int j = 0; j < 64; ++j)
      [...]
```

Written this way, the overhead of the parallel directive applies to each iteration of the outer loop. The LLVM implementation tries to avoid this by compiling *#pragma omp teams distribute parallel for* into the former code where the associated loop is strip-mined by the number of teams, even though currently not expressible in OpenMP. LLVM calls this form 'SPMD-mode'.

3.5 Scheduling

The possibility of worksharing any level also allows adding a schedule clause on any level, including dynamic schedules. OpenMP's distribute construct allows only static schedules since dynamic schedules would require expensive synchronization between teams.

Additionally, we propose schedule(none), which is useful for shuffle instructions (Sect. 3.7). In contrast to a static schedule, this ensures that there is only a single chunk. Behavior is undefined if there are more logical iterations than tasks, to support the generation of efficient code. Non-participating executions only have to be masked out. If the loop is normalized (i.e., starting at 0 and incremented by 1), then the loop counter variable is identical to omp_get_thread_num(), and the runtime call (or introducing special variables such as threadidx.x in CUDA) can be avoided.

3.6 Compiler-Transformation-Based Directives

While the teams distribute and parallel for directives follow the *start parallelism* and *work-distribute* approach, the simd and loop directives do not. These directives do both at the same time but at the cost of less programmer control.

Our proposed parallel directive can first initialize a vector context for a number of lanes, as shown here.

```
#pragma omp parallel level(simd(8)) private(partial_sum)
{
  #pragma omp for bind(simd) schedule(static,8)
  for (int i = 0; i < 32; ++i)
    partial_sum += A[i];
  [...]
}
```

The code first initializes all elements of the vector `partial_sum` with 0; then each lane sums up $\frac{32}{8} = 4$ values from array `A`, a typical start of an implementation of a reduction. This resembles the SIMT execution model, there is no good reason why the SIMT programming model should be reserved for GPUs only. For LLVM, the command line flag `-fopenmp-target-simd` was proposed that would make the simd construct map to the individual lanes of a warp [18].

Combining starting parallelism and work distribution can be done with the `parallel for` combined construct. To get the descriptive semantics of the loop construct, one would simply use `#pragma omp parallel for sync()`.

3.7   Warp-Level Primitives

Another feature that CUDA supports but OpenMP does not is shuffle instructions, even though support has been proposed [20]. One of the difficulties is that a parallel directive may not be mapped to a hardware layer that supports them; and even if it does, warp sizes vary between devices. The following shows a solution based on our proposal.

```
#pragma omp parallel sync(shuffle,barrier) lastprivate(sum)
{
  [...]
  #pragma omp barrier
  for (int j = 0; j < omp_get_num_threads(); ++j)
    sum += omp_get_value_from_sibling(partial_sum, j);
}
```

Each warp lane has its private copy of `partial_sum`, which are collecting partial sums, as in the preceding section but without limitation to a specific warp size. Worksharing loops have an implicit barrier ensuring that all partial sums have been computed. On Nvidia devices since Volta, it maps to the `__syncwarp` instruction or does nothing if the lanes are in lockstep. The partial sums then are added up for the final result. Here this is done by all lanes, but only the last task needs to do it because of `lastprivate`. In CUDA, the library function `omp_get_value_from_sibling` can use the `__shfl_idx_sync` primitive. A more efficient implementation could use `__shfl_down_sync`, either because the compiler recognizes the pattern or by exposing it as a function call.

Compared to the solution in [20], this has the downside that it has no fallback in case shuffle instructions are not supported; and implementing `omp_get_value_from_sibling` by other means would be inefficient. A version that supports fallback using memory one level up would be the following, but it relies on compiler optimizations to promote `s[omp_get_thread_num()]` to a register.

```
float sum = 0;
float s[omp_get_max_threads()] = {0};
#pragma omp parallel sync(shuffle,barrier) shared(s) lastprivate(sum)
{
  #pragma omp for
  for (int i = 0; i < n; ++i)
    s[omp_get_thread_num()] += A[i];
  sum = 0;
  #pragma omp barrier
  for (int j = 0; j < omp_get_num_threads(); ++j)
    sum += s[j];
}
```

3.8   Level Partitioning

Previous examples assumed that a level occupies exactly one hardware level or collapses multiple levels into a virtual level. We propose the possibility to also split a hardware level. Intel's GPU hardware natively supports changing the warp size [6], but on Nvidia's GPUs it is fixed to 32 lanes. However, we can divide a lane by two as shown below.

```
#pragma omp parallel level(lanes) reserve(level(lanes(16)))
  #pragma omp parallel level(lanes(16))
    [...]
```

For the implementation this does not change a lot other than that it has to keep track of thread numbers and what nested directives bind to. For instance, Nvidia's warp-level instructions provide arguments to bind only to a subset of warp lines but still execute on all lanes. The `__shfl_*_sync` family of functions have `width` parameters to treat all warp subsections of that size as separate entities.

3.9   Versioning

Programmers can write multiple kernels optimized for different hardware. OpenMP already offers the means to do this with the metadirective and `declare variant` directive. For instance, a `device={isa("nvptx")}` filter can be used to execute an optimized kernel for CUDA-based targets only where levels such as "warp" are available, and `device={arch("navi")}` selects a GPU generation from AMD. Additionally, a robust application can fall back on a generic version of a kernel using the sync clause for hardware-independence.

4   Language Extensions for Hierarchical Memory

In addition to instruction stream processors, hierarchy levels may have memory that is used transparently as a cache, be accessible faster from the processing unit than from sibling units (a NUMA domain), not accessible at all from sibling units (a scratch-pad), or each unit may use independent storage for the same virtual address[3].

Using this nomenclature, OpenMP target device storage is a scratch pad (unless enabling unified shared memory), and the memory on it must be allocated by using either `omp_target_alloc` or the map clause. This could motivate also supporting the map clause for lower-level memories such as block-shared memory. Any access the mapped memory is redirected to the local memory, replacing the manual solution of declaring a temporary array in the outer construct and copying the data into it.

The more difficult problem is when each sibling can receive only part of the entire data because of memory constraints. Also, when the data is written as well, how the data is written back at the end of the construct has to be defined.

The following illustration tiles a 2-dimensional array where each tile is distributed to a different device.

```
float A[1024][1024];
#pragma omp parallel level(devices:0-3)                    \
    map(to(d):A[(d/2)*511:513][(d%2)*511:513])             \
    map(from(d):A[(d/2)*512:512][(d%2)*512:512])
```

The map clause is parameterized by a device number **d**, so each device can receive a different array section. The sections overlap so devices can access the immediate neighbors for reading, commonly referred to as a ghost surface. A second map clause with a from-modifier specifies what elements to transfer back to parent memory that must have unique sources. A reduction clause could be used to combine elements in case the array sections are overlapping. To avoid wasting memory, the compiler will need to pack the transferred data into a new data layout and rewrite the address computations within the construct. If the memory is a NUMA domain instead of a scratch-pad (so access from sibling devices are still possible, but slower), a similar syntax could be used to define data affinity.

Note that the target directive is not necessary here because `level(devices)` already declares our intention to offload. Heterogeneous devices manifest as junctions in the hierarchy diagram, such as Fig. 1. Without explicit device specification an implementation would likely execute this example on the host CPU.

---

[3] In the the OpenMP 6.0 draft called `groupprivate` memory, a generalization of `threadprivate`.

For more complicated mapping scheduling, the only generic solution might be to implement the mapping manually by the programmer, for example, `A_dist[4][513][513]`, and then map each `A_dist[d]` to a different device. In contrast to XcalableMP [9], which was explicitly designed for distributed memory (PGAS), our approach assumes that there is always a parent memory large enough to hold its child memories.

5   Related Work

The original hardware level names as invented by Nvidia were the grid, blocks, and threads. Later programming models use different names to emphasize its vendor-independence: OpenMP calls them league/team/thread, OpenACC uses kernel/gang/worker, and OpenCL uses the names NDRange, work-group, and work-item. In contrast to OpenMP which explicitly flattens the iteration space using the `collapse` clause, OpenCL's and CUDA's levels are multidimensional with up to three dimensions. In the following we discuss how CUDA, SYCL, and OpenACC handle increasingly deeper hardware hierarchies.

5.1   CUDA

Nvidia introduced *Thread Block Clusters* in CUDA 11.8 with Compute Capability 9.0 as a new level between grid and block [4,14]. It is supported only with the Hopper generation and only with up to 8 blocks, which suggests it is using the common memory of a multiprocessor (see Fig. 1). According to the documentation, however, they are required to be executed only on the same GPC. Access to Thread Block Cluster memory is not a language extension but has to be done using the Cooperative Groups API.

Cooperative Groups [4] is Nvidia's API to generalize the different abstraction levels inspired by `tiled_extent` from C++AMP. It predefines six different levels, including multi-grid, which spans multiple devices, but also allows user-defined partitioning like we proposed in Sect. 3.8. A Cooperative Group supports group-level operations such as barriers and shuffle methods (Sect. 3.7).

5.2   SYCL

SYCL 2020 added the notion of subgroups to the language [7]. A subgroup usually represents the SIMD lanes of a warp but is specified only to be 'related' work-items. Memory levels such as in Sect. 4 are selectable for atomic using the `sycl::memory_scope` enumeration. There is no specification of arbitrary depth, but vendors can and do introduce extensions that allow optimizing for their hardware, such as Xilinx `sycl::ext::xilinx::partition_ndarray`.

To support shuffle instructions, Intel proposed the ESIMD extension, which allows vector intrinsics instead of the implicit SIMT approach [5]. That is, the user has to write the instructions that operate on subgroup lanes, usually using a C++ `simd` class—a vector with as many elements as the SIMD width; it also supports inline assembly. Hierarchical partitions as shown in Sect. 3.8 are supported using a `simd_view` class. A noteworthy feature is to call ESIMD code from a SIMT context, by passing the code to the `invoke_simd` function. In the called function scalar parameters are pass as `simd` objects, unless declared as uniform.

5.3 OpenACC

OpenMP 3.3 introduced nesting multiple gang levels [15]. The outer gang levels have to specify how many levels of gang parallelism are to be reserved for nested constructs. This does not map to heterogeneous levels as in this proposal, but to the three dimensions of a CUDA grid.

6 Conclusion

OpenMP 1.0 started with a simple premise of flat, symmetric shared-memory parallelism. As computing resources become more powerful, they are also becoming more diverse and complex, but the specification can react only after the new hardware emerges. Devices must also match OpenMP's rigid execution model and hardware. FPGAs do not, and hence an FPGA device will never be able to comply with the OpenMP specification, despite OpenMP priding itself on having been implemented for many different kinds of hardware [2]. With our proposal, there are fewer guarantees that an implementation must provide and greater flexibility for future hardware without releasing a new OpenMP specification.

Additionally, it has the advantage of being descriptive (just define the requirements of a level via the sync clause), similar to the loop construct without a loop, but also prescriptive when needed for performance optimization using a hardware-specific level in the level clause. Programs that allocate compute hours on supercomputers generally require showing that the program has been optimized to the target hardware (e.g., [17,19]). With more complex hardware this will be increasingly harder to do if OpenMP does not provide the means to do so, and applications will have to use vendor-proprietary ecosystems (CUDA, HIP, DPC++, etc.) instead.

Reusing the well-known `parallel` and `for`/`DO` constructs would be the most straightforward since we are reusing its principles of starting an SPMD region, then distributing work between them, but there may be too many legacy behavior conflicts may make introducing new directive names necessary. It is also a major undertaking to revise OpenMP's current nomenclature of target, league, teams, contention groups, threads, and simd. In any case, a major advantage over the current approach is the orthogonal relations between levels using properties, compared with the heterogeneous but fixed levels and their pairwise defined relations that were intended to match a now-outdated generation of hardware.

Acknowledgments. The idea of reusing the parallel directive instead of teams was first brought up by Bronis de Supinski.

This research was supported by the Exascale Computing Project (17-SC-20-SC), a collaborative effort of the U.S. Department of Energy Office of Science and the National Nuclear Security Administration, in particular its subproject SOLLVE.

A   Nvidia Grace Hopper Superchip Hierarchy

In this section, we illustrate the complexity and hierarchical depth of contemporary high-performance hardware using Nvidia's most recent GPGPU design, the Hopper architecture [13], as an example. GPGPU hardware from other vendors such as Intel and AMD generally expose a similar hierarchy and implement the same programming model assumed by OpenMP, SYCL, OpenACC, etc., but will also be different enough to require different optimization strategies. For instance, Nvidia hardware has 32 lanes per warp, while AMD has 64, and Intel's GPU accelerators are configurable between 1 and 32 lanes per warp. Other typical differences are the number of levels, the amount of memory per level, and the number of tasks supported on each level. In contrast, specialized hardware such as FPGAs and dedicated AI accelerators may diverge significantly.

The current OpenMP programming model does not account for these differences and uses a one-model-to-match-them-all approach which cannot accurately represent the diversity of accelerator architectures. Moreover, compute hardware can be expected to become more complex in unpredictable ways in the future.

Figure 1 shows the H100 in a hypothetical configuration that might be sold as the Nvidia HGX Grace Hopper system or be part of the LANL Venado cluster. Unlike previous chips, Nvidia also offers its H100 'Hopper' architecture chips in combination with an ARM-based CPU called 'Grace' integrated into the elegantly named 'Grace Hopper' superchip [12]. Nvidia points out that the Grace CPU does not have NUMA for "high developer productivity", but in a typical setting where multiple processors are connected via NVLink, including Nvidia's own HGX offerings, each superchip is effectively its own NUMA domain. Otherwise, the Grace CPU matches the architectures that are taken account with the `parallel for` construct and `proc_bind` clause and the `simd` construct.

In contrast, the Hopper GPU has many more levels than the `teams distribute` and `parallel for` constructs can represent. An H100 chip is not just a flat collection of multiple SMs but builds a hierarchy itself. Most of them may not be relevant for either the programming model or performance, making them transparent to the programmer, except for the L2 cache, which splits the GPU into halves.

A H100 multiprocessor (SM) is a multicore processor itself and can process 4 instruction streams in parallel, each with its own warp scheduler and register file. The instruction streams can come from either the same or different Cooperative Thread Arrays (CTAs) if the memory constraints allow, but a currently resident task will never move to another SM. Since the four schedulers share the same local memory, data transfers between the warps on the same SM is significantly faster than between warps on different SMs. An algorithm may be able to take this into account; but since the same memory is also used for a per-block shared

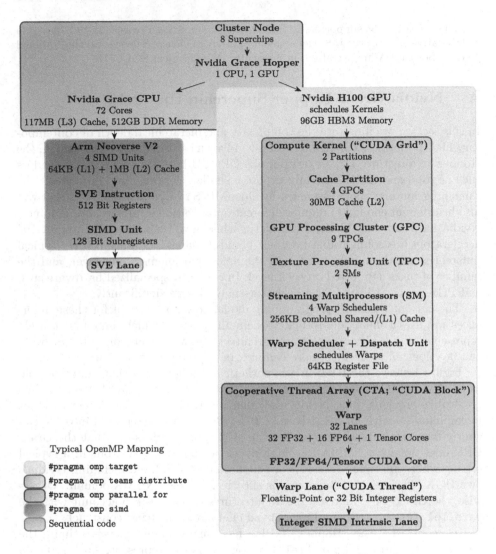

Fig. 1. Hierarchical parallelism of a fictitious Nvidia H100 cluster.

memory, it is architecturally possible to directly access another block's scratch pad memory when executing on the same SM using the abstraction called '*distributed* shared memory'. In OpenMP, it is currently not possible to access this memory.

A Cooperative Thread Array itself is split into warps of 32 lanes each, but whether they are executed in parallel depends on the hardware. In contrast to AMD and Intel, handling of divergent lanes of the same warp is done by the hardware (instead of instructions that explicitly set the execution mask) and, beginning with the Volta architecture, features 'independent thread scheduling' [11]. That is, the hardware is allowed to decide itself when to mask out a lane and when to continue its execution. As a result, which lanes are executed in lockstep is not predictable in software anymore, and Nvidia added `__syncwarps` and additional `_sync`-suffix instructions to CUDA to give software some control over the processes.

With 32 FP32 cores, the H100 can execute all warp lanes at once in the case of a single-precision instruction, but since only 16 FP64 cores are available, it takes two rounds for all 32 lanes of a double-precision instruction to execute. Neither CUDA nor OpenMP exposes this detail, but some algorithms might be able to exploit this detail knowing that using two warps each using just 16 lanes may result in the same performance as a full warp or that lanes that are not in the same group of 16 can diverge without performance penalty. Incidentally, this similarly applies to the Grace CPU, which processes a single 512-bit SVE instruction independently in 4 SIMD units.

In addition to the SIMT programming model, CUDA supports a limited selection of traditional SIMD intrinsics, but only for integer operations [14]. For instance, the `__vadd2` intrinsic treats a 32-bit integer register as a vector register containing two 16-bit integers and adds them independently. Similarly, `__vadd4` adds four 8-bit integers. We are not aware of any compiler that emits these vector instructions without explicitly using the intrinsics, even when using `#pragma omp simd`.

References

1. Dongarra, J., Geist, A.: Report on the Oak Ridge National Laboratory's Frontier System. Technical Report. ICL-UT-22-05, University of Tennessee (2022)
2. Fan, X., de Supinski, B.R., Sinnen, O., Giacaman, N. (eds.): IWOMP 2019. LNCS, vol. 11718. Springer, Cham (2019). https://doi.org/10.1007/978-3-030-28596-8
3. Franchetti, F., de Mesmay, F., McFarlin, D., Püschel, M.: Operator language: a program generation framework for fast kernels. In: Taha, W.M. (ed.) DSL 2009. LNCS, vol. 5658, pp. 385–409. Springer, Heidelberg (2009). https://doi.org/10.1007/978-3-642-03034-5_18
4. Harris, M.: Cooperative Groups: Flexible CUDA Thread Programming. Nvidia blog post (2017). http://developer.nvidia.com/blog/cooperative-groups/
5. Intel: "Explicit SIMD" SYCL extension. https://github.com/intel/llvm/tree/sycl/sycl/doc/extensions/experimental/sycl_ext_intel_esimd
6. Intel: oneAPI GPU Optimization Guide 2023.1. https://www.intel.com/content/www/us/en/docs/oneapi/optimization-guide-gpu/2023-1/intel-xe-gpu-architecture.html
7. Khronos: SYCL 2020 Specification (revision 7). http://registry.khronos.org/SYCL/specs/sycl-2020/html/sycl-2020.html
8. Kruse, M., Finkel, H.: A proposal for loop-transformation pragmas. In: de Supinski, B.R., Valero-Lara, P., Martorell, X., Mateo Bellido, S., Labarta, J. (eds.) IWOMP 2018. LNCS, vol. 11128, pp. 37–52. Springer, Cham (2018). https://doi.org/10.1007/978-3-319-98521-3_3
9. Lee, J., Tran, M.T., Odajima, T., Boku, T., Sato, M.: An extension of XcalableMP PGAS lanaguage for multi-node GPU clusters. In: Alexander, M., et al. (eds.) Euro-Par 2011. LNCS, vol. 7155, pp. 429–439. Springer, Heidelberg (2012). https://doi.org/10.1007/978-3-642-29737-3_48

10. Low, T.M., Igual, F.D., Smith, T.M., Quintana-Orti, E.S.: Analytical modeling is enough for high-performance BLIS. Trans. Math. Softw. (TOMS) **43**(2), 1–18 (2016)
11. Nvidia: Tesla V100 GPU Architecture V1.1. Technical report. (2017). http://www.nvidia.com/object/volta-architecture-whitepaper.html
12. Nvidia: Grace Hopper Superchip Architecture V1.01. Technical report (2022). http://resources.nvidia.com/en-us-grace-cpu/nvidia-grace-hopper
13. Nvidia: H100 Tensor Core GPU Architecture V1.03. Technical report. (2022). http://resources.nvidia.com/en-us-tensor-core
14. Nvidia: CUDA Toolkit Documentation V12.1 Update 1 (2023). https://docs.nvidia.com/cuda/
15. OpenACC-standard.org: The OpenACC Application Programming Interface Version 3.3 (2022). https://www.openacc.org/specification
16. OpenMP Architecture Review Board: OpenMP C and C++ Application Program Interface Version 1.0 (1998)
17. PRACE: Guide for Applicants to Tier-0 Resources. Call for Proposals (2016). http://prace-ri.eu/hpc-access/project-access/project-access-open-calls/guide-for-applicants-to-tier-0-resources/
18. Tian, S.: Add new clang argument '-fopenmp-target-simd'. LLVM code review (2021). https://reviews.llvm.org/D110286
19. US Department of Energy: INCITE Call for Proposals. http://www.doeleadershipcomputing.org/proposal/new-proposals-instructions/
20. Wang, A., Yi, X., Yan, Y.: Supporting data `Shuffle` between threads in OpenMP. In: Milfeld, K., de Supinski, B.R., Koesterke, L., Klinkenberg, J. (eds.) IWOMP 2020. LNCS, vol. 12295, pp. 98–112. Springer, Cham (2020). https://doi.org/10.1007/978-3-030-58144-2_7

Exploring the Limits of Generic Code Execution on GPUs via Direct (OpenMP) Offload

Shilei Tian[1]($^\boxtimes$)(iD), Barbara Chapman[1](iD), and Johannes Doerfert[2]($^\boxtimes$)(iD)

[1] Stony Brook University, Stony Brook, NY 11794, USA
{shilei.tian,barbara.chapman}@stonybrook.edu
[2] Lawrence Livermore National Laboratory, Livermore, CA 94550, USA
jdoerfert@llnl.gov

Abstract. GPUs are well-known for their remarkable ability to accelerate computations through massive parallelism. However, offloading computations to GPUs necessitates manual identification of code regions that should be executed on the device, memory that needs to be transferred, and synchronization to be handled. Recent work has leveraged the portable target offloading interface provided by LLVM/OpenMP, taking GPU acceleration to a new level. This approach, known as the direct GPU compilation scheme, involves compiling the *entire* host application for the GPU and executing it there, thereby eliminating the need for explicit offloading directives. Nonetheless, due to limitations of the current GPU compiler toolchain and execution, seamlessly executing CPU code on GPUs with certain features remains a significant challenge. In this paper, we examine the limits of CPU code execution on GPUs by applying the direct GPU compilation scheme to LLVM's `test-suite`, analyze the encountered errors, and discuss potential solutions for enabling more code to execute on GPUs without any changes if feasible. By studying these issues, we shed light on how to improve GPU acceleration and make it more accessible to developers.

Keywords: OpenMP · GPU · compiler testing

1 Introduction

GPUs are renowned for their exceptional computational power, primarily attributed to their ability to leverage massive parallelism. Offloading computations to GPUs has proven to be an effective approach for accelerating various applications. However, this process typically requires manual identification of code regions suitable for GPU execution, as well as managing data transfers and synchronization between the CPU and GPU. To address this challenge, recent work [20,21] has proposed the direct GPU compilation scheme, which leverages the portable target offloading interface offered by LLVM/OpenMP. This scheme involves compiling the *entire* host application for the GPU and executing it there, eliminating the need for explicit offloading directives.

© The Author(s), under exclusive license to Springer Nature Switzerland AG 2023
S. McIntosh-Smith et al. (Eds.): IWOMP 2023, LNCS 14114, pp. 179–192, 2023.
https://doi.org/10.1007/978-3-031-40744-4_12

Despite the potential benefits of the direct GPU compilation scheme, there are limitations to executing CPU code on GPUs seamlessly due to current toolchain and execution constraints. In this paper, we examine the limits of CPU code execution on GPUs by applying the direct GPU compilation scheme to LLVM's test-suite. Through our analysis, we identify and categorize a series of encountered errors into eight distinct types, which encompass issues with test cases, bugs in the compiler and runtime, and the absence of certain features that led to the failure of test case compilations. In addition, we delve into potential solutions that could enable a wider range of codes to be executed on GPUs, ideally without necessitating any alterations to user codes, provided it's feasible. The study's primary objective is to elucidate the potential areas of improvement in GPU acceleration, thereby making it more user-friendly and accessible to developers.

The paper is organized as follows. In Sect. 2, we provide an overview of the direct GPU compilation scheme, which is the approach we use in this study. In Sect. 3, we describe our methodology and implementation details. Section 4 presents the results of our study, along with a detailed analysis. We review related works in Sect. 5. Finally, we conclude the paper in Sect. 6.

2   Background

OpenMP 4.0 introduced the `target` construct, which allows code regions to be executed on target devices such as GPUs [3] and FPGAs [10]. An example of CUDA code and its equivalent OpenMP version is shown in Fig. 1. In addition to the `target` construct (as well as its combined variants), OpenMP provides the `declare target` directive that specifies that all associated variables and functions are to be mapped onto the target devices and thus are usable in device code [18]. The `device_type(nohost)` clause on a `declare target` construct forces the compiler not to generate host versions of the enclosed variables and functions.

While this approach provides a simpler programming model than traditional CUDA or OpenCL, it still requires users to wrap the code with the `target` construct. In particular, users need to identify the regions of code that would benefit from GPU acceleration and explicitly mark them with the `target` construct.

The proposed approach by Tian et al. [20] enables the compilation of an existing host application for GPU execution with minimal modification to the user code by leveraging the portable target offloading interface provided by LLVM/OpenMP. Users can provide simple stub code to delegate function calls to the host using the host remote procedure call (RPC) framework for functions that can not be executed directly on a GPU. Later, the approach was extended by augmenting the compiler with a custom link-time optimization pass, which can automatically generate RPC calls without the need for stub code from users, and expand source parallelism to the entire GPU device [21].

The compilation and execution path of this approach is illustrated in Fig. 2. In the following we will briefly introduce the compilation of the direct GPU compilation scheme.

```
__device__ int g;
__device__ void foo();

__global__ void baz() { foo(); }

void bar() {
  baz<<<...>>>();
}
```

(a) An example of CUDA code. The function `baz` is a *kernel* that is the entry point of a GPU program and can be launched from host. The function `foo` is a device function that can be called in a kernel.

```
#pragma omp begin declare target device_type(nohost)
int g;
void foo();
#pragma omp end declare target

void bar() {
// The following region will be outlined to a new function, and will be
// launched from the host, similar to the function baz in the CUDA
// example.
#pragma omp target
  { foo(); }
}
```

(b) Equivalent OpenMP code using target offloading to Fig. 1a. Even though there is no explicit kernel specified by users, an OpenMP compiler will outline the target region and generate a kernel implicitly.

Fig. 1. An example of CUDA code and its equivalent OpenMP code.

2.1 Device Code Representation

The direct compilation framework facilitates executing the entire program on the GPU by marking all user code associated with the `declare target` directive, essentially prepending a `begin declare target device_type(nohost)` before any user source file. The framework offers a user wrapper header (shown in Fig. 3), which can be pre-included using `clang`'s `-include` command line option when compiling user code.

2.2 Loader

The GPU execution still follows a "host-centric" approach where the execution of a "GPU program" must be initiated from the host. Traditionally, the `main` function in the host code has been the entry point for user applications. However, since the entire user code is now considered device code, a new entry point for the host code is needed. The direct compilation framework provides a main wrapper (also depicted in Fig. 2) that acts as the new host entry point. The main wrapper

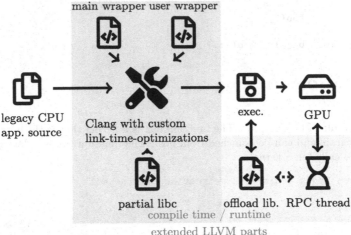

Fig. 2. Overview of the compilation and execution path of the direct GPU compilation framework introduced by Tian et al. [20] and the extended work [21]. The figure is from the work [21].

first maps all program arguments to the device so that the user code can access them and then invokes the user's `main` function. To avoid conflicts with the existing `main` function, the user's `main` function is renamed to `__user_main` (as illustrated in Fig. 3). The new host entry point must be compiled and linked with all other user source files into the executable by the user.

```
#pragma omp begin declare target device_type(nohost)
int main(int, char *[]) asm("__user_main");
```

Fig. 3. User wrapper header to take all user code as device code and rename `main` function to `__user_main`.

3   Methodology

This section introduces a new compiler driver wrapper designed to simplify the use of the direct compilation scheme. It then discusses the comprehensive handling of different `main` functions, followed by the test suite and system configuration employed in the exploration of the limits of generic code execution on GPUs using the direct compilation scheme.

3.1   Compiler Driver Wrapper

As described in Sect. 2, the direct GPU compilation scheme involves three steps: 1) compiling user source files with a user wrapper header included; 2) compiling the loader; and 3) linking the object files of user code and loader. However, the additional second step makes it difficult to seamlessly integrate the compilation scheme into build systems like CMake without significant changes to the configuration or build script.

To address this limitation, we have developed a solution by implementing a compiler driver wrapper, called `clang-gpu` and `clang-gpu++`, for C and C++ compilation, respectively. When the driver is used in compilation-only mode (`-c`), the wrapper forwards all arguments to the invocation of `clang/clang++` as well as all necessary extra compilation flags. Otherwise, the wrapper first compiles the loader and then adds the loader object file to the invocation of `clang/clang++` as an additional input file. With this approach, users can use `clang-gpu` and `clang-gpu++` as a regular compiler in build systems without requiring any changes.

3.2   Handling Different `main` Functions

In a host environment, a program must contain a global function named `main`, which serves as the designated start of the program. In C++, this function has one of two forms: `int main();` or `int main(int argc, char *argv[]);`. The C language also allows the form `void main();`.

As mentioned in Sect. 2, the user's `main` function is renamed to `_user_main` to avoid ambiguity. However, this approach assumes that all users' `main` functions are in the form of `int main(int argc, char *argv[]);`, which may not always be the case and can lead to a compile error due to a conflict declaration of a function.

To address this issue, we implemented a compiler pass that "canonicalizes" the `main` function to the form `int main(int argc, char *argv[]);` and renames it accordingly. This approach ensures that the loader can correctly invoke the user's `main` function, regardless of its original form.

3.3   Test Suite and System Configuration

We used LLVM's `test-suite` to test the correctness and performance of the compilation scheme. This suite includes benchmarks and test programs, and provides tools to collect metrics such as benchmark runtime, compilation time, and code size. The suite includes several categories of tests, including:

- `SingleSource`: Contains single-file test programs.
- `MultiSource`: Includes entire programs with multiple source files.
- `MicroBenchmarks`: Programs using the `google-benchmark` library. The programs define functions that are run multiple times until the measurement results are statistically significant.
- `External`: Contains descriptions and test data for code that cannot be directly distributed with the test-suite. The most prominent members of this directory are the SPEC CPU benchmark suites.
- `Bitcode`: These tests are mostly written in LLVM bitcode.

– CTMark: Contains symbolic links to other benchmarks forming a representative sample for compilation performance measurements.

We chose not to perform runtime performance evaluation in this paper, as this has been extensively studied in prior work [20,21]. We did not use the Bitcode tests, as these are written in LLVM bitcode, which is target dependent and can not be directly used for GPU testing.

Our system consisted of an NVIDIA A100 Tensor Core GPU (40GB) with AMD EPYC 7532 processors (32 cores with hyper-threading disabled) and 256 GB DDR4 RAM. We used CUDA 11.8.0 and compiled the entire test suite using the default configuration for release build. Figure 4 shows how we configured, built, and executed the test suite.

```
$ cmake -G Ninja -S llvm-test-suite                                        \
    -DCMAKE_C_COMPILER=clang-gpu -DCMAKE_CXX_COMPILER=clang-gpu++
$ ninja -k 0
$ llvm-lit -v .
```

Fig. 4. Commands used to configure, build, and run the test suite. The compiler driver wrappers are used as compilers for C/C++ and there is no extra CMake configuration arguments nor changes in CMake files required.

4   Results and Analysis

The results of each subdirectory are presented in Fig. 5. In the subsequent sections, we delve into a detailed analysis of the different errors encountered, discussing its root causes and potential solutions.

4.1   Test Case Issue

We identified some issues in the test suite, such as the incorrect use of parallel for in the test case SingleSource/Benchmarks/SmallPT/smallpt.cpp, which caused a compile error (as shown in Fig. 6). This issue was not previously revealed because OpenMP was not enabled when compiling the SingleSource subdirectory. Another example is in MultiSource/Applications/sgefa/driver.c, where malloc is declared as char *malloc();, causing conflicting types for the function.

After fixing those issues, we got seven more passing tests: four in MultiSource/Applications and three in MultiSource/Benchmarks.

4.2   Compiler/Runtime Bug

We uncovered several bugs throughout the compiler, spanning front-end code generation, middle-end optimization, backend code generation, and runtime

Sub Directory	Passed	Failed	Rate (%)
SingleSource	1641	185	89.9
MultiSource	125	75	62.5
CTMark	3	7	30
MicroBenchmarks	0	18	0

(a) Number of test cases and their compilation results in each subdirectory.

Sub Directory	Passed	Failed	Rate (%)
SingleSource	1641	0	100.0
MultiSource	5	120	4.0
CTMark	0	3	0.0

(b) Execution results of passed cases in Fig. 5a.

Fig. 5. Number of passed and failed test cases in each sub directory.

```
#pragma omp parallel for schedule(dynamic, 1) private(r)
fprintf(stderr,"Rendering (%d spp)\n",samps*4);
```

Fig. 6. Incorrect use of **parallel for** in the test case **SingleSource/Benchmarks/SmallPT/smallpt.cpp** that causes compile error.

library. These bugs were discovered when assertions were triggered during compile or link time, indicating that certain errors were not caught beforehand and that certain assumptions made during development did not hold.

For example, while compiling the test case CTMark/ClamAV, clang crashed because the user code did not specify a size for a variable length array (VLA) in a way that was handled. The source excerpt is shown in Fig. 7. Despite of fact that the size of the array dents is a compile-time constant, rather than a literal, this error should have been detected earlier and an appropriate error message should have been produced, especially since VLAs are not currently supported when targeting GPUs (will be discussed in Sect. 4.6).

Another bug we encountered during our investigation was related to the LLVM Attributor framework. This bug manifests as an assertion error when compiling the test case CTMark/tramp3d-v4, as depicted in Fig. 8.

The majority of runtime failures shown in Fig. 5b were caused by illegal memory access. These failures can arise from various issues, including miscompilation or a faulty device runtime library. Further investigation is required to pinpoint the exact cause. Meanwhile, the other runtime failures were caused by issues in the automatic RPC implementation, where external functions were invoked on the host but the pointer arguments were not handled correctly.

In addition to the aforementioned bugs, we observed limitations in handling inline assembly and compiler intrinsics that are specifically target-dependent. Operations such as AVX512, which are specific to certain targets, are not portable by default. If inline assembly used in the code is not supported by the target, the compiler backend will crash instead of emitting an error. We will delve into this topic further in Sect. 4.8.

```
FAILED: CTMark/ClamAV/CMakeFiles/clamscan.dir/libclamav_readdb.c.o
...
clang-17: llvm-project/clang/lib/CodeGen/CodeGenFunction.cpp:2188:
clang::CodeGen::CodeGenFunction::VlaSizePair
clang::CodeGen::CodeGenFunction::getVLASize(const clang::
    VariableArrayType*):
Assertion 'vlaSize && "no size for VLA!"' failed.
```

(a) The assertion hit by clang.

```
/* MultiSource/Applications/ClamAV/libclamav_readdb.c */
static int cli_loaddbdir_l(...) {
  ...
  const unsigned MAX_DIRENTS = 20;
  struct dirent dents[MAX_DIRENTS];
  ...
```

(b) The corresponding source code caused the crash.

Fig. 7. clang crashed because an assertion is hit (top) for the source code shown in the bottom. Given the target does not support VLAs, an error should have been raised earlier.

```
FAILED: CTMark/tramp3d-v4/CMakeFiles/tramp3d-v4.dir/tramp3d-v4.cpp.o
...
clang-17:
llvm-project/llvm/lib/Transforms/IPO/AttributorAttributes.cpp:1536:
{anonymous}::AAPointerInfoFloating::updateImpl(llvm::Attributor&)::
<lambda(llvm::Value*, llvm::Value*, bool&)>:
Assertion '!PtrOI.isUnassigned() && "Cannot pass through if the input Ptr
    was not visited!"' failed.
```

Fig. 8. clang crashed because an assertion is hit in LLVM's Attributor framework.

4.3   External Global Variable

Some header files contain external global variables, such as extern std:: ostream cout; from <iostream> and extern char *optarg; from <unistd. h>. While in the extended work [21] external function calls are replaced with host RPC calls automatically by the compiler, external global variables are not handled in the same way. To address this, one possible solution is to replace access to an external global variable with host RPC calls, similar to the approach used for external functions. However, it may be difficult to handle pointers such as extern char *optarg;. Alternatively, with the emerging unified memory design where both CPU and GPU use the same memory, this will no longer be an issue.

4.4   Variadic Function

Variadic functions, such as fprintf, are commonly used in CPU code. However, they are not supported in GPU due to the lack of support from application binary interface (ABI). The extended work [21] managed to support external variadic functions in two steps: first, by creating a non-variadic wrapper on the device solely for host RPC calls, and second, by creating a non-variadic wrapper on the host side that recovers the call site. However, this approach may not work if users handle variadic arguments explicitly in the code, as shown in Fig. 9.

```
// CTMark/sqlite3/sqlite3.c
static int getDigits(const char *zDate, ...){
  va_list ap;
  ...
  va_start(ap, zDate);
  do{
    N = va_arg(ap, int);
    min = va_arg(ap, int);
    max = va_arg(ap, int);
    nextC = va_arg(ap, int);
    pVal = va_arg(ap, int*);
    ...
  }while( nextC );
  ...
  va_end(ap);
  return cnt;
}
```

Fig. 9. An example of explicit handling of variadic arguments in the test case `CTMark/sqlite3`.

To solve this issue, a proper ABI for variadic functions needs to be defined. Some exploration has already been done in this area. For instance, NVIDIA GPUs can support the `printf` variadic function. In this case, the front end creates a structure at the call site that accommodates all variadic arguments, and then lowers the function call to `void vprintf(const char *fmt, void *args);`, where the second argument is a pointer to the structure. Figure 10 demonstrates how this procedure works.

This approach can be extended to support the explicit handling of variadic functions, where both the caller and callee are compiled by the same compiler.

```
int a;
float b;
char *c;



printf("%d %f %s", a, b, c);
```
  (a) Original function call to `printf`.

```
int a;
float b;
char *c;
struct {int a; float b; char *c;} s;
s.a = a; s.b = b; s.c = c;
vprintf("%d %f %s", &s);
```
  (b) Pseudo code after lowering by `clang`.

Fig. 10. The lowering of `printf` in `clang` for NVIDIA GPUs.

4.5   C++ Exception Handling

Exceptions are a mechanism for handling exceptional circumstances, such as runtime errors, in programs by transferring control to special functions called handlers. An exception is thrown using the `throw` keyword from inside a `try` block. Exception handlers are declared with the keyword `catch`, which must be placed immediately after the `try` block. However, no GPU compilers supports arbitrary C++ exception handling.

Full support for exceptions requires features such as stack unwinding, which are not yet available on GPUs. Moreover, the inherent dynamically divergent execution can cause problems on specific (lock step) targets. A reasonable alternative solution is to lower the `throw` expression to a built-in trap that aborts GPU execution. The `catch` statement then becomes a no-op, effectively equivalent to using the `-fno-exceptions` compiler flag except that the syntactic `throw` and `catch` statements would still be allowed.

4.6   Variable Length Array

Currently, GPU targets impose a limitation on stack allocation, requiring a statically known size. This constraint poses a challenge when dealing with variable length arrays that necessitate dynamic-sized stack allocation. Although NVIDIA has introduced a preview feature in PTX 7.3 that supports dynamic stack allocation [12], the compiler does not yet provide full support for this feature. To overcome this limitation, an alternative solution is to replace dynamic stack allocation with dynamic heap allocation. To ensure proper memory management, it becomes necessary to insert cleanup code that handles the deallocation of these dynamically allocated variables as their scope is left.

4.7   Unsupported Data Type

There are data types, such as `long double`, that are not supported by GPUs. Similar to the host side when the target CPU does not support certain types, software emulation can also be applied on GPUs. Moreover, more data types are likely to be supported in the future as GPUs evolves. For now, `clang` will allow `long double` and other unsupported types to appear, e.g., as part of struct declarations, but it will not allow use of them, e.g., as part of arithmetic operations.

4.8   Inline Assembly

As mentioned earlier, both inline assembly and compiler intrinsics are inherently target-dependent and lack portability by default. To address this challenge, a potential solution is to translate the assembly code into the corresponding target-specific assembly code. This approach has been successfully employed in binary translation projects such as Apple's Rosetta 2 and Intel's Houdini, enabling cross-architecture execution. Similarly, for compiler intrinsics, a wrapper layer can be introduced to map them to a code sequence that is valid on the target architecture. This approach allows the intrinsic functions to be adapted and utilized in the context of the specific target architecture. A relevant study by Doerfert et al. [6] proposes techniques for mapping intrinsics to target-specific code sequences, offering a means to achieve compatibility across architectures. The OpenPOWER group provides functional equivalents of Intel MMX, SSE, and AVX intrinsic functions commonly used in Linux applications [17].

5   Related Work

Several prior works have investigated the execution of host programs on GPUs. Silberstein et al. [16] proposed direct access to the host's file system from GPU code and implemented an RPC protocol to facilitate data transfers between the CPU and GPU. Damschen et al. [4] explored transparent acceleration of binary applications using heterogeneous computing resources without manual porting or developer-provided hints. Matsumura et al. [9] introduced an automated stencil framework that transforms and optimizes stencil patterns in C source code, generating corresponding CUDA code. Mikushin et al. [11] presented a parallelization framework that detects parallelism and generates target code for both X86 CPUs and NVIDIA GPUs. To support functions that cannot be natively executed on GPUs, they replaced function calls in LLVM with an interface that uses a foreign function interface to execute the requested functions on the host. Jablin et al. [8] proposed a fully automatic system for managing and optimizing CPU-GPU communication, comprising a runtime library and compiler transformations. Pakin et al. [15] proposed reverse-acceleration model where the accelerators orchestrate the computation, offloading work that can not be accelerated to the general-purpose processors. Tian et al. [20] were the first to attempt running the entire host program on a GPU using OpenMP target offloading. They augmented the compiler with a custom link-time optimization pass to generate RPC calls automatically, eliminating the need for stub code from users and expanding source parallelism to the entire GPU device. Their work later has been extended in [21], where the compiler was augmented with a custom link-time optimization pass, which can automatically generate RPC calls without the need for stub code from users, and expand source parallelism to the entire GPU device.

In recent years, researchers have focused on compiler and runtime optimization for OpenMP after the introduction of target offloading in OpenMP 4.0. Bertolli et al. [2,3] enabled OpenMP offloading to GPUs in LLVM. Flang, the PGI Fortran front-end, also supports OpenMP offloading through the LLVM OpenMP runtime [13]. Antão et al. [1] introduced front-end-based optimizations for NVIDIA GPUs, reducing register usage and avoiding idle threads. Doerfert et al. [5] presented the TRegion interface, enabling more kernels to execute in SPMD mode. Tian et al. [19] introduced runtime support for concurrent execution of OpenMP target tasks. Yviquel et al. [22] presented a framework for using the OpenMP programming model in distributed memory environments, combining OpenMP directives and MPI communication. Huber et al. [7] developed OpenMP-aware program analyses and optimizations for efficient execution of CPU-centric parallelism on GPUs. Ozen and Wolfe [14] demonstrated its implementation of the `loop` directive on NVIDIA GPUs.

6 Summary

In this paper we investigated the feasibility and effectiveness of executing CPU code on GPUs using the direct GPU compilation scheme. We highlighted the challenges and limitations in the current GPU compiler toolchain and hardware support. In addition, we discussed potential solutions to enable broader GPU execution capabilities. The findings can contribute to advancing GPU acceleration and facilitating the utilization of GPUs for a wider range of code without significant modifications from application developers.

This work highlights the effectiveness of the compilation scheme introduced in [20,21], which enables straightforward execution of CPU codes on GPUs, to test "GPU compilers" using a vast collection of existing CPU code. In this initial study alone we detected multiple compiler bugs and categorized other the shortcomings; both will lead to improved capabilities and robustness.

Acknowledgement. This research was supported by the Exascale Computing Project (17-SC-20-SC), a collaborative effort of two U.S. Department of Energy organizations (Office of Science and the National Nuclear Security Administration) responsible for the planning and preparation of a capable exascale ecosystem, including software, applications, hardware, advanced system engineering, and early testbed platforms, in support of the nation's exascale computing imperative. The views and opinions of the authors do not necessarily reflect those of the U.S. government or Lawrence Livermore National Security, LLC neither of whom nor any of their employees make any endorsements, express or implied warranties or representations or assume any legal liability or responsibility for the accuracy, completeness, or usefulness of the information contained herein. This work was in parts prepared by Lawrence Livermore National Laboratory under Contract DE-AC52-07NA27344 (LLNL-CONF-827970). We also gratefully acknowledge the computing resources provided and operated by the Joint Laboratory for System Evaluation at Argonne National Laboratory.

References

1. Antão, S.F., et al.: Offloading Support for OpenMP in Clang and LLVM. In: Workshop on the LLVM Compiler Infrastructure in HPC (LLVM-HPC@SC), 14 November 2016, pp. 1–11, IEEE Computer Society, Salt Lake City, UT, USA (2016). https://doi.org/10.1109/LLVM-HPC.2016.006
2. Bertolli, C., et al.: Integrating GPU support for OpenMP offloading directives into Clang. In: Workshop on the LLVM Compiler Infrastructure in HPC (LLVM-HPC@SC), 15 November 2015, pp. 1–11, ACM, Austin, Texas, USA (2015). https://doi.org/10.1145/2833157.2833161
3. Bertolli, C., et al.: Coordinating GPU threads for OpenMP 4.0 in LLVM. In: Workshop on the LLVM Compiler Infrastructure in HPC (LLVM-HPC@SC), 17 November 2014, pp. 12–21. IEEE Computer Society, New Orleans, LA, USA (2014). https://doi.org/10.1109/LLVM-HPC.2014.10

4. Damschen, M., Riebler, H., Vaz, G., Plessl, C.: Transparent offloading of computational hotspots from binary code to Xeon Phi. In: Design, Automation & Test in Europe Conference & Exhibition (DATE), 9–13 March 2015, pp. 1078–1083, ACM, Grenoble, France (2015). https://dl.acm.org/doi/10.5555/2755753.2757063

5. Doerfert, J., Diaz, J.M.M., Finkel, H.: The TRegion interface and compiler optimizations for OpenMP target regions. In: Fan, X., de Supinski, B.R., Sinnen, O., Giacaman, N. (eds.) IWOMP 2019. LNCS, vol. 11718, pp. 153–167. Springer, Cham (2019). https://doi.org/10.1007/978-3-030-28596-8_11

6. Doerfert, J., et al.: Breaking the vendor lock: performance portable programming through openMP as target independent runtime layer. In: International Conference on Parallel Architectures and Compilation Techniques (PACT), 8–12 October 2022, pp. 494–504, ACM, Chicago, Illinois (2022). https://doi.org/10.1145/3559009.3569687

7. Huber, J., et al.: Efficient Execution of OpenMP on GPUs. In: International Symposium on Code Generation and Optimization (CGO), 2–6 April 2022, pp. 41–52, IEEE, Seoul, Republic of Korea (2022). https://doi.org/10.1109/CGO53902.2022.9741290

8. Jablin, T.B., Prabhu, P., Jablin, J.A., Johnson, N.P., Beard, S.R., August, D.I.: Automatic CPU-GPU communication management and optimization. In: ACM SIGPLAN Conference on Programming Language Design and Implementation (PLDI), 4–8 June 2011, pp. 142–151, ACM, San Jose, CA, USA (2011). https://doi.org/10.1145/1993498.1993516

9. Matsumura, K., Zohouri, H.R., Wahib, M., Endo, T., Matsuoka, S.: AN5D: automated stencil framework for high-degree temporal blocking on GPUs. In: International Symposium on Code Generation and Optimization (CGO), February 2020, pp. 199–211, ACM, San Diego, CA, USA (2020). https://doi.org/10.1145/3368826.3377904

10. Mayer, F., Knaust, M., Philippsen, M.: OpenMP on FPGAs—a survey. In: Fan, X., de Supinski, B.R., Sinnen, O., Giacaman, N. (eds.) IWOMP 2019. LNCS, vol. 11718, pp. 94–108. Springer, Cham (2019). https://doi.org/10.1007/978-3-030-28596-8_7

11. Mikushin, D., Likhogrud, N., Zhang, E.Z., Bergstrom, C.: Kernelgen - the design and implementation of a next generation compiler platform for accelerating numerical models on GPUs. In: International Parallel & Distributed Processing Symposium Workshops (IPDPSW), 19–23 May 2014, pp. 1011–1020, IEEE Computer Society, Phoenix, AZ, USA (2014). https://doi.org/10.1109/IPDPSW.2014.115

12. NVIDIA: Parallel Thread Execution ISA Version 8.1. https://docs.nvidia.com/cuda/parallel-thread-execution/index.html#stack-manipulation-instructions-alloca (2023)

13. Özen, G., Atzeni, S., Wolfe, M., Southwell, A., Klimowicz, G.: OpenMP GPU Offload in Flang and LLVM. In: Workshop on the LLVM Compiler Infrastructure in HPC (LLVM-HPC@SC), 13 November 2018, pp. 1–9, IEEE, Dallas, TX, USA (2018), https://doi.org/10.1109/LLVM-HPC.2018.8639434

14. Ozen, G., Wolfe, M.: Performant portable openMP. In: ACM SIGPLAN International Conference on Compiler Construction (CC), 2–3 April 2022, pp. 156–168, ACM, Seoul, South Korea (2022). https://doi.org/10.1145/3497776.3517780

15. Pakin, S., Lang, M., Kerbyson, D.J.: The reverse-acceleration model for programming Petascale hybrid systems. IBM J. Res. Develop. **53**(5), 8 (2009). https://doi.org/10.1147/JRD.2009.5429074

16. Silberstein, M., Ford, B., Keidar, I., Witchel, E.: GPUfs: integrating a file system with GPUs. In: Architectural Support for Programming Languages and Operating Systems (ASPLOS), 16–20 March 2013, pp. 485–498, ACM, Houston, TX, USA (2013). https://doi.org/10.1145/2451116.2451169
17. System Software Work Group, OpenPOWER Foundation: Vector Intrinsics Porting Guide. https://openpowerfoundation.org/specifications/vectorintrinsicporting guide/ (2018)
18. Tian, S., Chesterfield, J., Doerfert, J., Chapman, B.: Experience report: writing a portable GPU runtime with openMP 5.1. In: McIntosh-Smith, S., de Supinski, B.R., Klinkenberg, J. (eds.) IWOMP 2021. LNCS, vol. 12870, pp. 159–169. Springer, Cham (2021). https://doi.org/10.1007/978-3-030-85262-7_11
19. Tian, S., Doerfert, J., Chapman, B.M.: Concurrent execution of deferred openMP target tasks with hidden helper threads. In: Chapman, B., Moreira, J. (eds.) Languages and Compilers for Parallel Computing. LCPC 2020. Lecture Notes in Computer Science, vol. 13149. Springer, Cham (2020). https://doi.org/10.1007/978-3-030-95953-1_4
20. Tian, S., Huber, J., Parasyris, K., Chapman, B.M., Doerfert, J.: Direct GPU compilation and execution for host applications with OpenMP Parallelism. In: Workshop on the LLVM Compiler Infrastructure in HPC (LLVM-HPC@SC), 13–18 November 2022, pp. 43–51, IEEE, Dallas, TX, USA (2022). https://doi.org/10.1109/LLVM-HPC56686.2022.00010
21. Tian, S., Scogland, T., Chapman, B., Doerfert, J.: GPU First - Execution of Legacy CPU Codes on GPUs (2023)
22. Yviquel, H., et al.: The OpenMP Cluster Programming Model. In: Workshop of the International Conference on Parallel Processing (ICPP), 29 August 2022–1 September 2022, pp. 1–11, ACM, Bordeaux, France (2022). https://doi.org/10.1145/3547276.3548444

OpenMP Infrastructure and Evaluation

Improving Simulations of Task-Based Applications on Complex NUMA Architectures

Idriss Daoudi[1]($\boxtimes$) (iD), Thierry Gautier[2], Samuel Thibault[3] (iD),
and Swann Perarnau[1] (iD)

[1] Argonne National Laboratory, Lemont, USA
idaoudi@anl.gov
[2] INRIA Grenoble - LIP - ENS Lyon, Lyon, France
[3] INRIA Bordeaux - Université de Bordeaux, Bordeaux, France

Abstract. Modeling and simulation are crucial in high-performance computing (HPC), with numerous frameworks developed for distributed computing infrastructures and their applications. Despite node-level simulation of shared-memory systems and task-based parallel applications, existing works overlook non-uniform memory access (NUMA) effects, a critical characteristic of current HPC platforms.

In this work, we introduce a modeling for complex NUMA architectures and enhance a simulator for dependency-based task-parallel applications. This facilitates experiments with varied data locality models: we refine a communication-oriented model leveraging topology information for data transfers, and devise a more intricate model incorporating a cache mechanism for last-level cache data storage. Dense linear algebra test cases are used to validate both models, demonstrating that our simulator reliably predicts execution time with minimal relative error.

Keywords: NUMA architectures · Modeling · OpenMP tasks · Simulation

1 Introduction

Task-based runtimes, originating with Cilk in 1998 [4], have evolved to accommodate shared-memory machines [16], heterogeneous architectures with accelerators [2,3,18], and distributed-memory systems [2,6,11,17]. The 2008 OpenMP standard version 3.0 integrated the independent task model, expanding in 2013 to incorporate dependent task model and accelerator targeting.

To achieve optimal performance on shared-memory machines, schedulers need to tackle non-uniform memory access (NUMA) effects [26,32]. Despite these advancements, technical constraints often hinder reproducibility of results on such platforms. Some studies [30] addressed these issues through simulation, enabling realistic and reproducible scheduling research [1] and facilitating quick prototyping before implementing on real systems.

For (OpenMP) task-based applications, a high-quality simulation of shared-memory could lead to efficient runtimes, benefiting from a robust, reproducible

S. McIntosh-Smith et al. (Eds.): IWOMP 2023, LNCS 14114, pp. 195–209, 2023.
https://doi.org/10.1007/978-3-031-40744-4_13

methodology. Prior studies [30] emphasized the need for NUMA-aware simulators that consider cache effects for accurate performance prediction.

Our earlier work [13] introduced a preliminary simulator, named sOMP, using SimGrid [9] to predict the performance of task-based applications on shared-memory architectures by modeling a simple NUMA structure and data locality impacts. This tool allowed the non-cycle-accurate simulation of task-based applications using a trace of their sequential execution obtained with OMPT. Nevertheless, it neglected cache effects and failed to model complex NUMA architectures, diminishing the relevance of some application predictions. This paper expands on that work in several ways:

- We model **complex and more intricate** NUMA and cache architectures;
- We refine the task execution simulation to take into account **overlapping between** *communications* **and computations**.
- We introduce **L3 caching in the simulation**, which strongly improves simulation accuracy;
- We study the **cost of the simulation**.
- We show that we can easily experiment with a **proof-of-concept** cache-aware scheduler thanks to the refined models.

Following a review of existing literature, we delve into the principles of simulation and our modeling of NUMA architectures. We revisit a prior model ignoring data locality, extend another model considering NUMA locality, and introduce an enhanced model factoring in cache locality. Simulation accuracy across different application algorithms (Cholesky, QR and LU factorization algorithms), matrix sizes, and Intel and AMD platforms is then demonstrated. Lastly, we discuss the simulator's cost and its applications for cache-aware scheduling research.

2 State of the Art

Many simulators have been designed for predicting performance in a variety of contexts in order to analyze application behavior. Simulators like BigSim [34], xSim [15], Dimemas [19], MERPSYS [12], CloudSim [8], and GreenCloud [23] predict performance across various applications and contexts. Some focus on specific architectures, like hybrid MPI/OpenMP applications and task-based simulations on multicore processors [21,27–29,31]. While these offer precision, no particular memory model is implemented, as in the case of Simany [22].

Efforts have also been made to study task-based applications performance, involving modeling NUMA access on large compute nodes [14,20] and accelerators [30]. Some studies, like SimGrid [25] and simNUMA [24], align with our work technically or in modeling, but none currently predict performance of task-based applications with data dependencies on NUMA architectures considering both NUMA and cache locality effects.

Our previous work [13] presented the sOMP simulator, which leverages the SimGrid framework to simulate task-based application execution with NUMA effects. Despite good predictions for Cholesky factorization, the project had several limitations:

- NUMA architectures modeling was very simplistic;
- data transfers cost was trivially added the computations cost;
- cache effects were ignored.

Therefore, several trade-offs were made. For example, large tile sizes were needed to compensate for unsimulated cache effects. For the more complex QR factorization and on AMD platforms, the simulations were unreliable. This paper extends sOMP to incorporate cache effects and refines platform modeling and data transfers, greatly improving prediction accuracy and exploring potential scheduling research opportunities.

3   Context and Principles

This study addresses scenarios where scheduling researchers aim to optimize task-based runtime system scheduling heuristics for specific applications and platforms. However, real execution experiments are subject to system noise, non-reproducibility due to software or firmware upgrades, and limited platform access due to high energy costs.

To overcome these challenges, it's desirable to experiment with heuristics in a simulated environment offering **perfect reproducibility** and flexibility to run on any platform. This simulation needs to accurately model the platform behavior to align the scheduling heuristics with the platform's actual performance. In multicore systems, NUMA and L3 cache effects are crucial for scheduling heuristics and need to be accurately simulated. This paper focuses on meticulously modeling the NUMA architecture, incorporating L3 cache simulation, and verifying the performance aligns with native execution. Other performance influencers like thermal constraints, dynamic voltage and frequency scaling, and OS noise, though relevant, are beyond this paper's scope.

To implement these principles, we relied on our previously developed tool sOMP, which will be improved in this work. sOMP was built using SimGrid, a powerful non-cycle-accurate simulator.

SimGrid. Initially designed for simulating distributed-memory platforms to study heterogeneous platforms scheduling algorithms [9], is employed here for shared-memory architectures. The latter's L3 caches and NUMA coherency mechanisms essentially render them distributed systems, which will be discussed in Sect. 4. SimGrid isn't a cycle-accurate simulator. Computations are interpreted as overall calculation quantities, consuming time relative to machine performance (GFlop/s), and communications as data quantities transferred based on bandwidth (GB/s) and latency (ns). Instead of a costly cycle-by-cycle simulation, our aim is a less expensive overall behavior simulation, while still accurately observing phenomena like NUMA and cache effects, contention, and concurrency.

sOMP. The simulator, presented in our previous work [13] and tailored for task-based applications with data dependencies, predicts their performance on architectures modeled in the SimGrid XML format using native execution-generated trace files. After parsing these files, sOMP submits tasks to a queue managed by a scheduler, akin to a standard OpenMP runtime. We enhance sOMP by introducing L3 cache simulation support and refining platform profiling for increased accuracy.

Overview of the Profiling and Simulation Principles. The overall principle of our profiling and simulation experiments is as follows, given a task-based application to be run on a target platform:

1. Platform specifics such as L3 caches, NUMA nodes, and architectural link bandwidths are discerned through manufacturer documentation and benchmarking. The platform modelization is expressed in an XML file. This step in presented in Sect. 4;
2. Unmodified OpenMP applications are executed sequentially (on a single core) on the platform with varied parameters (e.g., the tile size) to observe behavior under different conditions, recording the overall application execution makespan as a reference;
3. During these executions, an execution trace is generated using OpenMP's OMPT support, from which we extract the task graph and task execution duration;
4. Using the collected information, a parallel simulation of the execution is performed, substituting tasks with virtual time accounting for cost-effective simulation, and combining it with models that take into account NUMA and cache effects. This step is presented in Sect. 5.

With these simulations, scheduling researchers can reliably experiment with their heuristics, modifying task schedulers, data placement, or platform specifics to investigate the effects on their scheduling heuristic. In the following sections, we describe some of these steps in more detail for our experiments.

4   NUMA Architectures Modeling

We see a NUMA architecture as a distributed machine in this work: several computation units are interconnected, forming a NUMA node. Depending on the machine, one or more NUMA nodes (also interconnected) form a socket that can be coupled to one or more other sockets, each having its own memory controller. The sockets are connected with UPI (Intel) or Infinity Fabric (AMD) links.

An overview of NUMA architectures was presented in our previous work [13] for an Intel platform: specifically, an Intel Xeon Gold 6240 with 36 cores (Cascade-Lake microarchitecture) and two NUMA nodes, 18 cores each. The latter is represented with SimGrid components: the cores and the memory controllers are modeled as SimGrid hosts, the intrasocket interconnect is modeled as a SimGrid *backbone*, and the intersocket UPI link is modeled as a SimGrid link between routers.

While this model proves adequate for the relatively straightforward architecture of this particular Intel processor, it is not applicable to more intricate processors that exhibit a hierarchically structured and interconnected arrangement of components. Such complexities cannot be overlooked due to their direct bearing on the accuracy of the simulation.

4.1   Modeling Complex NUMA Architectures

In the first contribution of this work, we consider a second more intricate processor: a dual-socket AMD EPYC 7452 with 64 cores (AMD Infinity microarchitecture) and 16 NUMA nodes, four cores each.

This architecture, based on the *zen 2* microarchitecture, is more complex than the Intel platform, featuring two sockets with four dies connected by an Infinity Fabric network. Each die contains two NUMA nodes, therefore, two caches and eight cores.

Hence, our previous Intel platform model [13] was insufficient, prompting extension for this study. Figure 1 shows our proposed SimGrid model for the AMD platform. The Infinity Fabric network is modeled as a router network based on AMD documentation. Each die, as shown on the top left, comprises a SimGrid backbone symbolizing the in-die Infinity Fabric interconnect linking the die-to-die network, RAM, and two L3 cache + 4 CPU core sets. Each L3 cache + 4 core set, known as a CCX, embeds a faster backbone than the in-die Infinity Fabric interconnect. This closely follows the actual *zen 2* architecture and is necessary to accurately reflect the varying access speeds of cores to different L3 caches and account for bandwidth contention in the die-to-die interconnect.

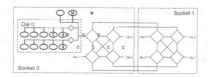

Fig. 1. AMD platform model using SimGrid components (the details of only die 0 are shown; other dies are modeled identically).

4.2   Bandwidth Measurements

The critical aspect of our modeling approach hinges upon the precise measurement of machine parameters, specifically the link bandwidths interconnecting the components under study. Our preceding work [13] primarily relied on bandwidth values as stipulated by the manufacturers. However, these prescribed values exhibited limitations due to their failure to incorporate the overhead associated with coherency protocols. Furthermore, they were not wholly indicative of the attainable bandwidth, thus underscoring the need for rigorous benchmarking. To this end, we employed the Intel Memory Latency Checker v3.8 for the task of quantifying the bandwidths associated with the memory controller and intersocket links. By manipulating the buffer size of this tool, we were able to retain data in the L3 cache. This adjustment, in turn, facilitated the measurement of the available bandwidth connecting the cores and the shared L3 cache, thereby enabling us to determine the intra-CCX interconnect bandwidth.

However, this tool doesn't measure other topology link bandwidths, leading us to create a simple reader-writer microbenchmark for measuring bandwidth between L3 caches. This allowed us to directly measure parameters used by Sim-Grid to characterize a communication link: overall link bandwidth (*shared*), uni-lateral link bandwidth (*splitduplex*), and per-flow link bandwidth (*fatpipe*). We obtained *fatpipe* bandwidth through a single writer+reader pair, while aggregated bandwidth from multiple pairs provided *splitduplex* bandwidth. Similarly, with writers and readers spread across two L3 caches, we determined the *shared* bandwidth.

5   NUMA and Cache Effects Modeling

This section presents three simulation models to provide three levels of refinement: a *TASK* model presented in Sect. 5.1, a NUMA model in Sect. 5.2, and a NUMA and cache model in Sect. 5.3. We present the results for the three models in Sect. 6.

5.1   Recap: The TASK Model

The initial sOMP approach presented in our previous work [13] simulates only task durations, not data transfers, using SimGrid for virtual clock accounting and task dependency adherence. It assumes non-preemptible tasks tied to CPU cores, typical in task-based runtime systems. This model, referred to as the *TASK* model, records average task durations from single-core application executions. These durations are then used to simulate parallel executions.

Discussion. Parallel execution modeling is inherently complex as task durations lengthen with more cores due to data locality. Data exchanges between sockets increase, eventually hitting bandwidth limitations. Thus, the previous sOMP version proposed a model simulating NUMA data locality effects. This model separates task execution into computation and communication components. The computation part replays the average task durations from single-core executions (as the *TASK* model does), thereby excluding data locality effects. The communication simulation, added subsequently, enables sOMP to account for varying locality effects across different scheduling strategies.

5.2   NUMA Effects Modeling: The COMM Model

The previous version of sOMP [13] extended the *TASK* model to account for NUMA data communications induced by task dependencies using SimGrid transfers over the platform model, thus accounting for NUMA effects. In this subsection, we outline the second contribution of this work: this approach is improved to include communications overlap with computations.

Data Transfers Modeling. In the prior sOMP version [13], data communication cost was simply added to computation cost. Yet, a task on a CPU core often executes arithmetic and memory instructions (like load/store) interleaved. Depending on the implementation and CPU behavior, memory instruction latency may be overlapped by arithmetic instructions. Hence, over the duration $T(t_i)$ of task t_i, the time for memory instructions $T_M(t_i)$ is more or less overlapped with the arithmetic part of the task $T_C(t_i)$. Formally, we have:

$$max(T_C(t_i), T_M(t_i)) \leq T(t_i) \leq T_C(t_i) + T_M(t_i). \tag{1}$$

Our dense linear algebra tasks consist of single calls to BLAS operations. Overlap between computation and communication is considerable for some tasks, like *dgemm*, but less so for others, like the QR factorization tasks. We establish overlap ratios through experimentation, selecting values that minimize precision error. As such, we set overlap ratios of 60% for Cholesky, 4% for QR, and 10% for LU. If communication time is less than the overlap ratio of computation time, it is entirely overlapped; if greater, the excess is added to computation time. Memory instructions considered in $T_M(t_i)$ are those handling task input and output operands or scratch buffers. To align with SimGrid's distributed-memory platform orientation, we model task memory accesses as data transfers for task operands, meaning matrix tiles or tiled scratch buffers, grouped for tractable simulation times. Task memory accesses are modeled as concurrent by access mode, with all read or write operations concurrent. However, communications of different access modes are made sequential, since a task usually reads its data, performs the computations, and then writes the result back to memory. $T_M(t_i)$ can thus be written as

$$T_M(t_i) = \max_{j=1}^{n} T_{commR}(a_{i,j}) + \max_{j=1}^{n} T_{commW}(a_{i,j}), \tag{2}$$

where n is the number of memory accesses, $a_{i,j}$ is the jth operand of task t_i, and $T_{commR}(a_{i,j}$ (resp. $T_{commW}(a_{i,j}))$ is the time to read (resp. write) $a_{i,j}$ depending on its NUMA location and the core performing task t_i. As a result, the set of tasks executing at the same time on the different cores induces a corresponding set of communications that progress concurrently on the platform. SimGrid can then determine, at each timestep of the simulation, the bandwidth sharing between the communications [10] and thus account for contention on the simulated links.

Discussion. The *COMM* model enhances simulations by considering data NUMA locality. Data flows between architecture components, affected by architecture parameters and traversed links, impact execution time. Accounting for NUMA data locality and modeling transfers as communications creates contention and concurrency effects.

However, data locality isn't static during real execution. Cache effects come into play alongside NUMA effects. When a task on a CPU core uses matrix tiles, they remain in the corresponding L3 cache. If another task on the same core needs those tiles, they can be fetched from the cache instead of the NUMA node RAM, saving time and bandwidth. The previous $COMM$ model, not considering these effects, always simulates data fetching from the NUMA nodes' RAM, leading to a pessimistic simulation.

This issue is addressed by enhancing the $COMM$ model with a caching mechanism to consider data reuse between tasks.

5.3   Cache Effects Modeling: The COMM+CACHE Model

The third contribution of this work extends the $COMM$ model into a new $COMM+CACHE$ model, by tracking in which L3 caches one can fetch copies of matrix tiles efficiently and modeling the communications between the RAM, the L3 caches, and the CPU cores.

Implementation of L3 Caches. The tile size in dense algebra is often chosen to fit tasks' datasets into the L3 cache but not the L2 cache, maximizing cache utilization. We model only the L3 caches, as including L2 would significantly increase simulation times without improving precision, as they aren't shared between cores and don't exhibit notable locality behavior.

In our L3 cache implementation, we consider the actual cache size and tile size. The cache comprises slots, calculated by $\frac{CacheSize}{TileSize}$. Data insertion in the cache follows a least recently used (LRU) behavior for evictions, approximating actual cache associativity while ignoring aspects like conflict misses.

During task execution, the data associated with the task is locked in the cache. Despite its simplicity and low simulation cost, this model provides satisfactory accuracy for dense linear algebra kernels.

Cache Transfers. In the improved version of sOMP, we record not only the matrix tiles' NUMA node RAM locality but also their presence in the L3 cache. This complex notion of locality acknowledges that the required tiles can be fetched from various locations - local L3 cache, remote L3 cache, or local or remote NUMA node.

We model data transfers from remote cache or RAM to the local cache, and then from the local cache to the core, as communications. If the same tile is needed for a subsequent task executed on a neighboring CPU core, only a transfer from the local cache to the core is triggered, assuming the tile hasn't been evicted. This effectively models the decongestion of intersocket links, reflecting actual platform behavior.

If a task alters a matrix tile, we remove the tile from all other L3 caches. Subsequent tasks requiring the updated tile will have to reload it. Evicted modified tiles must be transferred back to their corresponding NUMA node RAM.

In the QR factorization, we model the reuse of per-core scratch workspaces with one matrix tile per CPU core that tasks only write to, thus accurately representing the L3 caches' storage of the corresponding CPU cores' workspaces.

Discussion. The *COMM+CACHE* model refines data locality over the model from Sect. 5.2, which assumes all data to be remote. By simulating the occupancy of L3 caches and data transfers between L3 caches and RAM, we enhance the accuracy of predicting application behavior. As tile sizes fit in the L3 cache but not L2, we model only the former, striking a balance between simulation precision and cost. This modeling is suitable for tiled dense linear algebra, while sparse linear algebra would require a more intricate task behavior modeling.

6   Results

Our experiments were conducted on the processors mentioned in Sect. 4. The Intel system's limited locality effects contrast with AMD's complex interconnect of numerous NUMA nodes and caches.

OpenBLAS 0.3.10 and LLVM OpenMP runtime were used, with thread binding on the core places and frequency governors set to powersave mode, to avoid uneven behavior of the software and hardware governors. Experiments in this paper, unless specified otherwise, utilized a matrix size of 16384×16384 (double precision), namely, 1 GB of data, and approximately 6000 tasks for the Cholesky case. The matrix size, larger than the L3 caches but allowing for substantial data reuse, will therefore require accurate simulation of cache-to-cache transfers.

A task tile size of 512×512 was chosen, optimal for working sets fitting in L2+L3 caches but not L2 alone. Performance was evaluated against the number of cores used, selected in proximity order (the hwloc [5] logical order) to observe topological effects, first within individual sockets and subsequently across multiple sockets.

6.1   Application Case

The KASTORS [33] benchmark suite, designed to evaluate the OpenMP dependent task paradigm from OpenMP 4.0 specifications, forms the basis for our experiments. We assess three dense matrix factorization algorithms from the suite's PLASMA [7] subset: Cholesky, QR, and LU factorizations.

The Cholesky factorization incorporates four task types:$\theta(n)$ dpotrf, $\theta(n^2)$ dtrsm, $\theta(n^2)$ dsyrk, and $\theta(n^3)$ dgemm. Predominantly comprising efficient dgemm tasks involving three matrix tiles, it exhibits substantial data reuse between tasks.

QR factorization involves $\theta(n)$ dgeqrt, $\theta(n^2)$ dormqr, $\theta(n^2)$ dtsqrt, and $\theta(n^3)$ dtsmqr tasks. Dominated by less efficient dtsmqr tasks involving four matrix tiles and one scratch tile, it presents less data reuse, leading to increased cache evictions.

Lastly, LU factorization (with pivoting) includes $\theta(n)$ dgetrf, $\theta(n^2)$ dswptr, $\theta(n^3)$ dgemm, and $\theta(n^2)$ dlaswp tasks. Predominantly composed of dgemm tasks, it exhibits less data reuse, with pivoting introducing variation in behavior.

6.2   Methodology

To measure the accuracy of the simulations by comparing simulation time (T_{sim}) with real execution time (T_{native}), we do not consider the absolute values of the metric but set one that defines the relative precision error of sOMP compared with native executions:

$$PrecisionError(\%) = \frac{(T_{native} - T_{sim})}{T_{native}}. \tag{3}$$

The following graphs depict the precision error of simulated versus native execution times for varying core counts, with polynomial regression curves (5th order) indicating trends. Positive precision errors denote optimistic "undersimulation" and negative errors, pessimistic "oversimulation", hence, curves nearer to 0 signify greater precision. We initially present simulation precision results, then demonstrate simulation's time efficiency compared to real application execution, and finally, illustrate the simulator's importance in assessing scheduling policies using a cache-aware scheduling instance.

6.3   Precision Results

Figure 2 presents the Cholesky case results on the Intel platform. The *TASK* model only considers task computation time and its precision decreases beyond 18 cores, equivalent to the first NUMA domain (or socket). Beyond this, the *TASK* model exhibits approximately +3% precision error due to its disregard for data locality and transfers.

The *COMM* model improves simulations beyond 18 cores by accounting for memory latencies due to platform contention, but becomes too pessimistic with many cores, as it overlooks data reuse in caches. The *COMM+CACHE* model, considering L3 cache data movements, consistently achieves under 1% average precision error across all core counts.

The *TASK* model performs well on the Intel platform due to its single NUMA domain per socket, yielding a 0.8% average precision error, implying minimal NUMA-related effects. However, on the AMD EPYC 7452 as shown in Fig. 3, with 16 NUMA nodes and 16 L3 caches, the *TASK* model's precision error increases to around +3% on the first socket and up to +10% when utilizing all cores. The increased data transfers due to multiple NUMA nodes on the AMD machine necessitate more accurate modeling.

The *COMM* model lacks accuracy due to underestimation of intersocket communications, leading to up to -10% error. The *COMM+CACHE* model consistently provides reliable results, with less than 2% error, highlighting the importance of accurately modeling data reuse and L3 cache interconnections. A simplified version of this model, named "*COMM+CACHE* simple platform", ignoring the machine's hierarchical topology, becomes overly optimistic due to neglecting die-to-die network contention.

The QR factorization results in Fig. 4 show that the *TASK* model is overly optimistic, and the *COMM* model is pessimistic. The *COMM+CACHE* model

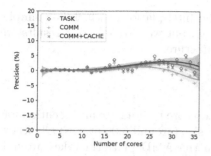

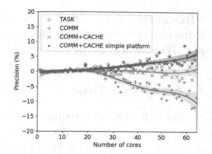

Fig. 2. Precision error of Cholesky simulations on the Intel platform.

Fig. 3. Precision error of Cholesky simulations on the AMD platform.

accounts for L3 caching effects, but fails to consider bandwidth variation effects on the application kernels when many cores are used, making it optimistic in these scenarios. A more refined model **within SimGrid**, intertwining execution time and memory transfers, could address this but is beyond this paper's scope.

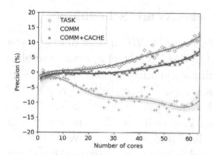

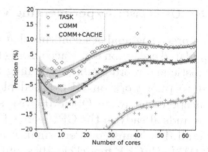

Fig. 4. Precision error of QR simulations on the AMD platform.

Fig. 5. Precision error of LU simulations on the AMD platform.

Figure 5 presents LU factorization results, where precision errors of models significantly vary for few-core executions due to native measurements' unpredictable performance, primarily due to pivoting in LU factorization. As core count increases, these inconsistencies diminish, and the *COMM+CACHE* model accurately simulates the computation/communication behavior. The *TASK* model remains overly optimistic, and the *COMM* model, overly pessimistic.

Our models have demonstrated consistent accuracy across various linear algebra algorithms and different matrix sizes. For matrix sizes of 12288×12288, 16384×16384, 20480×20480 and 24576×24576, which means an increase in task and data transfer volumes due to larger matrices, the *COMM+CACHE* model remains reliable with an average precision error of 1.4% for Cholesky, 4.5% for QR, and 1.4% for LU. These results validate our experimentally determined overlapping factors, confirming simulation accuracy regardless of problem size changes.

To summarize, we get good results on the Intel platform, which is a simple architecture not showing ample NUMA effects, but we also get good results on the AMD platform despite its complex architecture.

6.4 Simulation Time

The simulator typically requires 1 s on a laptop core to simulate an execution for a 16384×16384 matrix with a 512×512 tile size (around 6,000 tasks) Cholesky factorization, while the actual execution on the AMD platform takes around 75 s on one core or 1.6 s on 64 cores. This is due to our use of coarse, not cycle-accurate, simulation, where all actual computations and read/write operations are replaced by single simulation steps.

Simulation time grows linearly with task number and with core count for the *COMM* and *COMM+CACHE* models due to increased concurrent communications. However, this increase is independent from the computations of the real execution and remains reasonable, and the reduced precision error is usually worth the simulation time increase.

6.5 Use Case: Experimenting with Cache-Aware Schedulers

The preceding analysis confirms that the *COMM+CACHE* model offers precise simulated execution times accounting for both NUMA and cache effects, enabling realistic and reproducible scheduling research for optimizing cache affinity, similar to prior work on GPU-based platforms [1,30]. We introduced a proof-of-concept cache-aware OpenMP task scheduler that prioritizes tasks with data operands already in the CPU core's L3 cache. This reduces L3 cache misses and overall data transfers. Performance results, displayed in Fig. 6, reveal that the COMM+CACHE model closely simulates native executions. Utilizing the refined scheduler in the simulator exhibits a performance improvement that escalates with the number of cores used, demonstrating the heuristic's scalability benefits on a large multicore system. The *COMM+CACHE* model uniquely exhibits this effect in simulation due to the performance improvement resulting from

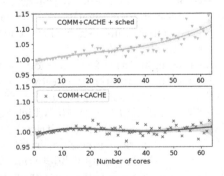

Fig. 6. Simulated performance with a cache-aware scheduler on AMD platform.

cache effects. This experiment highlights the advantage of simulation. It allowed us to swiftly prototype a proof-of-concept scheduler, observe gains without the scheduler's cost impacting performance, and balance these costs and gains. This simulation-led prototyping approach enables refinement of heuristics, faster performance results, and reproducible investigation of scheduling bugs.

7 Conclusion and Future Work

In this study, we presented significant enhancements to simulate parallel task-based applications on shared-memory architectures using three models. We improved our previous work with an enhanced *COMM* model to better account for computation / communication overlap and NUMA effects. Then, they newly introduced *COMM+CACHE* model further improves this by incorporating a cache mechanism to handle data movement and cached data access. Coupled with precise modeling of the target architecture, this model achieves superior precision, underlining the importance of accurate modeling of machine components and hierarchy.

Rather than relying on error-prone manual determination of socket topology, we collected bandwidth and latency measurements from target platforms. We plan to design an automatic tool for determining platform topology and bandwidths, similar to SimGrid's automatic network discovery.

To characterize the overlap between arithmetic and memory instructions, we intend to use performance counters to observe kernel behavior and refine overlap ratios, requiring a rework of SimGrid's task execution model.

We aim to extend our evaluation to more applications and platforms, particularly those that are memory-bound. With our simulator accurately reproducing target platform behavior, it provides a reproducible experimentation platform for task-based runtime systems and schedulers, alleviating challenges associated with technical conditions on CPU-based platforms.

Acknowledgements. This research was supported by the Exascale Computing Project (17-SC-20-SC), a joint project of the U.S. Department of Energy's Office of Science and National Nuclear Security Administration, responsible for delivering a capable exascale ecosystem, including software, applications, and hardware technology, to support the nation's exascale computing imperative, and the U.S. Department of Energy, Office of Science, Office of Advanced Scientific Computer Research, under Contract DE-AC02-06CH11357.

References

1. Agullo, E., Beaumont, O., Eyraud-Dubois, L., Kumar, S.: Are static schedules so bad? a case study on Cholesky factorization. In: IPDPS (2016)
2. Augonnet, C., Thibault, S., Namyst, R., Wacrenier, P.A.: StarPU: a unified platform for task scheduling on heterogeneous multicore architectures. Concurr. Comput. Pract. Exp. **2009**(23), 187–198 (2011). Special Issue: Euro-Par

3. Ayguadé, E., Badia, R.M., Igual, F.D., Labarta, J., Mayo, R., Quintana-Ortí, E.S.: An extension of the StarSs programming model for platforms with multiple GPUs. In: Proceedings of the 15th Euro-Par Conference. Delft, The Netherlands (2009)
4. Blumofe, R.D., Joerg, C.F., Kuszmaul, B.C., Leiserson, C.E., Randall, K.H., Zhou, Y.: Cilk: an efficient multithreaded runtime system. J. Parallel Distrib. Comput. 37(1), 55–69 (1996)
5. Broquedis, F., et al.: hwloc: a generic framework for managing hardware affinities in HPC applications. In: International Conference on Parallel, Distributed and Network-Based Processing (PDP2010), pp. 180–186. Pisa, Italia (2010)
6. Bueno, J., Martinell, L., Duran, A., Farreras, M., Martorell, X., Badia, R.M., Ayguadé, E., Labarta, J.: Productive cluster programming with OmpSs. In: Proceedings of the 17th international conference on Parallel processing - Volume Part I. Euro-Par 2011 (2011)
7. Buttari, A., Langou, J., Kurzak, J., Dongarra, J.: Lapack working note 191: a class of parallel tiled linear algebra algorithms for multicore architectures (2007)
8. Calheiros, R.N., Ranjan, R., Beloglazov, A., De Rose, C.A.F., Buyya, R.: CloudSim: a toolkit for modeling and simulation of cloud computing environments and evaluation of resource provisioning algorithms. Softw. Pract. Exp. 41(1), 23–50 (2011)
9. Casanova, H.: Simgrid: a toolkit for the simulation of application scheduling. In: CC Grid, pp. 430–437 (2001)
10. Casanova, H.: Modeling large-scale platforms for the analysis and the simulation of scheduling strategies. In: 18th International Parallel and Distributed Processing Symposium, 2004. Proceedings. p. 170 (2004)
11. Charles, P., et al.: X10: an object-oriented approach to non-uniform cluster computing. SIGPLAN Notices 40(10), 519–538 (2005)
12. Czarnul, P., et al.: MERPSYS: an environment for simulation of parallel application execution on large scale HPC systems. Simul. Model. Pract. Theory 77, 124–140 (2017)
13. Daoudi, I., Virouleau, P., Gautier, T., Thibault, S., Aumage, O.: sOMP: simulating OpenMP task-based applications with NUMA effects. In: IWOMP 2020, pp. 197–211 (2020)
14. Denoyelle, N., Goglin, B., Ilic, A., Jeannot, E., Sousa, L.: Modeling non-uniform memory access on large compute nodes with the cache-aware roofline model. IEEE Trans. Parallel Distrib. Syst. 30(6), 1374–1389 (2019)
15. Engelmann, C.: Scaling to a million cores and beyond: using light-weight simulation to understand the challenges ahead on the road to exascale. Futur. Gener. Comput. Syst. 30, 59–65 (2014)
16. Galilee, F., Cavalheiro, G., Roch, J.L., Doreille, M.: Athapascan-1: on-line building data flow graph in a parallel language. In: PACT (1998)
17. Gautier, T., Besseron, X., Pigeon, L.: KAAPI: a thread scheduling runtime system for data flow computations on cluster of multi-processors. In: Proceedings of the 2007 International Workshop on Parallel Symbolic Computation. PASCO 2007 (2007)
18. Gautier, T., Lima, J.V., Maillard, N., Raffin, B.: Xkaapi: A runtime system for data-flow task programming on heterogeneous architectures. In: IPDPS. IEEE (2013)
19. Girona, S., Labarta, J.: Sensitivity of performance prediction of message passing programs. J. Supercomputing 17, 291–298 (2000)
20. Haugen, B.: Performance analysis and modeling of task-based runtimes, Ph.D. thesis (2016)

21. Haugen, B., Kurzak, J., YarKhan, A., Luszczek, P., Dongarra, J.: Parallel simulation of superscalar scheduling. In: ICPP, pp. 121–130 (2014)
22. Heinrich, F.: Modeling, prediction and optimization of energy consumption of MPI applications using SimGrid, Theses, Université Grenoble Alpes (2019)
23. Kliazovich, D., Bouvry, P., Khan, S.U.: Greencloud: a packet-level simulator of energy-aware cloud computing data centers. J. Supercomput. **62**, 1263–1283 (2012)
24. Liu, Y., et al.: SimNUMA: simulating NUMA-architecture multiprocessor systems efficiently. In: ICPDS (2013)
25. Mohammed, A., Eleliemy, A., Ciorba, F.M., Kasielke, F., Banicescu, I.: Experimental verification and analysis of dynamic loop scheduling in scientific applications. In: ISPDC. IEEE (2018)
26. Olivier, S.L., Porterfield, A.K., Wheeler, K.B., Spiegel, M., Prins, J.F.: OpenMP task scheduling strategies for multicore NUMA systems. Int. J. High Perform. Comput. Appl. **26**(2), 110–124 (2012)
27. Rico, A., Duran, A., Cabarcas, F., Etsion, Y., Ramirez, A., Valero, M.: Trace-driven simulation of multithreaded applications. In: International Symposium on Performance Analysis of Systems and Software (2011)
28. Shudler, S., Calotoiu, A., Hoefler, T., Wolf, F.: Isoefficiency in practice: configuring and understanding the performance of task-based applications. SIGPLAN Notices **52**(8), 131–143 (2017)
29. Stanisic, L., et al.: Fast and accurate simulation of multithreaded sparse linear algebra solvers. In: ICPDS. Melbourne, Australia (2015)
30. Stanisic, L., Thibault, S., Legrand, A., Videau, B., Méhaut, J.F.: Faithful performance prediction of a dynamic task-based runtime system for heterogeneous multi-core architectures. Concurr. Comput. Pract. Exp. **27**(16), 4075–4090 (2015)
31. Tao, J., Schulz, M., Karl, W.: Simulation as a tool for optimizing memory accesses on NUMA machines. Perform. Eval. **60**(1), 31–50 (2005)
32. Virouleau, P., Broquedis, F., Gautier, T., Rastello, F.: Using data dependencies to improve task-based scheduling strategies on NUMA architectures. In: ECPP (2016)
33. Virouleau, P., et al.: Evaluation of OpenMP dependent tasks with the KASTORS benchmark suite. In: DeRose, L., de Supinski, B.R., Olivier, S.L., Chapman, B.M., Müller, M.S. (eds.) IWOMP 2014. LNCS, vol. 8766, pp. 16–29. Springer, Cham (2014). https://doi.org/10.1007/978-3-319-11454-5_2
34. Zheng, G., Kakulapati, G., Kalé, L.V.: Bigsim: A parallel simulator for performance prediction of extremely large parallel machines. In: IPDPS, p. 78. IEEE (2004)

Experimental Characterization of OpenMP Offloading Memory Operations and Unified Shared Memory Support

Wael Elwasif[✉][iD]

Oak Ridge National Laboratory, Oak Ridge, TN 37831, USA
elwasifwr@ornl.gov

Abstract. The OpenMP specification recently introduced support for unified shared memory, allowing implementation to leverage underlying system software to provide a simpler GPU offloading model where explicit mapping of variables is optional. Support for this feature is becoming more available in different OpenMP implementations on several hardware platforms. A deeper understanding of the different implementation's execution profile and performance is crucial for applications as they consider the performance portability implications of adopting a unified memory offloading programming style. This work introduces a benchmark tool to characterize unified memory support in several OepnMP compilers and runtimes, with emphasis on identifying discrepancies between different OpenMP implementations as to how they various memory allocation strategies interact with unified shared memory. The benchmark tool is used to characterize OpenMP compilers on three leading High Performance Computing platforms supporting different CPU and device architectures. The benchmark tool is used to assess the impact of enabling unified shared memory on the performance of memory-bound code, highlighting implementation differences that should be accounted for when applications consider performance portability across platforms and compilers.

Keywords: OpenMP · Unified Shared Memory · Offloading

Notice: This manuscript has been authored in part by UT-Battelle, LLC under Contract No. DE-AC05-00OR22725 with the U.S. Department of Energy. The United States Government retains and the publisher, by accepting the article for publication, acknowledges that the United States Government retains a non-exclusive, paid-up, irrevocable, world-wide license to publish or reproduce the published form of this manuscript, or allow others to do so, for United States Government purposes. The Department of Energy will provide public access to these results of federally sponsored research in accordance with the DOE Public Access Plan (http://energy.gov/downloads/doe-public-access-plan.

1   Introduction

The OpenMP device offloading model has been designed based on explicit disjoint data environment for execution on the host and offloading devices. This approach manifests itself in the different rules governing the mapping of variables that exist in one environment to their corresponding counterparts in other data environments within the program. Recent advances in hardware and system software have increasingly allowed for both the host and connected offloading device to directly access each other's memory. The OpenMP standard introduced support for unified shared memory starting in version 5.0 [15], allowing for implementations to present the program with a single address space view of both the host and device memory. As this supports is incorporated into more compilers implementation running on different platforms with various level of hardware and system support for unified addressing and/or remote host/device memory access, the decisions made by the various implementations in supporting this functionality comes into focus as they have a profound impact on code performance and correctness.

This paper presents an assessment of support for unified share memory (USM) in OpenMP compilers running on three leading edge hardware platforms. The work presented here also looks into how memory allocated using different allocators is handled by the various studied compilers and their associated runtimes. The goal here is to present an experimental characterization of compiler and runtime behavior, highlighting different behavior (if any) when USM is enabled in the code. The work also aims to highlight the different ways compilers and runtimes handle different classes of memory, across the platforms in the study. Towards that goal, a synthetic memory-bound benchmark is used to isolate the impact of memory access on code execution, pinpointing change in behavior due to the use of different allocators and USM. The benchmark is used to access both vendor and open source compilers on three platforms, the Cray EX Crusher system and the IBM Summit supercomputer at the Oak Ridge National Laboratory as well as the Cray EX Perlmutter supercomputer at the National Energy Research Scientific Center (NERSC).

This paper is organized as follows, background and related work are presented in Sect. 2 while the benchmark used to study USM and memory allocators is presented in Sect. 3. Experimental results on the three target platforms are presented in Sect. 4. Discussions, conclusions, and possible future work are presented in Sect. 5.

2   Background and Related Work

Offloading computations to accelerator devices was introduced into the OpenMP standard starting with version 4.0. The programming model was based on the concept of discrete devices with separate distinct memory spaces, with the programmer explicitly managing data movement using OpenMP directives and runtime calls. This model can prove tedious and error prone for deeply nested data structures, where the programmer must manually create a mirror mapped copy of the data structure on the offloading device (such a problem is typically referred to as the deep copy problem). CUDA introduced the concept of managed memory starting in CUDA version 6.0 [11,12], providing an abstraction and runtiume support that allows memory to be accessed using the same underlying pointer with no need for explicit distinct host and device versions of the same data structure.

OpenMP expanded support for offloading in version 4.5, including the introduction of the `is_device_ptr` clause, which indicates that a pointer already exists in the device data environment, and that it could be used directly with no mapping. This facility was used (e.g. in [10] to allow data structures allocated using CUDA's `cudaMallocManaged()` to be used in OpenMP target regions without explicit mapping. This approach, however, requires that the CUDA managed memory allocator be used for offloaded data structures, which may require invasive changes to code bases and reduces code portability as different accelerator technologies are introduced. In [13], the LLVM compiler OpenMP runtime was modified, implementing the device allocation runtime call `omp_target_alloc()` using the CUDA managed memory API. The updated compiler was then used to benchmark unified memory support using several benchmark from the Rodinia test suite. This approach, still requires the use of the `is_device_ptr` clause, but replaces the platform specific CUDA memory alloction with an OpenMP runtime API, improving the portability of the resulting code.

The OpenMP specification added support for the **requires** directive in version 5.0, including the `unified_shared_memory` clause. This renders explicit use of the **map** clause optional in target regions. Compliant implementations can leverage underlying system software to support this functionality, allowing for a pure OpenMP code to seamlessly access data structures from the host or the device, without the need for custom allocators or platform-specific APIs. Support for this feature has recently been introduce into several OpenMP compilers, and this work attempts to provide a *breadth first* assessment of the existing implementations on several platforms, highlighting the interaction of this feature with different memory allocation schemes.

3 Benchmark Description

The code outline of the benchmark test function used in this study is shown in Listing 1. Full benchmark code is available in [5]. For each memory allocation and mapping configuration, the test runs 4 iterations of a *sequence* of memory initialization loops that execute on the host and the device. The first entry in this sequence is executed on the host (lines 12-15). In the following results, performance of this phase is referred to as CPU_0 for the very first execution instance, and CPU_2 for subsequent instances. This host-side execution is then followed by 4 iterations of device target region that re-initializes the memory (lines 17-35), with GPU_0 in the following results denoting performance of the first iteration, and GPU_{1+} denoting performance of subsequent iterations. Finally the

CPU version of the loop is again executed (lines 40-43), denoted by CPU_1 in the following results. It follows that CPU_1 represents the first execution of the CPU loop *after* execution on the device, and CPU_2 represents the second execution in the subsequent outer loop iteration. The performance of different instances is used to indicate memory access behavior across the host and the device. Memory pages can be accessed *locally* if they already reside on the respective compute device before loop execution. Memory pages residing on the host or device may be accessed *in place* remotely by the other compute device (in this case no page migration occurs, and access is done remotely over the connecting links). Finally access to remote memory pages can trigger page faults that cause such pages to migrate to the compute device where the memory access loop is executing. Page faults and migration is an expensive operation, and this scenario would typically be reflected in the slowest performance of the three possible scenarios on the same compute device.

The benchmark test is enclosed in a function, with memory allocation and control over mapping behavior defined in a driver portion of the benchmark. Listing 2 shows two invocations of the test function, where memory is allocated using the AMD ROCm Open Software Platform [8] via the C++ Heterogeneous-Compute Interface for Portability(HIP) [9] `hipHostMalloc()` allocator. The test is executed twice, once setting (`managed_memory=true`) to disable explicit OpenMP mapping, and once with (`managed_memory=false`) to enable explicit OpenMP memory mapping. Enabling the OpenMP compiler's USM support is controlled using a compile-time macro (`USE_DSM`). Performance of various portions of the benchmark is evaluated using a measure of the bandwidth (in GiB/Sec) observed during memory operations, as well as during the execution of the kernels on the host and device (since the code has no meaningful compute-heavy segments). Time intervals are measured using two invocations of the (`omp_get_wtime()`) OpenMP routine, that surround the target segment.

This benchmark is used to explore how the OpenMP runtimes in the studied compilers deal with the following memory allocation categories, and how enabling USM affects this treatment

- **System memory:** Memory allocated using the native system allocator (using `malloc` for C or `new` in C++). In this work, only aligned system memory is considered (using the aligned `new` operator introduced in C++17). A variant of this scheme, where memory on the device is allocated using `omp_target_alloc()` and associated with the host pointer using the `omp_target_associate_ptr()` is also studied.
- **Managed memory:** Memory allocated using a native device runtime facility (e.g. using `hipMallocManaged()` for ROCm or `cudaMallocManaged()` for CUDA). Such memory typically support page migration between the host and the device, under control of the device driver.
- **OpenMP allocated memory:** Memory allocated using the `omp_alloc()` OpenMP runtime. This is usually drawn from system allocated memory, however the runtime can add extra traits as part of the allocation process. Only default allocation is considered in this paper (by passing the flag `omp_default_mem_alloc` as an argument to the OpenMP allocator.

```
1   #ifdef USE_USM
2   #pragma omp requires unified_shared_memory
3   #endif
4
5   void run_test(double *p,   // Memory allocated in driver
6                 const char *tag, // Output logging tag
7                 bool managed_memory = false, // e.g. CUDA/HIP managed memory
8                 bool associated = false) // Using omp_associate_ptr()
9                 {
10      // Outer loop
11      for (int j = 0; j < 4; ++j){
12          if (not managed_memory && not associated) {
13  #pragma omp target enter data map(always, to: p[:SIZE])
14          }
15          // CPU_0 (and CPU_2)  kernel
16  #pragma omp parallel for num_threads(NUM_THREADS)
17          for (size_t i = 0; i < SIZE; i++){
18              p[i] = 1.0;
19          }
20          // Inner loop - GPU1 - GPU4
21          for (int k = 0; k < 4; ++k) {
22              if (not managed_memory) {
23                  // Explicit data movement
24  #pragma omp target update to(p[:SIZE])
25  #pragma omp target teams distribute parallel for
26                  for (size_t i = 0; i < SIZE; i++){
27                      p[i] = 2.0;
28                  }
29              }
30              else {
31  #pragma omp target teams distribute parallel for is_device_ptr(p)
32                  for (size_t i = 0; i < SIZE; i++) {
33                      p[i] = 2.0;
34                  }
35              }
36              if (not managed_memory) {
37  #pragma omp target update from(p[:SIZE])
38              }
39          } // k loop
40          if (not managed_memory && not associated) {
41  #pragma omp target exit data map(delete : p[:SIZE])
42          }
43          // CPU_1 Kernel execution
44  #pragma omp parallel for num_threads(NUM_THREADS)
45          for (size_t i = 0; i < SIZE; i++){
46              p[i] = 1.0;
47          }
48      } // j loop
49  }
```

Listing 1: Benchmark testing code

```
1     {
2           double *p = NULL;
3           hipHostMalloc((void **)&p, SIZE * sizeof(double));
4           run_test(p, "hipHostMalloc", true);
5           hipHostFree(p);
6     }
7     {
8           double *p = NULL;
9           hipHostMalloc((void **)&p, SIZE * sizeof(double));
10          run_test(p, "hipHostMalloc", false);
11          hipHostFree(p);
12    }
```

Listing 2: Sample benchmark driver code

- **Pinned host memory:** Pinned memory allocated on the host device using facilities of the device runtime API (e.g. using `hipHostMalloc()` for ROCm or `cudaHostMalloc()` for CUDA).

4   Experimental Evaluation

In this sections, benchmark results using several OpenMP compilers are presented on three platforms. In the results presented here, entries represent the bandwidth observed for various stages of execution. CPU_0 entries correspond to the very first execution of the loop on the CPU, isolated to capture impact of system factors such as allocate on first touch that may not be present in subsequent executions. CPU_1 represents the bandwidth observed on the CPU immediately after the sequence of executions on the device. CPU_2 represents the bandwidth observed *before* a new sequence of GPU executions (but excluding CPU_0) (this means that CPU_2 immediately follows CPU_1 in the execution order). GPU_0 represents the bandwidth for the first kernel execution on the device, where GPU_{1+} represents the average bandwidth for subsequent instances on the device. *Map*, *HTOD* and *DTOH* represents the bandwidth observed during explicit mapping, copying memory from the host to the device, and copying memory from the device to the host, respectively. Column marked `omp_map` indicates whether explicit mapping and data movement clauses are active for the corresponding test case. Bandwidth measurements are averaged over all execution instances for the corresponding operation across all iterations in the outer loop in 1. Entries marked *inf* represent mapping and data transfer operation where no data was actually transferred, resulting in artificially high reported bandwidth. In all experiments, a single thread was used in the CPU loop. Tests used a double vector of size $2,000,000,000$ or 14.901 GiB. We should note that the entry marked `std::new` (`assoc_ptr`) corresponds to standard system memory allocation on the CPU, and a corresponding memory allocated on the device, and associated with the host pointer using the OpenMP `omp_target_associate_ptr()` runtime routine.

4.1   Results on Crusher

Crusher [3] is a 192 node Cray EX system hosted at the Oak Ridge Leadership Computing Facility (OLCF), with each compute node supporting 512 GB, 64-core AMD EPYC 7A53 cores and 4 AMD MI250X GPUs, each with 2 Graphics Compute Dies (GCDs) for a total of 8 GCDs per node. In results reported here, the following compilers were used: the Cray CCE compiler version 15.0.0, the AMD ROCm OpenMP compiler version 5.3.0, the LLVM upstream compiler development version 17.0.0 (commit e7b9c2f00fa0) and the GCC compiler (development branch `devel/omp/12` commit b150ba8eebc). The benchmark was compiled using the `-O3 -std=c++17 -fopenmp` flags with appropriate default offloading flags for each compiler.

It should be noted that on Crusher, page migration is controlled via the `HSA_XNACK` environment variable [1], which is turned off by default. In the following tables, only results where the use of USM is matched with the proper setting for `HSA_XNACK` are reported. Both the CCE and ROCm compilers perform a check for `HSA_XNACK` at run time, and generates a run time error and abort execution if `##pragma omp requires unified_shared_memory` is enabled and `HSA_XNACK` is not properly set. GCC on the other hand, sets `HSA_XNACK` to 1 if the code requires the use of USM. Table 1 shows results for CCE with USM on and off, Table 2 shows the results for the ROCm compiler, 3 show results for LLVM, and Table 4 shows GCC results. In the following results, page migration is indicated by significant changes in the performance of successive executions of the memory access loop *on the same device*. This can be seen, for example, in the entry for `hipMallocManaged` with USM enabled in Table 1, where GPU_0 shows a bandwidth of 3.63 GiB/Sec and subsequent executions on the device (GPU_{1+}) shows a bandwidth of 1044.12 GiB/Sec.

While a detailed analysis of all results is beyond the scope of this work, the following observations can be made.

- With USM enabled, the CCE compiler appears to *not* enable page migration whether or not explicit memory mapping and copying directives are used in the OpenMP target regions (except for `hipMallocManaged`). This can be seen for memory allocated via `std::new` or the OpenMP default allocator, as compared to the behavior for `hipMallocManaged` where page migration takes place during the GPU_0 loop. With explicit mapping, observed bandwidth results indicate that memory remain on the CPU, and the mapping and data movement operations appear to be a noop.
- For the ROCm compiler, `omp_default_alloc` generated a page fault runtime error with USM enabled when the benchmark was run on Crusher, using the GPU kernel driver version 5.16.9.22.20.7654. A subsequent run on another identical test system, with a newer version of the GPU kernel driver (version 6.0.5) using the same ROCm 5.3.0 toolchain produced no errors. This result is reported in the `omp_defaul_alloc` (No Err) entry in Table 2.
- For the LLVM, ROCm, and GCC compilers, memory allocated via the OpenMP allocator or `std::new` migrate back and forth between the host

Table 1. Benchmark Bandwidth (GiB/Sec) on Crusher using CCE 15.0.0.

allocator	omp map	CPU_0	CPU_1	CPU_2	GPU_0	GPU_{1+}	Map	HTOD	DTOH
USM on XNACK on									
hipMallocManaged	N	3.82	2.92	23.74	3.63	1044.12			
omp_default_alloc	Y	3.82	23.73	23.78	20.35	21.02	inf	inf	inf
hipHostMalloc	N	23.73	23.76	23.75	25.36	25.37			
hipHostMalloc	Y	23.73	23.75	23.75	25.35	25.36	inf	inf	inf
hipMalloc	N	3.05	17.97	17.98	1074.36	1171.82			
std::new	Y	3.92	23.77	24.23	25.35	25.35	inf	inf	inf
std::new (assoc_ptr)	Y	3.92	23.76	23.77	1159.23	1160.74	inf	23.46	23.46
std::new	N	3.80	23.78	23.77	24.18	25.35			
USM OFF XNACK OFF									
hipMallocManaged	N	23.29	23.32	23.32	25.35	25.36			
omp_default_alloc	Y	23.77	23.76	23.77	1155.42	1156.80	14.90	14.88	14.78
hipHostMalloc	N	23.75	23.78	23.78	25.35	25.36			
hipHostMalloc	Y	23.75	23.76	23.79	1156.36	1156.90	23.75	23.76	23.47
hipMalloc	N	3.10	17.68	17.72	1062.29	1168.62			
std::new	Y	23.76	23.77	23.77	1157.07	1156.75	14.86	14.86	14.76
std::new (assoc_ptr)	Y	3.77	23.77	23.77	1157.04	1156.48	inf	14.87	14.78

Table 2. Benchmark Bandwidth (GiB/Sec) on Crusher using ROCm 5.3.0.

allocator	omp map	CPU_0	CPU_1	CPU_2	GPU_0	GPU_{1+}	Map	HTOD	DTOH
USM on XNACK on									
hipMallocManaged	N	5.1	2.79	15.8	3.64	1040.20			
omp_defaul_alloc	Y	RE	RE	RE	RE	RE	RE	RE	RE
omp_defaul_alloc (No Err)	Y	5.21	2.82	15.88	3.69	1154.76	inf	inf	inf
hipHostMalloc	N	16.24	16.25	16.26	25.33	25.34			
hipHostMalloc	Y	16.24	16.25	16.26	25.34	25.35	inf	inf	inf
hipMalloc	N	2.53	6.48	6.48	941.8	1175.82			
std::new	Y	5.15	2.82	16.06	3.64	1176.69	inf	inf	inf
std::new (assoc_ptr)	Y	5.36	15.93	15.96	1158.46	1161.29	inf	17.54	18.03
std::new	N	5.11	3.26	16.08	3.02	1038.29			
USM OFF XNACK OFF									
hipMallocManaged	N	14.84	14.92	14.91	25.34	25.35			
omp_defaul_alloc	Y	15.78	15.93	15.93	1139.63	1141.79	17.04	16.88	17.96
hipHostMalloc	N	15.93	15.81	15.94	25.33	25.34			
hipHostMalloc	Y	16.06	15.83	15.97	1143.16	1131.52	18.59	18.48	19.33
hipMalloc	N	2.5	6.48	6.46	955.27	1168.51			
std::new	Y	16.07	15.87	16.06	1128.37	1134.52	17.78	17.59	17.99
std::new (assoc_ptr)	Y	5.12	15.84	15.98	1145.07	1138.96	inf	17.64	17.98

Table 3. Benchmark Bandwidth (GiB/Sec) on Crusher using LLVM 17.0.0-dev.

USM on XNACK on

allocator	omp map	CPU_0	CPU_1	CPU_2	GPU_0	GPU_{1+}	Map	HTOD	DTOH
hipMallocManaged	N	5.18	2.78	15.75	3.64	765.13			
omp_defaul_alloc	Y	5.43	3.26	15.8	3.04	678.41	inf	inf	inf
hipHostMalloc	N	15.82	15.88	15.71	24.66	24.67			
hipHostMalloc	Y	15.21	15.79	15.44	24.66	24.67	inf	inf	inf
hipMalloc	N	2.51	6.46	6.45	878.6	1009.68			
std::new	Y	5.2	3.27	15.85	3.08	765.37	inf	inf	inf
std::new (assoc_ptr)	Y	5.42	15.66	15.51	1000.8	1001.6	inf	18.50	19.00
std::new	N	5.2	3.27	15.85	3.08	764.91			

USM OFF XNACK OFF

hipMallocManaged	N	14.26	14.55	14.43	24.62	24.64			
omp_defaul_alloc	Y	15.58	15.93	15.51	1138.24	1144.77	17.1	16.57	17.77
hipHostMalloc	N	15.64	15.73	15.68	24.61	24.62			
hipHostMalloc	Y	15.7	15.75	15.55	1170.62	1170.65	23.72	23.75	25.22
hipMalloc	N	2.51	6.43	6.41	1044.89	1175.61			
std::new	Y	15.64	15.77	15.63	1155.75	1149.11	17.6	17.55	17.94
std::new (assoc_ptr)	Y	5.12	15.73	15.45	1155.89	1141.90	inf	17.68	17.96

Table 4. Benchmark Bandwidth (GiB/Sec) on Crusher using GCC 12.2.1-dev.

USM on XNACK on

allocator	omp map	CPU_0	CPU_1	CPU_2	GPU_0	GPU_{1+}	Map	HTOD	DTOH
hipMallocManaged	N	5.00	2.86	17.27	3.92	358.13			
omp_defaul_alloc	Y	4.96	3.32	17.54	3.42	358.61	inf	inf	inf
hipHostMalloc	N	16.48	16.48	16.46	21.25	21.28			
hipHostMalloc	Y	17.51	17.47	17.45	21.24	21.29	inf	inf	inf
hipMalloc	N	2.56	6.54	6.53	843.10	903.41			
std::new	Y	5.10	2.85	17.28	3.91	900.32	inf	inf	inf
std::new (assoc_ptr)	Y	17.40	3.34	17.13	3.41	3.42	inf	RE	RE
std::new	N	17.41	3.34	17.13	3.41	900.51			

USM OFF XNACK OFF

hipMallocManaged	N	17.41	17.44	17.44	21.23	21.28			
omp_defaul_alloc	Y	17.29	17.29	17.29	948.74	948.73	20.37	20.44	22.79
hipHostMalloc	N	16.25	16.27	16.26	21.23	21.29			
hipHostMalloc	Y	17.56	17.58	17.56	895.70	883.19	23.74	23.76	25.28
hipMalloc	N	2.55	6.62	6.61	882.69	955.73			
std::new	Y	17.46	17.09	17.09	947.6	948.15	17.94	17.66	18.61
std::new (assoc_ptr)	Y	4.95	17.37	17.54	947.68	947.24	inf	17.76	18.41

and the GPU when USM is enabled, whether or not explicit mapping is used. Explicit mapping is a noop for these compilers.

- With USM enabled, the LLVM compiler shows a 50.13% drop in performance for std::new with explicit mapping for GPU_{1+}. This performance drop appears to be present for all configurations where data is copied or migrates to the GPU, with the highest drop of 68.7% for omp_default_alloc.
- With USM enabled, the GCC compiler's std::new assoc_ptr resulted in a runtime error from the underlying libgomp runtime library when copying data between the host and the device.
- The behavior of omp_default_alloc is similar to that of std::new for all compilers with USM enabled. There is however a performance gap for GPU_{1+}, where bandwidth observed using std::new outperforming that for omp_default_alloc for the LLVM and GCC compilers. This performance gap is 12.8% for LLVM and 251% for GCC, and for LLVM there's another gap of 31.9% between std::new and the performance obtained via explicit device allocation using hipMalloc.
- With USM enabled, ROCm shows an improvement of 13.3% in GPU_{1+} for std::new when explicit mapping is used. This improvement is not seen in the LLVM and GCC compilers, where memory migrates to the GPU.
- In general, the variability in GPU_{1+} performance with USM on depends on the compiler, with CCE and ROCm providing a more consistent performance than LLVM and GCC.

4.2   Results on Summit

Summit [7] is an 4600 node IBM AC922 POWER9 system with each compute nodes supporting two IBM POWER9 processors and six NVIDIA Tesla V100 GPUs. For the experiments reported here, two compilers were used. The LLVM compiler development version 17.0.0 commit d366da97bd24 and the GCC compiler (development branch devel/omp/12 commit a410f603fca). The experiments used the same flags as was used on Crusher, with the appropriate required offloading flags. Table 5 shows results for the LLVM compiler while Table 6 shows the results for GCC. It should be noted that the nvhpc compiler on Summit (latest version 22.11) failed to compile the benchmark.

On summit, memory allocated on the CPU using system allocators is accessible from the GPU using the NVIDIA Address Translation Service (ATS) [14, 16]. The following points can be observed from the performance results:

- Using the LLVM with USM enabled, memory does not migrate to the GPU in any of the memory allocation scenarios except for CUDA managed memory allocated using cudaMallocManaged.
- With explicit mapping and USM enabled, the LLVM compiler's mapping and data update operations appear to be a noop, and memory remains on the CPU and is accessed *in place* remotely from the GPU.
- With USM enabled, the GCC compiler copies memory to the device whether or not explicit mapping is used.

Table 5. Benchmark Bandwidth (GiB/Sec) on Summit using LLVM 17.0.0-dev.

USM on allocator	omp map	CPU_0	CPU_1	CPU_2	GPU_0	GPU_{1+}	Map	HTOD	DTOH
cudaMallocManaged	N	9.96	7.38	28.69	5.03	770.2			
omp_defaul_alloc	Y	13.09	30.70	30.71	18.81	18.12	inf	inf	inf
cudaMallocHost	N	30.68	31.10	31.10	41.34	41.34			
cudaMallocHost	Y	31.24	31.22	31.22	41.31	41.35	inf	inf	inf
std::new	Y	13.21	31.05	31.08	21.23	20.97	inf	inf	inf
std::new (assoc_ptr)	Y	13.18	30.87	30.82	765.57	769.16	inf	12.28	17.35
std::new	N	13.22	31.01	31.01	20.92	20.70			
USM OFF									
cudaMallocManaged	N	9.94	7.36	28.83	5.1	767.8			
omp_defaul_alloc	Y	1.94	30.80	30.79	762.82	763.82	10.01	12.28	6.59
cudaMallocHost	N	30.8	30.81	30.81	41.34	41.35			
cudaMallocHost	Y	30.85	30.81	30.67	770.24	771.58	24.74	43.61	43.53
std::new	Y	1.94	31.05	31.05	760.95	769.86	10.11	12.28	17.30
std::new (assoc_ptr)	Y	13.22	31.00	30.99	769.81	770.53	inf	12.28	17.29
std::new	N	13.12	30.94	31.00	20.46	20.52			

Table 6. Benchmark Bandwidth (GiB/Sec) on Summit using GCC 12.2.1-dev.

USM on allocator	omp map	CPU_0	CPU_1	CPU_2	GPU_0	GPU_{1+}	Map	HTOD	DTOH
cudaMallocManaged	N	9.65	7.39	28.33	5.37	170.55			
omp_defaul_alloc	Y	2.06	29.5	29.39	167.88	170.00	15.10	12.29	10.05
cudaMallocHost	N	29.56	29.85	29.84	3.18	3.18			
cudaMallocHost	Y	29.67	29.79	29.7	170.93	171.49	24.66	43.61	43.53
std::new	Y	9.66	7.39	28.3	5.42	171.23	inf	inf	inf
std::new (assoc_ptr)	Y	9.68	24.25	23.45	0.92	1.17	inf	12.26	14.13
std::new	N	7.31	7.31	27.21	5.44	170.62			
USM OFF									
cudaMallocManaged	N	10.14	7.58	31.44	5.34	171.6			
omp_defaul_alloc	Y	1.94	27.73	27.59	157.35	169.41	10.19	12.4	4.75
cudaMallocHost	N	28.29	28.85	28.84	3.18	3.17			
cudaMallocHost	Y	28.93	28.98	28.99	160.94	171.63	24.78	43.61	43.53
std::new	Y	1.94	29.1	29.11	165.79	171.01	10.2	12.4	16.83
std::new (assoc_ptr)	Y	12.29	29.17	29.17	170.97	170.99	inf	12.4	16.87
std::new	N	12.3	29.53	29.4	0.05	0.05			

- The GCC compiler's behavior with both explicit mapping and USM enabled is different between memory allocated using `omp_default_alloc`, where mapping and data update operations are handled by the compiler, and `std::new` where mapping and data update operations appear to be noop, and memory pages migrate to the GPU during the execution of the GPU_0 loop. The behavior in this latter case is similar to the `cudaMallocManaged` and `std::new` with no explicit mapping. This behavior s different from GCC on Crusher, where explicit mapping was a noop in all cases, and memory pages migrated during execution of GPU_0.
- GCC results in the `std::new (assoc_ptr)` with USM enabled show a very low bandwidth for loops executing on the GPU, suggesting a possible defect that maybe related to the issue observed with GCC on Crusher for the same scenario.

4.3   Results on Perlmutter

Perlmutter [6] is a Cray EX system with two partitions, a 3072-node CPU partition based on the AMD EPYC 7763 processor, and a 1536-node GPU partition using the AMD EPYC 7763 procesor connected to 4 NVIDIA A100 40 GB GPUs, in addition to 256 nodes with 4 NVIDIA A100 80 GB GPUs. For experiments used in this work, three compilers were used, The LLVM compiler version 16.0.0, the GCC compiler (development branch devel/omp/12 commit a410f603fca), and the NVHPC compiler version 23.1. Table 7 shows results for the LLVM compiler, Table 8 shows results for the GCC compiler, and Table 9 shows results for NVHPC.

Table 7. Benchmark Bandwidth (GiB/Sec) on Perlmutter using LLVM 16.0.

allocator	omp map	CPU_0	CPU_1	CPU_2	GPU_0	GPU_{1+}	Map	HTOD	DTOH
USM on									
cudaMallocManaged	N	7.15	5.16	16.91	7.76	1305.29			
omp_defaul_alloc	Y	10.6	RE	RE	RE	RE	inf	inf	RE
cudaMallocHost	N	16.87	16.62	16.62	23.7	24.44			
cudaMallocHost	Y	16.33	16.43	16.17	21.76	24.53	inf	inf	inf
std::new	Y	10.47	RE	RE	RE	RE	inf	inf	RE
std::new (assoc_ptr)	Y	4.69	11.54	11.5	1293.64	1296.85	inf	12.76	14.53
std::new	N	5.58	RE	RE	RE	RE	RE	RE	RE
USM OFF									
cudaMallocManaged	N	7.12	5.33	17.02	7.86	1321.91			
omp_defaul_alloc	Y	4.24	17.28	17.23	1290.97	1297.08	18.96	19.33	14.46
cudaMallocHost	N	17.15	17.24	17.22	24.07	24.53			
cudaMallocHost	Y	17.42	16.29	16.38	1289.6	1282.8	24.2	24.83	24.48
std::new	Y	4.1	17.26	17.21	1283.64	1281.87	12.88	13.04	11.9
std::new (assoc_ptr)	Y	10.39	17.21	17.26	1286.12	1285.55	inf	13.46	11.98

Table 8. Benchmark Bandwidth (GiB/Sec) on Perlmutter using GCC 12.2.1-dev.

| USM on | | | | | | | | | |
allocator	omp map	CPU_0	CPU_1	CPU_2	GPU_0	GPU_{1+}	Map	HTOD	DTOH
cudaMallocManaged	N	7.10	5.25	17.07	11.53	371.52			
omp_defaul_alloc	Y	4.17	17.28	17.12	371.33	371.5	12.97	13.14	11.33
cudaMallocHost	N	17.58	17.54	17.4	8.36	8.30			
cudaMallocHost	Y	17.38	17.40	17.38	370.48	371.99	24.20	24.86	24.49
std::new	Y	6.82	5.20	17.01	11.14	372.39	inf	inf	inf
std::new (assoc_ptr)	Y	6.87	17.12	17.08	11.76	11.69	inf	13.03	4.25
std::new	N	7.00	5.27	17.17	11.53	372.51			
USM OFF									
cudaMallocManaged	N	6.95	5.21	17.28	11.08	371.36			
omp_defaul_alloc	Y	4.03	17.2	17.12	356.57	366.55	12.94	13.17	11.31
cudaMallocHost	N	17.57	17.55	17.46	8.32	8.23			
cudaMallocHost	Y	17.22	17.24	17.16	369.43	368.61	24.19	24.84	24.49
std::new	Y	4.34	16.42	16.43	365.10	365.00	12.94	13.10	11.99
std::new (assoc_ptr)	Y	10.43	17.36	17.33	371.50	365.71	inf	13.55	11.98

Table 9. The NVHPC compiler on Perlmutter.

| USM on | | | | | | | | | |
allocator	omp map	CPU_0	CPU_1	CPU_2	GPU_0	GPU_{1+}	Map	HTOD	DTOH
cudaMallocManaged	N	4.91	4.85	23.66	5.79	1285.52			
omp_defaul_alloc	Y	3.34	23.74	23.71	1282.93	1283.74	13.61	13.6	10.6
cudaMallocHost	N	23.72	23.74	23.76	24.33	24.54			
cudaMallocHost	Y	23.74	23.74	23.74	1283.39	1283.84	13.64	13.64	10.56
std::new	Y	3.47	23.68	23.66	1283.72	1283.92	13.49	13.53	10.52
std::new (assoc_ptr)	Y	9.11	23.7	23.71	1283.56	1283.95	inf	14.11	10.64
std::new	N	RE	RE	RE	RE	RE	RE	RE	RE
USM OFF									
cudaMallocManaged	N	4.96	4.94	23.64	5.87	1285.45			
omp_defaul_alloc	Y	3.22	23.72	23.7	1283.73	1284.94	13.77	13.75	10.53
cudaMallocHost	N	23.67	23.69	23.71	24.21	24.54			
cudaMallocHost	Y	23.69	23.76	23.75	1283.82	1284.08	13.72	13.72	10.48
std::new	Y	3.47	23.76	23.76	1283.81	1284.3	13.67	13.67	10.48
std::new (assoc_ptr)	Y	9.26	23.73	23.75	1283.86	1284.18	inf	14.24	10.57
std::new	N	RE	RE	RE	RE	RE	RE	RE	RE

The following observations can be made regarding the observed results

- Both the LLVM and NVHPC compilers did not generate an error due to the use of `##pragma omp requires unified_shared_memory` directive. However, both compilers generated runtime errors when no explicit mapping is used with system allocator `std::new`. This suggests non-compliance in these versions of the compilers, as the OpenMP specification states that the `unified_shared_memory` clause makes the `map` clause optional on target constructs.
- The GCC compiler successfully executed all tests with USM on, with memory pages migrating between the host and the device as appropriate (except for the case with associated device pointers). With USM enabled, the GCC compiler behavior on Perlmutter is analogous to its behavior on Summit. The two machines have the same accelerator architecture (with NVIDIA V100 on Summit and A100 on Perlmutter), but have different CPU architecture and different CPU-GPU connection, indicating a degree of portability of USM support in GCC when targeting the NVPTX backend.

5   Conclusions and Future Work

In this work, unified shared memory support in various OpenMP compilers is investigated. A synthetic benchmark was developed to characterize the performance of memory-bound operations as applied to memory allocated via the various allocators available on three platforms with offloading capabilities. Results suggest that while support for USM is becoming more available, there remains significant gaps and variability across compilers and platforms. While results presented in this work represent a snapshot in time for the current state of USM support, the benchmark described here should prove useful to track and characterize USM support in different OpenMP implementations, as such implementations mature and get deployed to new and emerging hardware platforms. Emerging platforms (such as the NVIDIA Grace Hopper Superchip [4] and the AMD MI300 [2]) with hardware support for coherent and unified memory access using discrete or single memory spaces are an obvious short term target for this tool.

While the OpenMP specification only states that unified shared memory renders the `map` clause optional, it is up to individual implementations to decide the manner in which this is implemented. Such decisions can have a profound impact on code performance. This can be seen on platforms with separate, discrete host and device physical memory - and where the hardware and low level system software allow for cross-device remote memory access *in place*. On such platforms, leveraging mechanisms for page migration to the appropriate compute device would provide a higher performance for code patterns with repeated access to the same memory page. While both strategies are compliant with the OpenMP specification, such difference in performance represents a significant performance portability challenge for applications that rely on USM.

It should be noted that compiler implementations and operating system support for USM is maturing rapidly, and issues identified in this study should probably be addressed in near term releases of the respective compilers. However, proper implementation documentation detailing various aspects of runtime memory management and interaction with various memory spaces remain needed.

Acknowledgments. This research used resources of the Oak Ridge Leadership Computing Facility at the Oak Ridge National Laboratory, which is supported by the Office of Science of the U.S. Department of Energy under Contract No. DE-AC05-00OR22725. This research used resources of the National Energy Research Scientific Computing Center (NERSC), a US Department of Energy Office of Science User Facility located at Lawrence Berkeley National Laboratory, operated under Contract No. DE-AC02-05CH11231.

References

1. AMD Instinct MI200 GPU memory space overview. https://gpuopen.com/learn/amd-lab-notes/amd-lab-notes-mi200-memory-space-overview/
2. AMD Instinct MI300 Details Emerge, Debuts in 2 Exaflop El Capitan Supercomputer. https://www.tomshardware.com/news/new-amd-instinct-mi300-details-emerge-debuts-in-2-exaflop-el-capitan-supercomputer
3. Crusher Quick-Start Guide. https://docs.olcf.ornl.gov/systems/crusher_quick_start_guide.html#
4. NVIDIA Grace Hopper Superchip Architecture Whitepaper. https://resources.nvidia.com/en-us-grace-cpu/nvidia-grace-hopper
5. OLCF Compiler Tests. https://code.ornl.gov/elwasif/olcf-compiler-tests
6. Perlmutter Architecture. https://docs.nersc.gov/systems/perlmutter/architecture/
7. Summit User Guide. https://docs.olcf.ornl.gov/systems/summit_user_guide.html
8. Advance Micro Devices: AMD ROCm Open Software Platfor. https://rocm.docs.amd.com/en/latest/
9. Advance Micro Devices: HIP: C++ Heterogeneous-Compute Interface for Portability. https://github.com/ROCm-Developer-Tools/HIP
10. Grinberg, L., Bertolli, C., Haque, R.: Hands on with openMP4.5 and unified memory: developing applications for IBM's hybrid CPU + GPU systems (part II). In: de Supinski, B.R., Olivier, S.L., Terboven, C., Chapman, B.M., Müller, M.S. (eds.) IWOMP 2017. LNCS, vol. 10468, pp. 17–29. Springer, Cham (2017). https://doi.org/10.1007/978-3-319-65578-9_2
11. Harris, M.: Unified memory in CUDA 6 (2013). https://developer.nvidia.com/blog/unified-memory-in-cuda-6/
12. Hindriksen, V.: CUDA 6 unified memory explained (2013). http://streamcomputing.eu/blog/2013-11-14/cuda-6-unified-memory-explained/
13. Mishra, A., Li, L., Kong, M., Finkel, H., Chapman, B.: Benchmarking and evaluating unified memory for openMP GPU offloading. In: Proceedings of the Fourth Workshop on the LLVM Compiler Infrastructure in HPC. LLVM-HPC2017, Association for Computing Machinery, New York, NY, USA (2017). https://doi.org/10.1145/3148173.3148184

14. NVIDIA Corp.: NVIDIA TESLA V100 GPU ARCHITECTURE (2017). https://images.nvidia.com/content/volta-architecture/pdf/volta-architecture-whitepaper.pdf
15. OpenMP Architecture Review Board: OpenMP application program interface version 5.0 (2018). https://www.openmp.org/wp-content/uploads/OpenMP-API-Specification-5.0.pdf
16. Sakharnykh, N.: Everything you need to know about unified memory (2018). https://on-demand.gputechconf.com/gtc/2018/presentation/s8430-everything-you-need-to-know-about-unified-memory.pdf

OpenMP Reverse Offloading Using Shared Memory Remote Procedure Calls

Joseph Huber$^{(\boxtimes)}$ and Jon Chesterfield

Advanced Micro Devices, Santa Clara, USA
{Joseph.Huber,Jonathan.Chesterfield}@amd.com

Abstract. The widespread adoption of general purpose GPU programming in high-performance computing (HPC) has led to an increased need for expanded GPU functionality. Currently there are several features that still require host services to be accomplished on the GPU, notably printing and dynamic memory allocation. The OpenMP 5.0 standard includes support for reverse offloading to allow the GPU to execute code on the host. This paper proposes a means of implementing reverse offloading within the LLVM toolchain.

The remote procedure call (RPC) is a common method for executing routines on a separate machine. This is adapted here for executing routines on heterogeneous hardware. We claim that shared memory supporting relaxed atomic load and store and acquire/release fences are sufficient to implement remote procedure calls. Furthermore, using reliable shared memory bypasses the usual failure modes associated with networking.

In this paper we introduce a generic shared memory RPC library that can be used to implement host services that works on AMDGPU, NVPTX, and x86-64 architectures. We then show how this can be used to implement OpenMP 5.0 reverse offloading at the runtime level. Finally, we examine some of the performance considerations and trade-offs when using this implementation.

Keywords: OpenMP · GPU · RPC · Runtimes

1 Introduction

Recent developments in HPC systems suggest a shift towards heterogeneous accelerators connected by high speed memory. This trend has only increased as GPU vendors like NVIDIA and AMD have begun selling accelerators with CPUs and GPUs in the same package. This general shift towards more general purpose GPU programming has been assisted with the development of unified shared memory features, blurring the lines between accelerator and host code. However, truly blurring the line is limited by the lack of general host services on many accelerator programs.

The remote procedure call (RPC) is a simple interface for executing a routine on an external machine. To the user, it appears as a simple function call while the details of the implementation are hidden behind the interface. The simplicity of

S. McIntosh-Smith et al. (Eds.): IWOMP 2023, LNCS 14114, pp. 226–238, 2023.
https://doi.org/10.1007/978-3-031-40744-4_15

this interface hides several well-known issues in common implementations. Works by Tanenbaum and Renesse [8] highlight the difficulties, while Vinoksi's [11] paper argues that RPC interfaces offer "convenience over correctness".

The design choice for RPC over a network is either to ignore failure mode at loss of correctness or to augment the interface of all function calls to report additional errors. Specific to shared memory heterogeneous systems, the communication between CPU and GPU is as reliable as other memory traffic, and failures are likely to be handled the same way other memory faults are handled, e.g. checkpointing, restarts, or replacing hardware. Therefore no change to the function interface is necessary or useful when changing the implementation to execute remotely.

Essentially any shared memory system supporting multiple threads of execution is likely to meet the minimum requirements for this implementation. We require only weakly ordered atomic loads and stores along with acquire/release memory fences. This interface can then be made general enough to implement host services and reverse offloading.

In this paper, we introduce a novel and general RPC mechanism for implementing host services via OpenMP 5.0 reverse offloading. First, we cover relevant background knowledge in Sect. 2. We will then cover related work in Sect. 3. Section 4 will cover the implementation of our RPC library and interface which will then be used in Sect. 5 to implement OpenMP 5.0 reverse offloading. We will then provide basic performance evaluations of the implementation in Sect. 6. Finally, future work and the conclusion will be discussed in Sect. 7 and Sect. 8.

1.1   Contributions and Limitations

The main contributions of this paper are as follows:

- A general-purpose RPC mechanism written in freestanding C++ for implementing host services.
- An overview of how this interface can be used to implement OpenMP reverse offloading.
- An evaluation of the latency of RPC calls from the GPU.

This paper outlines a proof-of-concept for implementing reverse offloading for OpenMP 5.0. Because of this, we explicitly leave for future work beyond this paper:

- The compiler front-end and back-end changes required to support reverse offloading.
- Integration into the existing LLVM/Clang OpenMP offloading runtime.

2   Background

Remote procedure calls (RPC) represent a broad array of methods to call procedures on external machines. This implementation defines an RPC mechanism split between a *client* and *server*. The *client* is the process that initiates a connection to the server and is considered *active*. The *server* is the process that listens for and handles connections from the client and is considered *passive*. We will refer to the pair of these as a *process*.

We will use the more-familiar CUDA terminology for GPUs in lieu of the OpenCL terminology commonly used in association with AMD GPUs. That is, a thread refers to a single work-item in the context of the GPU and a POSIX thread in the context of the CPU.

2.1 Shared Memory

In this paper, *shared memory* refers to memory that is accessible from both the GPU and CPU in a system asynchronously. In particular, writes to the memory may be seen by the other device during the execution of a compute kernel. In NVIDIA terminology, this refers to *host-pinned* allocations. Using Heterogeneous System Architecture (HSA) terminology, as used by AMDGPU, we instead call this *fine-grained* memory. A single address space is convenient but not necessary.

In order for our scheme to work we require a shared memory buffer that is accessible from both the client and the server. Furthermore, the shared buffer must support atomic operations that are visible to the other device. In practice this can be achieved using system-level relaxed atomic loads and stores with appropriate acquire/release fences. The hardware requirements for this are met by both NVIDIA and AMD GPUs starting with the sm_60 and gfx801 architectures respectively.

3   Related Work

This work is not the first to implement host services using shared memory. The AMD compiler provides printing services through an interface called *hostcall* or *hostexec* for HIP and OpenMP offloading compilations respectively. These use a lock free stack based on atomic compare and swap in combination with HSA signals to coordinate work. These implementations are not currently available on non-AMDGPU architectures and are therefore not sufficient for generic support for OpenMP reverse offloading.

The GCC 13 release introduced support for reverse offloading [3]. Their method uses a similar approach to preallocate a fixed number of slots in shared memory that threads can use to share data with the host. This is implemented as a ring buffer continuously flushed by the host. However, this implementation does not support many concurrent calls, nowait functionality, or mapping of memory private to the thread.

This work is an adaptation of the implementation outlined in [4]. The four distinct states tracked at compile time in the theoretical work are instead reduced to two states tracked at runtime in this one. The conceptual framework of the state machine is the same while the interface is unrelated and novel to this work.

Previous work has also explored RPC implementations in OpenMP itself. One implementation created a basic RPC mechanism to compile OpenMP programs directly on the GPU [10]. This implementation used compiler transforms to automatically generate RPC stubs to enable host routines.

4   Remote Procedure Calls

This section will describe in detail the implementation of our RPC library. A pseudocode implementation of the RPC interface is presented in Fig. 1. We elected to implement the core RPC interface in freestanding C++ rather than OpenMP as others have [9] so that the same implementation can be included by other offloading languages, such as CUDA or HIP. This will first describe the fundamental implementation of the underlying state machine in a one-to-one case with a single thread on both the GPU and CPU. We will then extend this interface to handle multiple producers. Finally, we will discuss how this can be extended to handle the GPU's SIMT model and multiple devices.

```
struct Process {
  atomic_int *inbox;
  atomic_int *outbox;
  void *packet;
};

struct Port {
  template <typename U> void recv(U use) noexcept;
  template <typename F> void send(F fill) noexcept;
  void close() noexcept;
};

struct Client : Process {
  template <int opcode> Port open() noexcept;
};

struct Server : Process {
  Port open() noexcept;
};
```

Fig. 1. Pseudocode for the RPC interface.

4.1   One-to-One Remote Procedure Calls

For the RPC interface we first allocate a fixed size buffer of memory that can be shared between the server and the client. We set aside shared memory for control flags and use a fixed-size buffer to implement our *packet* of data that will be exchanged between the two processes. The reason we use a fixed-size packet will be explained in Sect. 4.5.

The strategy is to provide mutual exclusion over the shared packet, organised such that ownership of the packet alternates exclusively between the client and the server.

In order to provide mutual exclusion we use two mailboxes. Each process' state contains a write-only outbox and a read-only inbox. We redundantly encode two of the possible four states to allow us to toggle binary ownership between the two processes. This nets us two primitive operations for controlling ownership, posting and waiting. To give ownership to the other side, we post the data by toggling the process' outbox. Similarly, we can wait until we have ownership of the buffer by polling the status of the inbox. For this work we decided to assign ownership of the shared buffer to the client if `inbox == outbox` and conversely assign ownership to the server if `inbox != outbox`.

These primitives are sufficient to implement the **send** and **recv** routines as described in Fig. 1. The **send** function allows one process to send a single packet to a **recv** call on the other end. The base implementation of these routines is shown in Fig. 2. To send data, we must first wait until we own the buffer, we can then use a callback to fill the packet with the desired data and pass ownership to the other side. Similarly, to receive data we wait until we own the buffer and then use the sent packet. Because a receive into a send does not require changing ownership of the buffer, we only need to give ownership back if we are expecting another incoming packet or are closing the server's port. The implementation supports asynchronous RPC calls by allowing the client to close a port after a send without waiting for a response from the server. This only requires that we check for ownership of the buffer when opening a port from the client as another thread may have released its lock without ownership.

```
template <typename F>
void Port::send(F fill) {
  int in = inbox.load(RELAXED);
  int out = outbox.load(RELAXED);

  while (!owns_buffer(in, out))
    in = inbox.load();

  memory_fence(ACQUIRE);
  fill(packet);
  memory_fence(RELEASE);
  out.store(!out, RELAXED);
}
```

```
template <typename U>
void Port::recv(U use) {
  int in = inbox.load(RELAXED);
  int out = outbox.load(RELAXED);

  if (last_op_was_recv) {
    memory_fence(RELEASE);
    out.store(!out, RELAXED);
  }

  while (!owns_buffer(in, out))
    in = inbox.load(RELAXED);

  memory_fence(ACQUIRE);
  use(packet);
  memory_fence(RELEASE);
}
```

Fig. 2. Implementation of the **send** and **recv** functions.

4.2   Many-to-Many Remote Procedure Calls

The above interface works in the case of a single client and server thread with persistent ownership of the data. However, GPUs are not known for their single threaded performance, so users will require support for concurrent RPC calls. To do this, we define the concept of a *port*.

The *port* interface is provided as multiple copies of the underlying state machine described in Sect. 4.1 as an array. A port is then simply an index into this array. Threads that wish to use the RPC mechanism must first open a port. The first level of mutual exclusion is that each instance can only be read or written by one of the client or server at any point in time. A second level of mutual exclusion is required to ensure that no two threads on a single device write to a given index. This is done with atomic test and set on device local memory.

Successfully opening a port establishes that the current thread on the current device is the exclusive owner of the corresponding shared memory. That thread can then proceed to the one-to-one state machine described above. Unlike the rest of the buffer, the lock is allocated in device memory as it is never accessed by the other device and local memory is likely to be faster than shared memory. Compare and swap is sufficient to take a lock with store to release. A more efficient solution avoiding the compare and swap is to use a set and retry loop if supported. Considerations for locks on GPU architectures are discussed in Sect. 4.5.

After the client successfully opens a port corresponding to some index and sends a packet, some time later the server will detect that there is work available at said index and attempt to acquire the server local ownership of that buffer. For multiple client and server threads, exactly which pair resolve to each other is not known ahead of time. The assumption is that any server thread can complete a task from any client thread.

One difference between the client and the server interface is the inclusion of an `opcode` in the port. When the client initiates the connection, it passes an integer to specify the operation it wishes the server to perform. That integer will be copied across to the server. The protocol assumes that the client will begin the connection with a `send` and the server must always begin with a `recv`. After the initial transaction any ordering is permitted so long as the opposite call is used by the other process.

To give a concrete example, given this construction the following steps are required to initiate an RPC call using the interface for a simple `send` and `recv` from the perspective of the client:

- The client searches for an available port and claims the lock.
- The client checks that the port is still available to the current device and continues if so.
- The client writes its data to the fixed-size packet and toggles its outbox.
- The client waits until its inbox matches its outbox.

- The client reads the data from the fixed-size packet.
- The client closes the port and continues executing.

The same operation viewed from the server is a `recv` and `send` instead:

- The server searches for an available port with pending work and claims the lock.
- The server checks that the port is still available to the current device.
- The server reads the opcode to perform the expected operation, in this case a receive and then send.
- The server reads the data from the fixed-size packet.
- The server writes its data to the fixed-size packet and toggles its outbox.
- The server closes the port and continues searching for ports that need to be serviced.

We provide Fig. 3 to illustrate the state transitions that occur for a more complicated `send`, `send`, `recv` operation. The interface described is sufficient to provide arbitrary data streaming between both devices. Note that client inbox and server outbox are pointers to the same memory. Likewise the client outbox and server inbox.

Client		Server		Server	
Inbox	Outbox	Inbox	Outbox	Client	Server
0	0	0	0	Sending	Idle
0	1	1	0	Waiting	Receiving
1	1	1	1	Sending	Waiting
1	0	0	1	Waiting	Receiving
1	0	0	1	Waiting	Sending
0	0	0	0	Receiving	Close

Fig. 3. The state transitions by the RPC interface when performing a `send`, `send`, `recv` operation. The time required for the outbox write to reach the other process' inbox is omitted for brevity.

4.3   Expanding to the SIMT Model

The above interface assumes we have independent parallelism. However, the GPU architectures use a SIMT execution model. This means that the smallest unit of independent parallelism is not a single thread, but rather a group of threads. So, in order to reliably claim a lock we must perform all the RPC calls with multiple threads active at the same time.

This is implemented by increasing the size of the packet to contain enough space for each hardware thread group to have its own slot. Additionally, the

SIMT model allows some threads to be inactive according to their mask. We therefore pass the mask alongside the opcode to indicate which slots should be processed. In order to conform to post-Volta independent thread scheduling requirements and to avoid deadlocks, we must ensure that the same mask that opens a port also closes it. This requires strictly enforcing convergence between the port interface.

4.4   Multiple Devices

Expanding the above machinery to multiple devices is done by simply providing multiple copies of the above machinery for each device. That is, each device would have its own shared process and the host would run a server on each one. This is primarily done because implementing a locking interface using the limited system level atomics would hinder performance and functionality. It would be possible to have a single group of server threads handle request's from multiple distinct GPUs through careful memory layout, but as they would likely need to know which specific GPU is requesting things like dynamic memory allocation this is not necessarily worthwhile.

4.5   Locking Concerns on GPUs

Special care must be given to the GPU execution model when implementing locks. The GPU may provide very little in the ways of forward progress guarantees. Under the OpenCL programming model, no thread may rely on a thread from a different workgroup being scheduled at the same time. The HSA model provides slightly more ordering constraints [7] that are not useful in this context. In general, any thread that waits on another thread to release resources must wait until that thread is scheduled, which may never happen. This complicates lock free programming, the majority of the data structures in use assume a somewhat fair machine scheduler.

This hazard is primarily avoided here by ensuring that each work group or thread pairs with one on the other device and executes independently of all others on the current device. The remaining problem is that there is a finite number of allocated ports and threads will fail to open one when all are exhausted.

The RPC model implemented here holds open exactly one port during execution. A given GPU has an upper bound on the simultaneous concurrency it can support in hardware and one of the few guarantees provided [7] is that this upper bound is not exceeded by indefinitely suspending tasks. For contemporary GPUs this is of the order of low thousands. Deadlocks under the worst possible scheduling scheme can therefore be avoided by allocating a large enough area of shared memory, which works out to the order of a few megabytes. Alternatively that could be considered overly cautious and the underlying memory overhead reduced correspondingly.

5   Reverse Offloading

Beginning with OpenMP 5.0 [2], implementations of OpenMP target offloading are allowed to offload back to the host in a process called *reverse offloading*. Support for this feature has been sparse with the first limited implementation being officially present in the GCC 13.1 release. An example application is given in Fig. 4. The rest of this section will briefly explain how this can be implemented using the RPC interface described in Sect. 4.

```
int foo(int x, int *A);
#pragma omp declare target to(foo) device_type(host)

void offload(int *A, int N) {
#pragma omp target map(to: A[:N])
    {
      int x = 1;
      int y;
#pragma omp target device(ancestor: 1) map(to: A[x]) map(from: y)
      y = foo(x, A);
    }
}
```

Fig. 4. Example of OpenMP 5.0 reverse offloading.

5.1   Data Mapping

The OpenMP 5.0 standard currently does not define strict data mapping rules in the case of reverse offloading, instead allowing them to be defined by the vendor. Typically, data mapping in target regions is handled by a pointer table associating host and device pointers. For global data, we can therefore use the existing OpenMP mapping pointer table to look up the corresponding host pointer or allocate a new one if it does not exist. We can then use the address to initiate a memory copy from the device to the host. This works with the caveat that this memory transfer occurs on a distinct CUDA stream [5] or HSA queue [1].

However, not all data on the GPU is able to be copied in this way. Values that are in private, device local, or shared memory are not accessible by the CPU. Furthermore, firstprivate values and function arguments will need to be passed by-value. In order to support this, we extend the send and recv functions to allow streaming arbitrary sized data across the RPC interface by repeatedly sending or receiving packets. This is therefore sufficient to support all kinds of data mappings also possible on the host. The implementation could choose whether or not to do this operation with a memory copy or an RPC stream depending on the application. One caveat is that private or shared variables may not have unique addresses and will require the thread-id to be mapped uniquely.

5.2 Nowait

The OpenMP 5.1 standard allows for the `nowait` clause to be placed on target clauses in a reverse offloading context. This is trivially implemented in our RPC protocol. As explained in Sect. 4.2, the process can initiate a send and then close the port without waiting for that send to complete. Therefore, supporting `nowait` simply requires that we do not wait for confirmation from the server and instead immediately close the port. Other OpenMP synchronization primitives, such as a taskwait, can then be supported following the asynchronous RPC call.

5.3 Remote Calls

Reverse offloading simply requires that we call a function on the host machine. Making a remote call therefore requires the following features be supported when using our interface:

- An RPC client to communicate with the server.
- An RPC server continuously checking for ports to service.
- An opcode to copy arbitrarily sized data between the client and server.
- An opcode to invoke a function pointer with given arguments.
- A mapping between host pointers and device pointers.
- An outlined function implementing the target region on the host and a global on the device initialized to its address on the host.

We can use these tools to implement a proposed lowering of the example in Fig. 5.

```
int foo(int x, int *A);
#pragma omp declare target to(foo) device_type(host)

struct args { int x; int *A; int *y; };

void *__omp_outlined_foo;
#pragma omp declare target to(__omp_outlined_foo) device_type(nohost)

void __omp_outlined_foo(void *args) {
  *args->y = foo(args->x, args->A);
}
#pragma omp declare target to(__omp_outlined_foo) device_type(host)

void __omp_outlined_offload(int *A, int N) {
    int x = 1;
    int y;
    __omp_rpc_copy_to(A);
    __omp_rpc_alloc(&y);
    __omp_rpc_invoke(__omp_outlined_foo, args{x, A, y}, sizeof(args));
    __omp_rpc_copy_from(&y);
}
#pragma omp declare target to(__omp_outlined_offload) device_type(nohost)
```

Fig. 5. High level proposed lowering of the reverse offloading region.

6   Evaluation

We implemented a proof-of-concept runtime implementing reverse offloading as described above. Evaluation was done to simply test the validity of the proposed interface without strict adherence to an implementation. We tested a region similar to the one in Sect. 5.3 and verified functionality with thread-local data. Our implementation uses RPC streaming to implement all memory copies because it does not have access to the OpenMP offloading runtime mapping table. Implementations of this test and the following performance analysis can be found at the associated public repository [6]. All timings shown are taken as the average of 10000 repetitions.

Relative latency of multi-threaded RPC calls.

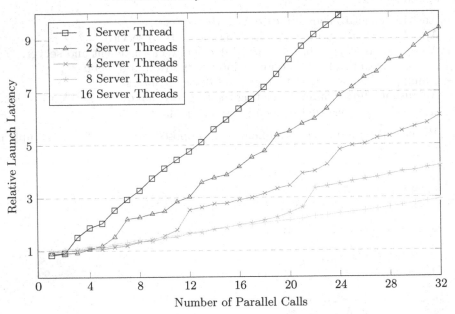

Fig. 6. Latency of a reverse offloading region on the GPU relative to launching a target region on the CPU.

We performed very basic performance tests to examine the usability of this interface. For our performance evaluation we used an AMD gfx1030 GPU system with a 24-core AMD PRO 5965WX threadripper and 128 GB of RAM. This interface was also tested on an NVIDIA sm_70 GPU for functionality. We first wanted to see how the latency of the reverse offloading compared to the latency of a standard target region. For this we measured the latency of an empty reverse offload target region launch on the device relative to a standard empty target region launch on the host. The results are plotted against the number of SIMT warps or wavefronts launched in parallel in Fig. 6. We observe that the basic RPC call is on-par with a target region launch, however it quickly becomes slow given increased parallelism. For this paper, we implemented the simplest possible port allocation scheme as a linear scan for available ports. This could be improved with more parallelism on the server and more efficient allocation of ports.

Mapping some data requires streaming it across the RPC interface. This will be very slow relative to the maximum bandwidth that can be achieved on the interconnect. We used the data streaming interface implemented in the RPC interface and sent increasingly large buffers of data to the other side. We launched the kernel with a single GPU thread to remove any contention. The observed bandwidth on our system was on average about 23 MB/s in each case for a 64-byte packet. This is quite slow relative to what the PCI-e bus is capable of, but is sufficient for most use-cases as we can assume large amounts of data can be mapped via standard device to host memory copies.

7   Future Work

The work outlined in this paper simply proposed an implementation of a generic interface that can be used to provide arbitrary RPC functionality using only a buffer of shared memory. We showed how this could be used to implement reverse offloading as according to the OpenMP 5.0 standard. Future work can be done to provide this interface in the LLVM/OpenMP offloading runtime and support the required code-generation and front-end actions.

Furthermore, this interface can be used to implement any host services on the GPU or other accelerator with shared memory. It would therefore be possible to use this interface to create a library performing actions typically not available on the GPU, such as `malloc` and `printf`.

Future optimizations could be done to the implemented RPC interface. The discussion in this paper also excludes some that are already used in the associated implementation [6] for brevity. In order to improve parallel RPC performance we could use a more intelligent method to scan the open ports. One method is to use a hash to choose a sufficiently random starting index, possibly based on hardware specific values such as NVIDIA's symmetric multiprocessor ID intrinstic.

The limited bandwidth results can be resolved for large copies by allocating memory and possibly calling into language runtime specific `memcpy` calls. As it is always possible to stream data through the pre-allocated buffer, this can be done without introducing any failure modes by falling back to the slow path.

8   Conclusion

In this work we presented a novel implementation of a remote procedure call (RPC) using only shared memory with minimal atomic support. Our interface provides a client and server that can communicate through port that can send and receive fixed-size packets between a client and a server. This interface can be used to send data between the CPU and GPU to implement a remote call on the host. We can use this support to implement the reverse offloading interface outlined in the OpenMP 5.0 standard.

We claim that these RPC calls are not prohibitively slow as the latency of launching a target region on the host is similar to launching a target region on the device. Data private to the thread that could normally not be accessed by the CPU by standard runtime calls can also be copied using the RPC interface and is sufficiently fast for the data sizes we expect to find in non-global memory.

References

1. HSA platform system architecture specification 1.2. http://hsafoundation.com/wp-content/uploads/2021/02/HSA-SysArch-1.2.pdf
2. OpenMP application programming interface version 5.0 (2018). https://www.openmp.org/spec-html/5.0/openmp.html
3. GCC 13 release serieschanges, new features, and fixes. https://gcc.gnu.org/gcc-13/changes.html (2023)
4. Chesterfield, J.: Shared memory remote procedure calls. In: 50th International Conference on Parallel Processing Workshop. ACM (2021). https://doi.org/10.1145/3458744.3473357
5. Harris, M.: Nvidia technical blog (2022). https://developer.nvidia.com/blog/how-overlap-data-transfers-cuda-cc/
6. Huber, J.: OpenMP reverse offloading. https://github.com/jhuber6/OpenMP-reverse-offloading (2023)
7. Sorensen, T., Evrard, H., Donaldson, A.F.: GPU schedulers: how fair is fair enough? In: 29th International Conference on Concurrency Theory (CONCUR2017), pp. 1–17 (2018)
8. Tanenbaum, A., Renesse, R.V.: A critique of the remote procedure call paradigm (1988)
9. Tian, S., Chesterfield, J., Doerfert, J., Chapman, B.: Experience Report: writing A Portable GPU Runtime with OpenMP 5.1. In: International Workshop on OpenMP. Bristol, UK (2021)
10. Tian, S., Huber, J., Parasyris, K., Chapman, B., Doerfert, J.: Direct GPU compilation and execution for host applications with openMP parallelism. In: 2022 IEEE/ACM Eighth Workshop on the LLVM Compiler Infrastructure in HPC (LLVM-HPC), pp. 43–51 (2022). https://doi.org/10.1109/LLVM-HPC56686.2022.00010
11. Vinoski, S.: Convenience over correctness. IEEE Internet Comput. **12**(4), 89–92 (2008). https://doi.org/10.1109/MIC.2008.75

Author Index

S. McIntosh-Smith et al. (Eds.): IWOMP 2023, LNCS 14114, p. 239, 2023.
https://doi.org/10.1007/978-3-031-40744-4

Printed in the United States
by Baker & Taylor Publisher Services